Praise for *Secrets of Female Entre*

"I can see this book being talked about for de
many people will use it to plan their own s
to read and highly recommended to everyone.

Avril Henry – Director, AH Revelations and Expert in Generation X & Y
Author of *Leadership Revelations – An Australian Perspective*

"*Secrets of Female Entrepreneurs Exposed!* should be required reading for anyone committed to starting up and building an extraordinary business – no matter if it's their first time in business or their tenth start-up. These women ignite the reader with their passion as well as practical advice."

Michelle Carden – Co-Founder, The Aspire Group of Companies
Winner WA Business News 40under40 Awards

"In case you think this book is just for women, think again. It contains numerous stories of courage, persistence and at times...genius, from which *everyone* can draw inspiration."

Matthew Brooks – Business Journalist

"I've loved reading this book! As a young mother of two small children I thought I was incapable of being in business. However, the stories in this book, especially from other mums, really inspired me and I now know if these women can do it, so can I."

Bianca Costigan – Aspiring Entrepreneur and Mother of Two

"It is about time someone put together a book like this. It's a triumph for all women in business. The stories it contains are both inspirational and informative. Well done Dale and Katherine."

Lisa Messenger – Managing Director of Messenger Marketing Pty Ltd
Finalist 2005 Telstra Business Woman of the Year Awards (NSW)

"Having studied entrepreneurial psychology for the last 20 years, I've discovered that there are many common traits which make a person succeed in business. These traits are clearly explained by the highly successful women whose stories make up this book, so study it closely, it's a shortcut to success."

John Rawson – Founder of Demtel International and Success Gym

"This book is the ultimate tool for women in business! Be inspired, be amazed and be motivated. Grab your copy, take notes and spring into action. What are you waiting for!?"

Amy Wilkins – Television Presenter and Co-creator of Active Kidz

"Reading about how these 'real' women have built their businesses inspired me to take my own business to the next level. Understanding the challenges they have experienced on their journeys helped me to realise that we all face the same obstacles, and that with a clear vision and a passion to see it happen, any of us can achieve success in our lives."

Jennifer Jefferies – Life Balance Expert, Author & Professional Speaker

"Having already read the *Secrets of Male Entrepreneurs Exposed!* book, I found this one to be just as insightful, if not more. Being a woman in the corporate world, I am excited about the calibre of Australian talent we have right here in our own backyard. I now have real life examples of successful women that are true pioneers. I sincerely value that."

Louise Murphy – Executive Assistant

"Though I have never met any of the people in this book personally, after reading their chapters I now feel like I really know each of them. I'm now looking forward to the day when I start my own business and become the master of my own destiny."

Myra Van Every – 23-year-old Aspiring Entrepreneur

SECRETS OF FEMALE ENTREPRENEURS EXPOSED!

"Get out of your own way."

SECRETS OF FEMALE ENTREPRENEURS EXPOSED!

Featuring written material by ★ Sonia Amoroso ★ Joanne Mercer ★ Suzi Dafnis ★ Margaret Lomas ★ Sue Ismiel ★ and many more

DALE BEAUMONT

WITH KATHERINE BEAUMONT & FOREWORD BY BESSIE BARDOT

FIRST EDITION 2006

Copyright © 2006 Dream Express International Pty Ltd

All rights reserved. No part of this publication may be reproduced, stored in a retrieval system, or transmitted in any form or by any means, electronic, mechanical, photocopying, recording or otherwise, without the prior written permission from the publisher.

National Library of Australia
Cataloguing-in-Publication entry:

Beaumont, Dale   Beaumont, Katherine
  Secrets of Female Entrepreneurs Exposed

  ISBN 0-9757974-4-1

  1. Business. 2. Women – Business. 3. Interviews – Australia.
  4. Beaumont, Dale. I. Title.

Published by Dream Express Publishing
A division of Dream Express International Pty Ltd
PO Box 567, Crows Nest, NSW 1585 Australia
Email: info@SecretsExposed.com.au
Website: www.SecretsExposed.com.au

Distributed in Australia by Gary Allen

For further information about orders:
Phone: +61 2 9725 2933
Email: customerservice@garyallen.com.au

Editing by Simone Tregeagle [simone@inkcommunications.com.au]
Layout and typesetting by Bookhouse [www.bookhouse.com.au]
Cover design by Jay Beaumont [www.thecreativehouse.com]
Illustrations by Grant Tulloch [info@secretsexposed.com.au]
Printed and bound by McPhersons Printing [www.mcphersonsprinting.com.au]

To my very special and extremely strong mum. Ever since I was young you told me I picked you to be my mother. After twenty-something years I think you're right. Thanks for everything and love ya heaps!

Dale Beaumont

To the four phenomenal women in my life: Mum, Jenn, Glenda and Ingrid. I am grateful for the lessons you have taught me, the belief you have had in me, your honesty and unconditional love.

Katherine Beaumont

Acknowledgments

As with any major project, there are a number of very special people who contributed to making this book happen, so we'd like to take a short moment to say 'Thank You'.

First, to the seventeen amazing entrepreneurs featured in this book, the biggest THANK YOU for accepting our invitation to be a part of this exciting project, and for your faith and patience in seeing it through. It has been wonderful to get to know you and experience the positive impact that each of you has on everyone whose lives you touch.

Next, thanks again to Jay Beaumont (Dale's brother) for all your help with designing the book covers, and to Craig Eve and Adam Davis for your support in building the 'Secrets Exposed' website. To Simone Tregeagle (from Ink Communications) our most amazing editor – thank you so much for your absolute belief in the vision for these books, and to Cheryl Jenkins and Bianca Costigan for your many hours of proofreading.

Thank you to our very talented publicist, Matthew Dillon (from KAPOW Media), for never ceasing to amaze us. And to our special friends for helping us write the hundreds of questions: Sharlene Naidu, Brent Williams, Ryan Butler, Armina Soemino – you guys are fantastic!

And finally, to the unsung heroes of this book – the totally terrific assistants of the entrepreneurs featured – Kim Edwards, Sophie Baker, Phillip Allcott, Tracey Booth, Paul Lacy, Sarah Irwin and Christine Nicholson. Our sincere thanks to each and every one of you for answering our many phone calls, replying to the dozens of emails and bringing it all together. Without your support this book would not have happened.

CONTENTS

PREFACE

If I were in your position right now I'd be wondering if I really needed to read this section. However, if I could ask you to resist the temptation to skip ahead for just a few minutes, I'd like to share with you a few of the reasons why this book has been created and how you can use it to impact your life.

When I was growing up I heard somewhere that there are two ways to live your life: the first is through 'trial and error' and the second is through 'other people's experience'. At the time I dismissed it as just another one of those sayings that sounds good, but doesn't make much sense. Then, like most teenagers I finished school with stars in my eyes thinking, 'This is great! My education is over – no more books, no more lectures, no more people telling me what to do'. How wrong I was. After a few months of bouncing around, not quite sure of what to do next, I stumbled across the idea of personal development and started to hear concepts such as:

- Formal education will earn you a living, but self-education will make you a fortune.
- Work harder on yourself than you do on your job.
- You will be the same person five years from now, except for the people you meet and the books you read.
- Don't wish that your job were easier, wish that you were better.
- You are your own greatest asset, so you must invest in yourself.

Since November 2000, I have been totally committed to becoming my own most valuable asset. After attending hundreds of seminars, listening to thousands of hours of CDs and reading shelves of books, I have discovered that the people who truly succeed aren't any smarter, better looking or harder working than anyone else – they just think differently and have learnt to incorporate different values into their lives.

I am now in the very fortunate position of being able to travel internationally to present personal development seminars to teenagers and I am often asked, 'What is the one thing you need to know to be successful?' My answer is always the same: 'The one thing that you need to know is that there is not *one* thing that you need to know to be successful'. I've learnt that success is multifaceted and that mastering one principle of success or area of your life isn't going to take you to the top – the more you master, the more successful you will become. But if I *did* have to identify one of the most important success strategies, it would be this: *'Find out what successful people do and do the same thing until you get the same results'.*

That's what this book is all about. The only difference is, instead of you going out and finding successful people, we've brought them to you.

You see, whatever you want in life, whatever you are shooting for, chances are that someone else is already living it. They have already invested years of their life and probably hundreds of thousands of dollars, they've made lots of mistakes, learnt from them and eventually succeeded. So why would you want to waste your own time, money and effort through 'trial and error' when you can fast-track your success by learning from 'someone else's experience'? As Sir Isaac Newton said, 'If I have seen further it is because I have been standing on the shoulders of giants'.

Every time you pick up a book, attend a seminar or interview a successful person, you are compressing years of life experience into a few hours. With any of the 'Secrets Exposed' books, you can multiply that by between twelve and seventeen people and you're looking at around 250+ years of experience and wisdom ready and waiting for you. It won't prevent you from making mistakes of your own, far from it, but it will help you to make more calculated and purposeful decisions, rather than big, misguided and ignorant ones.

There is no shortage of information about how to achieve proficiency or even greatness in any area of life these days. Go to any bookstore or library and you'll find the shelves sagging with titles from experts, all with their own theories and ways of doing things. But what I have discovered is lacking in almost all of these books is INSPIRATION. What's missing is role models and mentors – the stories of people we can all look up to. People who started out exactly like you – with a dream in their hearts and with all the same fears and insecurities. Given the choice between reading a text-book or a dozen success stories about people who have actually done something, I'd take the success stories any day of the week. I'm not saying that theoretical information isn't important, of course it is, but having presented hundreds of talks to all different types of audiences, I can confidently say that it's always the stories that move people. It's the whole, "If he or she did it, then so can I" that gets inside people's hearts. When we're inspired we get motivated and then we take positive action which leads to results.

The 'Secrets Exposed' books are not intended to be a one-stop-shop. They are an introduction to the wealth of knowledge available to you and to some of the real success stories of people who have reached the top in their chosen field of endeavour. That's why at the back of each book you will find most of the contributors' contact details and some of their other products and services that are available to help you continue your journey.

So, how did the whole idea for the 'Secrets Exposed' books come about?

Well, in 1998, when I was around seventeen, my nan gave me a copy of a book titled *Collective Wisdom,* by Brett Kelly. In it were transcripts of face-to-face interviews with a whole lot of prominent Australian personalities. And it was a fantastic read. Since then I have seen a handful of random 'success story' books, but the challenge I find with most of them is that they are either transcripts of interviews, that never really make complete sense in the printed form, or they are written by writers who paraphrase someone else's story. The result tends to be a diluted message that doesn't really allow you to get a sense of the individual's personality or character.

In around 2001 I read my first *Chicken Soup for the Soul* book and realised that there were dozens and dozens of related titles designed to meet the needs of different people's areas of interest. I thought that was pretty neat.

It wasn't until January 2004 that the 'Secrets Exposed' idea boiled over. I was in my hotel room in Singapore relaxing after six straight days of presenting to hundreds of teenagers. I was reflecting on the ideas that had been shared with them. One of the most important was to seek out those who have already achieved what you want and ask them lots of questions. I was plagued by the thought that only a small percentage would act on that very valuable advice and that most would never take the step due to a lack of confidence, fear of rejection or an inability to contact the people they needed.

That's when it hit me... 'What if I could find the people and put together a number of books covering a range of different areas?' I knew it would take a lot of effort, so for the next three days, I sat in my hotel room and developed the basis of an entire system to make it happen.

Based on my experience with other books, I decided that these books had to be non-time specific and be written (not spoken) by the people them-selves. This way the answers would be planned and well thought-out, providing richer content and more interesting reading. I also wanted to make sure that there was an even balance between practical 'how to' infor-mation and inspirational stories that gave an insight into the highs and lows of people's real journeys. I also wanted to ensure that a percentage of every book sold was donated to a charity relating to the nature of that partic-ular book.

When I arrived home I got into action. However, between working out of a tiny one-bedroom flat and trying to manage two other demanding busi-nesses, my plans were a little slow in the beginning and I had to be resourceful. So I bought a plastic tub and turned the boot of my car into a mobile office! Anytime I could find a spare hour or two, I'd park myself at the gym or a nearby coffee shop and make calls from my mobile phone.

Putting these books together has been both time-consuming and demanding, but it has also been a real privilege for me to have the opportunity to work with each of the people involved in the various books. Thank you, to each of you, for making it possible!

Well, I think you've heard enough from me. Now it's time for you to discover for yourself the wonderful wisdom contained in these pages. I hope that you enjoy the read as much as we've enjoyed putting it together. And who knows, maybe one day we will be reading your story?

Dream Big!

Dale Beaumont
Creator of the 'Secrets Exposed' Series
Sydney, Australia

FOREWORD

I know there are going to be many successful people reading this book who will wonder, 'Where on earth was all this priceless information when I was starting out?'

This book has truly captured the essence and heart of the entrepreneurial woman with its collective knowledge and fascinating insights. It has as much to offer the novice taking their first steps into the big wide world of business, as it does to remind and reinspire those already succeeding in the entrepreneurial world.

Being an entrepreneur, by default, means taking the bull by the horns and treading where most others fear to tread. More than anything else, this book offers a guiding hand over the inevitable rocks that we all face, and a crystal ball through which to benefit from the tried and tested advice of women who have actually walked the path before you.

Reading this book, I realised that many of my own experiences, fears and uncertainties would, without doubt, have been so much easier to deal with if I had the insights offered here. If I had realised that the obstacles I faced were simply part of the usual personal and business growing pains, I could have saved myself much time and many blocks of chocolate!

With its personal and easy to read format, it makes fun reading for even the busiest person who just wants to remind themselves about traits such as persistence, learning, time management and the many other common behaviours and values we must all share if we want to be in charge of our destinies.

So, whatever stage you are at, read this book, get back up, dust yourself off and remember you're not alone.

Better than 'good luck' – 'Good Learning'.

xxx Bessie Bardot

Professional Speaker, Best-Selling Author, Radio Presenter, Model and Businesswoman

INTRODUCTION

For centuries there has been a vast gap between those relative few who achieve high-level business success, and the rest of society – no more so than when it comes to women. But in recent decades we have seen many of the walls that have prevented women from participating (let alone excelling) in business come down. There are of course many historical and political reasons for this, but more recently it's been the public exposure of highly successful businesswomen that has inspired a new generation of spirited souls.

But simply knowing about the achievements of today's women business leaders, and learning about who they are and understanding how they've achieved their success are two very different things! This book aims to create a more personal relationship with some of the most successful business-women of today; to explore their rise to success, and share their ideas and philosophies on business and on life.

Following on from the enormous success of *Secrets of Male Entrepreneurs Exposed!*, in this book we've uncovered the secrets of seventeen women at the top of their game who are eager to pass on what they've learnt – and you'll see that we've covered a lot of ground:

- They range in age from 27 to 53.
- Their business turnover ranges from $1.6 million, through to an incredible $50 million.
- Fourteen of these women call Australia home, but they come from eight different countries.

- They represent a diverse range of industries, from real estate to pet tags, and everything in between.
- Some have several degrees, while others dropped out of high school.
- Some are single, some are divorced, and others are still happily married to their childhood sweethearts.
- Some have no children, others have several, and one gave birth just two days before writing this text.

As for the content, this book covers: goal setting, idea development, research skills, product creation, capital raising, sales and marketing, finance, branding, hiring staff, firing staff, joint ventures, leadership, franchising, stress management, web development, international expansion and much, much more.

So, is this book for you?

If you have a desire to:

- be your own boss and work the hours you choose
- dramatically increase your income-earning potential and possibly retire early
- build something of value that will assist future generations
- utilise your creative potential and grow as an individual
- be recognised for your skills, rather than for your position
- help to add value to the lives of your customers and your society

– then continue reading.

To assist you in your own entrepreneurial endeavours, at the back of the book we have included the contact websites of every contributor. You'll discover that many have their own books or educational materials, which we strongly endorse and encourage you to investigate further.

A number of contributors have also very generously offered valuable gifts to all of our readers. To receive them, all you need to do is visit the specified website, follow the steps and download the bonus gifts – absolutely *free*.

Finally, remember it's what you do *after you read this book* that is going to determine its real value to you. So, go out there, apply what you've learnt and when you reach a goal – no matter how big or small – let us know so we can share your success story.

ENJOY!

Dale and Katherine Beaumont

Email: info@SecretsExposed.com.au

PS. 10% of the profits from this book will be donated to The Breast Cancer Institute of Australia, an organisation committed to research and testing for early detection and to discover more advanced methods of treatment, helping to ensuring that in the not so distant future, breast cancer will be a thing of the past. For more information or to donate directly, please visit www.bcia.org.au.

SUZI DAFNIS

66 If I only focus on travelling around and producing events it just connects me to how exhausting that is, but if I focus on the result, which is thousands of people with improved lives, I can keep going any day. **99**

SUZI DAFNIS

Suzi Dafnis was born in 1966 in Sydney, to Greek immigrant parents and is the eldest of three children.

For most of her career, prior to starting her own business, Suzi worked in promotions and marketing positions in the music and fashion industries. She started Pow Wow Events International in 1994, together with partner Peter Johnston. The company was named after the American Indian term for 'a gathering of people, an exchange of good ideas'.

Pow Wow Events distributes books and other learning products, and organises seminars with top international authors and experts in sales, internet marketing, entrepreneurship, real estate and investing. Since 1994 it has delivered empowering educational experiences through live seminars and online events to more than 250,000 people. The company occupies more than 50 per cent of the market in the personal finance, personal development and business skills segment.

Suzi has been featured in many national publications, including *The Australian, The Sydney Morning Herald, Canberra Times, MyBusiness Magazine, Voyeur* (Virgin Blue's in flight magazine), as well as on numerous radio and television programs. She also appeared in the BRW Young Rich List in 2003, 2004 and 2005, where she was profiled among this country's great talents in business and entertainment. In 2005 she featured on Channel 7's revolutionary business program *Dragons' Den*.

Suzi is the National General Manager of the Australian Businesswomen's Network, which provides services for more than 10,000 businesswomen in Australia each year.

Suzi travels extensively for both business and pleasure, and is highly committed to her own personal development. She's an avid investor in real estate and small businesses.

When did you and your family first realise that you had an entrepreneurial flair?

Both of my parents worked for themselves and I think that had an influence on me, but it was probably something that I discovered as a teenager – I couldn't wait to get out of school and start making a difference. I got my first after-school job making sandwiches at a suburban shopping centre café. I wasn't even old enough to be legally employed but I wanted to have my own money and the freedom to spend it however I liked. To be able to work was very empowering to me.

My first business venture was Pow Wow Events International, which I started in 1994 (when I was 28 years old) to provide people with the tools to learn, without having to go back to formal educational institutions. I have a passion for transforming businesses and people, but I don't have a tertiary education and I knew that there were many people like me who wanted to continue to learn and grow, but not in a traditional learning environment such as university. Starting the company was the biggest learning experience I could have ever hoped for, it developed me as a leader, a marketer, a communicator and a manager of people, and through it I've learnt an enormous amount about myself, people, business and customer service – as well as reaping the financial rewards.

What education or experience did you have prior to starting Pow Wow Events?

I'd mainly worked in marketing and promotions in the fashion and music industries. I started at the ground level, doing basic secretarial and reception jobs to get a foot in the door, and like many Australians do, I travelled and worked in the UK and Europe before settling down and getting serious about my career.

The job I am still most fond of was when I was the marketing coordinator for Virgin Retail. I was in my early twenties and it was a fun, fast-growing

> 66...we wanted the business's future to be international and so we made it part of our vocabulary...99

business. The culture there was one that I've always hoped to emulate in my own business. My boss was my first real mentor and he encouraged me to learn marketing and gave me opportunities to grow and be accountable. I also had the opportunity to meet Richard Branson (my all-time role model) on a couple of occasions, which was a wonderful bonus.

What made you decide to set up Pow Wow Events, and is it true that you started in the spare room of your house?

My partner PJ and I both have a passion for personal education so we were looking to create non-traditional environments for people to learn business and personal development skills. We started in our spare room and stayed there for two years while cash flow was really tight. When we ended up with staff working out of our kitchen and living areas, we realised it was time to move into our first office – a whole 80 square metres in Crows Nest, Sydney – today we have an 1,800 square metre building in Rosebery, Sydney.

During those early years what were some of the things you did to make your company appear bigger than what it was?

We named the business Pow Wow Events International for a reason, we wanted the business's future to be international and so we made it part of our vocabulary from the very beginning.

Sitting in your spare room answering calls, you really need to have some strategies to cover up the fact that you a) may still be sitting in your pyjamas, and b) may be one of only two people doing everything. So we always adopted a very professional and business-like approach. We answered the phone very professionally (my reception experience coming in handy), we had email from the beginning, before it was common, and we got a website up early too, around 1996. It was only a few basic pages but it meant that we could advertise a web address, which gave people an impression about the professionalism of the company. We also created a client newsletter, which was a big investment in time and money, but it paid off.

In the beginning, what were some of the business skills you were lacking and what did you do about it?

At the start, the only skills I actually possessed were on the administrative and marketing side of things. The rest, such as managing a budget and staff, I had to learn until I could afford to employ people who knew how to do it better than me.

I love my staff and am very committed to helping them grow and learn, however managing people has been the biggest challenge for me. In the early days I used to take it personally when someone resigned, but I've learnt to see how their time with us can be productive and they will grow, but there will come a time when they want to move on.

What is one of the biggest business deals you've ever done and why did it work so well?

All of our great deals have been the result of good relationships. Our relationships with authors and speakers are usually very long term and I have found that the more open and honest I can be, the greater the trust that is built.

For example, Pow Wow Events has a very close relationship with the Rich Dad Company in the USA, which has spanned thirteen years. We have worked through many challenges, but remain great partners and great friends. With many of our relationships, we're one of the biggest resellers of the speaker's products and programs, and we contribute substantially to their bottom line. We still have relationships with suppliers that we first dealt with ten years ago – that's what makes business work for me, when your team goes beyond your employees – it's that extended team which allows you to have the confidence and power to do the bigger deals.

What do you think are some of the major benefits of having your own business?

Being as passionate as I am about business, I am sure I could easily write a whole book on this question alone. However, here's a quick summary of what I think are four of the main benefits of business ownership.

1. *You get to think differently* – I remember in 1998 Apple launched its 'Think Different' campaign. Its ads featured a montage of people such as Albert Einstein, Richard Branson, Amelia Earhart, Gandhi, Martin Luther King, and Picasso, and the voiceover said: 'They invent. They imagine. They heal. They explore. They create. They inspire. They push the human race forward'. In other words, they change the world. That's the way I feel about business. By daring to build your own business you are forced to think differently, and by doing so you touch the lives of thousands, or possibly even millions, of people.

2. *You get to be your own boss* – One of the main reasons I decided to start my own business was because I don't like limits, rules or being told what to do. That's my nature; I think it is in every entrepreneur's nature! In most jobs, regardless of how senior your role is, or how hard you work, you're expected to be somewhere at some time, and do something in exchange for a defined pay-cheque at the end of the week, fortnight or month. I started my own business so that I could have the freedom to create my life just the way I wanted it. Today, as my own boss I work harder (much harder) than I did when I was an employee, but I love it! The good thing is that I work because I *choose* to, not because I *have* to, and when I want time off, I take it. It's a great feeling.

3. *No glass ceiling and no ladders to climb* – Another upside of entrepreneurship, especially for women, is that there is no glass ceiling

and there is no corporate ladder. No one can put a cap on your earning potential and you don't have to play politics just to keep your job. Business doesn't care about your past, whether you're a man or a woman, your age or your background, it doesn't have prejudice – it is just a creative process and anyone can use business as a vehicle to obtain their own sovereignty.

4. *The alchemy of business* – With business you have the power to create something out of nothing. First there is an idea, then you add your knowledge, time, money and intention – and suddenly, you have a new 'something'. That's magic. I believe business is the ultimate creative endeavour. I've often thought that I'm not using my creativity, until I check in and remember that there was once nothing and now there are hundreds of thousands of people with experiences that resulted from something I created. It's very humbling.

In 2000 you left Australia to live in Phoenix to expand into the lucrative US market. What challenges did you experience leaving the Australian business?

Being away from the Australian business for up to eight months a year has been challenging because both PJ and I are still very much involved in certain aspects of the business's day-to-day activities. Leaving forced us to put management systems, budgets and project plans in place, which was great because we wouldn't have done it so quickly if we hadn't left.

The business was on an upward trend before we left and that growth carried on through the first two years following our departure. The last two years have been about consolidation. You can grow too fast and spin out of control and we were beginning to do that. All that was growing was the number of staff, but not the bottom line, so we've cut expenses and put systems in place to make us more productive and profitable.

> 66 You can grow too fast and spin out of control...99

What do you love most about business?

There's a lot that I love about business, but primarily it is the ability to create something out of nothing – to innovate, to market and to see a project from start to finish. Business allows me to be as creative as I want to be and it's also the best personal development program you can do –starting a business will test what you're really made of. I relish the personal development that comes from taking new steps, whether you succeed or fail, and moving to greater levels of leadership and knowledge.

Pow Wow Events just had its eleven-year anniversary, which was a big milestone. During the next year we will re-engineer our processes, business functions, roles and activities. Having been away from our domestic business for five years, I have learnt new skills, identified new market trends and new ways of doing business that we'll start to integrate in Australia. One of the great things about having offices in the USA is that we get to see another point of view and to experience opportunities that wouldn't come our way if we were solely based in Australia. This is what I love about business – that you can grow and expand with experience.

What is the biggest mistake you've ever made in business and what did you learn from it?

When we first opened Pow Wow Events in the USA, we left the Australian business in the hands of a general manager, but we hadn't set up the right reporting and financial systems and within four months money was flowing out the door – expenses were up, and productivity was down. We were forced to take back the reins, put in budgets, systems, key performance indicators, job specifications and procedures. What we learnt was that you can't grow a business based only on intuition and hard work. To truly leverage your time, you need to put measures in place that enable you to be able to take the pulse of the business from a distance while others operate it within a structure.

Another mistake we've made is complacency. We've been very deliberate about staying ahead of the market, but over the last four years a number of copycat companies have shown up, and we didn't pay attention to them. We've spent the last twelve months looking for our new 'edge'. We've realised that our complacency was making us lose the upper hand we had over our competition – and we won't make that mistake again.

What were some of the challenges you had to overcome on the journey to achieving your personal and business goals?

In the early years managing income was the biggest challenge. We were paying ourselves $100 a week, not out of the business but out of our savings, and we did everything ourselves for years to save on staff costs. In retrospect, I should have hired more senior and experienced staff to enable me to let go of many day-to-day activities. We didn't think we could afford them, so we waited four years before we hired our first senior person and six or seven years before we hired an executive assistant, which meant that we were doing work that others could have done for us while we concentrated on the business-building that only we could do as owners of the company.

I also now see the need to create systems. In his book *The E-Myth*, Michael Gerber suggests that any process that will be done more than once deserves a system. Systems allow business owners to have others perform jobs with minimum training. We have great systems today, but they are like a moving target and we have to pay constant attention to ensuring that the systems keep up with our growth and changes in the business.

These issues came up again when we opened our office in the USA, but because we'd learnt from our mistakes and experience, we were able to grow so much faster and smarter, and to get up to speed on productivity and income twice as fast. It took us just two years to do what had taken seven years the first time around.

...that you
a... ...uct of the
people you surround
yourself with. 99

Have there ever been times when you wanted to give up, and if so, what got you through?

Our very first venture lost us $40,000 and put us in a hole that took two years to get out of. We had to negotiate with creditors to pay them back over two years, to allow us to continue trying to get new business. It was a disaster. We did think of quitting but neither of us really wanted to go back to working for someone else. What kept me going was the vision of creating a unique business that empowers the human spirit. This is my personal vision and the reason that I continue to do what I do.

I still do feel like giving up some days when things don't go right; like when we are having issues with staff, or a deal doesn't quite go the way I'd hoped, or when I'm just physically exhausted from travelling for weeks on end. Sometimes I just feel like stopping and 'smelling the roses' a little, but I love the business and the results I get from it way too much to ever give up.

What is the most important thing you have learnt about succeeding in business?

What I've learnt is to not be arrogant. Success can bring arrogance and a notion that you actually know something, but you need to continually watch the market, and be prepared to innovate and adapt to changing circumstances.

Some people say that 'people are your best asset' but I think a better way of saying this is 'the right people are your best asset, but the wrong people (whether they are staff, suppliers or clients) can really mess things up!' I believe that you are a product of the people you surround yourself with.

To be a successful entrepreneur requires certain leadership skills: the ability to see the big picture, respect for others on the team, willingness to be wrong about things and to learn from mistakes, willingness to take risks, and a commitment to learning and growing. No matter how hard they may work, unless they take these skills into account, most people will not be successful in business. Starting a business doesn't make you an entrepreneur, but most people don't realise that. I have always tried to be a successful entrepreneur, I never wanted to be a good manager, but I do constantly strive to be a good leader. I am very demanding and have high standards, which can be a vice at times, but I think it's necessary if you want to be the best at something.

Your life partner, Peter Johnston (PJ), is also your business partner. What's it like working together and what advice would you give to others in a similar situation?

The most challenging part is switching off and taking breaks from the business. We are a great team and really complement each other, so the business's success has been the result of a great partnership. Many couples couldn't work together, but I can't imagine coming home and saying, 'So how was your day, honey?' Our goals and focus are very aligned. Regardless, we still need to work on having time out for the couple side of us, which we sometimes do by building days for us into our business travel.

For the last few years you have appeared in the BRW's Young Rich List. What is that recognition like for you?

It's an achievement that is both interesting and one that I am proud of. I can certainly say that I've been in excellent company in that list. It's a nice accolade, but at the end of the day being rich is not the end game for me. It's great to be acknowledged but there's more to my happiness than that.

I recall someone very successful, maybe it was Gerry Harvey of Harvey Norman, saying that he never gets complacent about being successful, because tomorrow it could all be gone. I know that sounds 'doomsday-ish', but I think people need to have a reality check about what business is

– it's a wonderful adventure with its ups and its downs, and I always look to learn and grow, to try new things and take calculated risks.

Who are the mentors that have inspired you and what important lessons have you learnt from them?

There have been many role models that have inspired me. The ones who inspire me from afar, include:

- Richard Branson, CEO of Virgin
- Anita Roddick of The Body Shop
- Steve Jobs who created Apple
- Ray Kroc who started McDonald's

The mentors who have inspired me more personally include my boss when I worked at Virgin, who was a young, extremely smart marketer who encouraged me to get into marketing, which I soon discovered was my real passion in business. Robert Kiyosaki, the author of *Rich Dad, Poor Dad*, has also become a mentor (whose business and investing advice I have taken on board), business partner and a truly great personal friend. In addition to these two amazing people, I have met countless inspiring entrepreneurs through the Australian Businesswomen's Network – both well-known people and quiet achievers who are changing the shape of business in Australia.

I'm very lucky to keep the company that I do, I have met some amazingly inspiring people who all share drive, determination and a 'never say never' approach. I've found that these people are very big picture – they think big, act big, and they have a commitment to their own education, growth and ongoing development.

If anyone can succeed in business no matter what their background or circumstances, what do you think holds people back from becoming successful entrepreneurs?

I don't actually believe that anyone *can* succeed in business, because very few do and ever will. Unfortunately, the statistics on the number of businesses that fail are terrible. I think the main thing that holds people back from success is what they don't know – whether it's how to manage money, how to market, what to market, how to manage staff, how to negotiate or how to sell – that's why I'm such a big advocate of personal education.

Is there a significant quote or saying by which you live your life?

The most important quote to me isn't so much a saying but a poem called *Commitment*. It is about how the moment one is truly committed, unforeseen circumstances come about to support the decision that you have made.

Until one is committed, there is hesitancy, the chance to draw back, always ineffectiveness. Concerning all acts of initiative (and creation) there is one elementary truth, the ignorance of which kills countless ideas and splendid plans: that the moment one definitely commits oneself, then Providence moves too. All sorts of things occur to help one that would never otherwise have occurred. A whole stream of events issues from the decision, raising in ones' favour all manner of unforeseen incidents and meetings and material assistance, which no man could have dreamt would have come his way. I have learned a deep respect for one of Goethe's couplets: 'Whatever you can do, or dream you can, begin it. Boldness has genius, power and magic in it'.

W H Murray (1951), *The Scottish Himalayan Expedition*

What advice would you give to an aspiring entrepreneur who wants to get started in a business of their own?

You just need to go for it. Start and don't worry about making mistakes. I'm not saying you won't make them, you will, everybody does, but it is our ability to handle them that makes us successful. Build up your knowledge so that it is easier to handle or prevent mistakes, it doesn't matter whether it's through books, tapes, seminars or a traditional business education. Find your mentors. Speak with people who are successful and don't take advice from people who aren't successful in the area that you want to be in. You need to have a good support network, so surround yourself with people who share your enthusiasm for what you want to do.

What is the Australian Businesswomen's Network and what does it do?

Since 1990, the Australian Businesswomen's Network has served women in business by providing networking opportunities, business education and role models/mentors. Since 1995, I have contributed time and energy to supporting this organisation because of the good work that it does. I work with a group of volunteers that make up the advisory board and committees to fulfil the vision of the organisation.

The main benefit is the support that women receive from the network. The community is 10,000 strong and comprises women in business in remote locations, rural areas and cities. Being a business owner can be very lonely, especially if you're in a small or micro business, so the network gives women a sounding board for ideas and provides peer mentoring in structured and affordable ways.

If you would like to know more please visit: www.abn.org.au.

Would you encourage more women to start their own businesses?

I encourage any woman who is brave enough to start. I really think that entrepreneurship is not a learned skill – you either have it or you don't, but if the spark of entrepreneurship is within you it can be expanded.

The advantages for a woman in starting her own business are that there is no glass ceiling, which means she doesn't face the prospect of remaining stagnant just because she's a woman, and she can also set her own agenda, create something out of nothing, and find the flexibility to work in the business while having a family by leveraging her time.

The disadvantages are that many women still bear most of the responsibility for caring for family and kids, and having a business on top of that can be exhausting. Australian women also don't have the support from government that American women do – there are far more initiatives for women starting and growing their own businesses in the USA than there are here.

What are some of the ways women can go about deciding what type of business to get involved in?

Passion is the key here. This could mean a passion for the product or service you will provide, for the results that it will bring, or for seeing something come to fruition. I have a friend who has a very successful, award-winning custom-wardrobe company – but she's not passionate about wardrobes! She is passionate about using the profits from her business to buy and renovate properties and create a nest egg for her family. I am passionate about seeing people transform their lives and that's exactly why Pow Wow Events exists. If I only focus on travelling around and producing events it just connects me to how exhausting that is, but if I focus on the result, which is thousands of people with improved lives, I can keep going any day.

> 66 I am like a 'pig in mud' when I'm learning and around others who are also driven... 99

Why is it so important for people to invest in their own self-education?

Self-education is a value that I hold very high and that's why I'm in the business I'm in and why I work with the Australian Businesswomen's Network. I finished school at eighteen and my family circumstances were such that I started working immediately and never completed a tertiary education. I have however completed many, many non-academic courses over the years and read hundreds of books that have all been a part of my learning, growth and success.

I can't imagine ever feeling like I know enough. The scope of what I don't know is huge, and I am like a 'pig in mud' when I'm learning and around others who are also driven to become smarter, better, stronger.

Having attended hundreds of seminars on business and personal development, can you list some of the most valuable lessons you've learnt from them?

Some of the most valuable lessons include:

Integrity – You need to be able to sleep with a clear conscience, so have integrity in your dealings with others and with yourself. Keep your relationships above board and work for the highest good.

Karma – I really believe that you reap what you sow. If you believe you are a victim of scarcity, there will never be enough money, clients or business. If you believe in abundance, you'll be generous and it will flow back to you.

Assets vs Liabilities – This is a big one, many business owners know how to generate cash but they don't know how to keep it. Using cash flow to buy assets, which in turn produce their own cash flow, means that your money is working for you, rather than you just working for your money. This was an idea that I mainly got from Robert Kiyosaki.

Marketing and Innovation – Without these components, you don't have a business. No matter how good you think your product is, if you cannot market it you will go broke. Innovation is not about inventing something new, it is the commitment to the ongoing improvement of what you do, whether it is the way you answer the phone, the way you market, or the way you recruit. Innovation is what differentiates exceptional companies from average ones.

Numbers – Business is a numbers game. If you don't understand financials, make sure somebody you trust does. No matter how fun it might be to take on a business activity, at the end of the day if it loses you money, it's not worth doing unless it's going to get you some other goal down the line. We've had some great fun projects that the team loved taking part in which cost us a lot of time and money.

Responsibility – Some people think that responsibility means taking on a lot of work. What it means to me is doing what you say you are going to do. As a business owner, I'm 100 per cent responsible for the success or failure of the business. Staff can and should be held accountable for their areas of the business, and my responsibility is to hold them accountable for what they say they will do, and to set an example by keeping my word.

How many books do you have in your library and what are your ten favourites?

I couldn't exactly say how many, but there are hundreds and hundreds scattered between my homes and offices in Sydney and Phoenix. I've got multiple copies of many books – one in each location, and with the advent of Apple's iTunes I now also have many audio books on my computer and iPod, which means I can be learning any time.

My favourites include:

1. *Rich Dad, Poor Dad* by Robert Kiyosaki – The bible for getting out of the financial rat race.
2. *Rich Dad's Cashflow Quadrant* by Robert Kiyosaki – A must for anyone who wants to grow a business.
3. *Good to Great* by Jim Collins – This one is very inspiring and important for those wanting to grow lasting companies.
4. *Losing My Virginity* by Richard Branson – He really is the master of branding and business culture.
5. *The E-Myth* by Michael Gerber – This is the key for anyone wanting to systemise their business so that it works without them.
6. *Influence* by Robert Cialdini – Dr Cialdini was the first speaker from the USA that Pow Wow Events worked with. His book is a classic and reveals the six most important marketing principles.
7. *The Power of Cult Branding* by Matthew W. Ragas and B J Bueno – Case studies of businesses that don't have clients, they have raving fans.
8. *Business As Unusual* by Anita Roddick – A wonderful role model and a social entrepreneur who explains her business.
9. *Permission Marketing* by Seth Godin – Any book by this marketing guru is worth reading.
10. *Guerrilla Marketing* by Jay Conrad Levinson – Another guru especially for marketing in small business.

Joanne M[?]

JOANNE MERCER

66 My favourites are a pair of diamante evening shoes in pink, which are part of our Joanne Mercer Italian Collection. I love their elegance and classic beauty. I am a big fan of boots, and have about ten pairs of long boots, which I know is ridiculous, but I can't bring myself to throw any out. 99

JOANNE MERCER

Joanne Mercer was born in Oldham, England, in 1965. In the first ten years of her life she moved countries six times before going to boarding school in Ashford, Kent. When she completed her schooling at the age of eighteen, she joined her parents who were by that time living in Melbourne, Australia.

While she was studying (arts, majoring in geography) at the University of Melbourne, Joanne held down three part-time jobs: working as a casual sales assistant in Miss Shop at Myer in the young fashion department; as a barmaid; and as a house cleaner for three families.

In 1987, after graduating, she started a traineeship with Myer where she had the opportunity to work in marketing, buying, distribution and personnel. She went on to spend two years as the customer service manager at the Myer Chadstone store and then moved into the buying office as a trainee in the footwear division. She was quickly promoted into the role of buyer for the Miss Shop footwear division and was soon running her own department with a turnover of $5 million. She later went on to become buyer of up-market and designer shoes at Myer.

In 1998, together with two partners, Joanne managed to secure venture capital funding to buy an existing retail business of 21 shoe stores trading in Melbourne. The purchase gave the trio the opportunity to launch their own business: Joanne Mercer footwear. Today, Joanne Mercer has 27 stores and a wholesale business with annual sales of over $22 million.

Joanne and her daughter, Samantha Jane, live in Brighton, Melbourne where they enjoy a wonderful life together. When she's not working (which isn't often), Joanne is a keen skier and she jogs regularly, which helps her to stay fit and keep up with Samantha.

When did you and your family first realise that you had an entrepreneurial flair?

Between the ages of seven and ten I lived in Toronto, Canada, and I remember as a seven-year-old watching a fun run that went past the housing estate where we lived. It was a humid Toronto day, and my brother and I set up a stall at the top of a steep hill selling cups of cordial for twenty cents each. The demand was incredible and we soon ran out of cordial, but because it was a Sunday morning, the shops were closed and we couldn't re-stock, so we started selling water for ten cents a cup. We made around $50 that morning!

By the time I was nine, I was babysitting within the housing estate and I was popular among the kids, so I always got plenty of work. I worked as much as I could, mostly to save enough money to go on holidays when I was older. When I was eighteen, I moved to Australia. The week after I arrived I got myself a job working in the Miss Shop in Myer's Melbourne store, and hence my passion for fashion developed.

What was your first significant business venture and what did you learn from it?

When I was sixteen and at boarding school in London, I used to go up to Portobello Road and buy beads to make earrings, which my friends and I sold through school. We came up with the idea through an association that we had joined called Young Enterprise, which was run by the local government in Ashford, Kent. The idea was to teach kids the basic concepts of business within a fun, youthful environment. Initially it was really just an excuse for my friends and me to escape boarding school and meet some boys from the local community, but it turned out to be a great learning curve and a fantastic introduction to the concepts of stock, cash flow and of course, profit! It also taught me that I loved retail, fashion and running my own show. The only negative was that absolutely no boys joined the club! Nonetheless, we were having fun and learning, and we kept our small business going for more than a year.

> 66 She likes to be fashionable and to wear the latest shoes, but she will not pay outrageous prices. 99

How did you get into the footwear industry and what made you decide to go into business for yourself?

I really wanted to be a fashion buyer, and I got my first opportunity as an assistant buyer with Myer when I was 23 – it was in ladies' designer shoes – my dream job and first real introduction to the shoe business. In 1997, Colin Brown and I were both working for John Naccarella; Colin was in men's shoes, I was in ladies' upmarket shoes and John was our general manager. We were all good friends and more importantly, had enormous respect for each other's skills. Over a coffee one day we made the decision to launch a footwear business together. We saw a gap in the ladies' footwear market in Australia, and we felt there was room for a new concept. We saw that the department stores were moving away from their traditional offering of service and quality shoes, and that there was space for a specialty chain offering great service, a fashionable environment and quality, comfortable shoes at value prices.

Women today want to look fashionable, they're not intimidated by their age, they don't want to be boxed or categorised and they will dress according to their aspirations. Typically our customer is busy and works or has temporarily stopped working to have kids. She likes to be fashionable and to wear the latest shoes, but she will not pay outrageous prices. She is aware of value and is able to make intelligent, informed decisions – and for all of these reasons she will choose our product over the rest.

In the beginning, what were some of the business skills you were lacking and what did you do about it?

I was lacking in financial and accounting skills. It's easy to fall into the trap of thinking that you don't need those skills, that it's your job to develop the product, and that you can employ someone else to handle the financial side of the business – but I am now a firm believer that you need to have a real grasp on what is going on from a financial perspective. None of the three founders of our company were financially skilled. We had strong retailing skills, but we were missing what I now consider to be a fundamental link, and the company virtually went broke three years into the business. We had cash flow issues, we were losing money and we were struggling to survive, then we hit a crisis point that I've always felt I should have seen coming. The venture capital fund backing the business lost confidence and were only minutes away from appointing an administrator when John and I managed to find a buyer for their shares. This is probably the most stressful experience I've had in the business. I think our passion and fear of failure is what enabled us, against all odds, to pull through a deal at the last minute.

I decided to do something and work on developing my knowledge by obtaining a Masters in Business Administration, which has taken me five years to complete. And while it has been a major effort it has really helped me and given me confidence when it comes to looking at balance sheets, cash flows and talking to the banks.

What made you decide to self title your company, as opposed to giving it a generic name?

It was actually my partner John's idea. Colin, John and I thought about many names before deciding to call our company Joanne Mercer. We did this because I was the product developer and could speak with authority about the shoes and the styling. I was also a woman in an industry that was surprisingly male-dominated. Most shoe manufacturers are male, and when I was a footwear buyer with Myer I was the only woman out of seven buyers in the division. It seemed to make sense to have a face behind the name and a spokesperson. The three of us were all equal shareholders, however, it was simply that I was the woman and the product person.

Surprisingly, 98 per cent of businesses never grow beyond one or two stores. How did you manage to roll out 27 stores across Australia in such a short period of time?

We bought an existing business of 21 stores called PB Shoes. This gave us a platform to launch our business via an existing infrastructure with stores, staff and a head office. While we didn't take on all of the head office staff and we actually closed down the majority of the PB stores, it gave us a vehicle through which to expand into the market a little more rapidly. Nowadays, we only trade in two of the original PB sites and we have moved our head office.

I also think it's about location, which proved to be one of the biggest challenges for our business in the early stages. Choosing the right location is absolutely critical, because any mistake is a five-year mistake – once that lease is signed there is very little that can be done about it if the store doesn't perform to expectations. John looks after leasing and we have learnt through bitter experience to never be optimistic about what we think a store might do in terms of sales turnover. Being very conservative when it comes to site selection is a must, and we now have a very tight performance model that the store must pass before we sign a lease. Even then, it is a Board decision that is passed by all shareholders prior to a final signature.

With the fashion world changing so rapidly, how do you keep up-to-date with trends?

I travel to Europe and America at least twice a year to get a feel for their market trends and I constantly look at magazines to keep up with what's in fashion. I am also a great believer in understanding our customer, so I like to look at what people are actually wearing today in Australia. We run surveys to understand what our customers are looking for, and it's not always the latest diamante thong from Gucci! Customers are usually pretty sensible with their shoe purchases and are looking for shoes that suit their lifestyles, rather than the latest fad from Europe – the fact that Ugg boots on stiletto

tully

heels are the latest fashion in London doesn't necessarily mean I will run them in our stores, the shoes must be relevant to our target market.

How much time do you spend in the design and selection of the shoes?

Not as much as I would like. I am still very much involved with the day-to-day running of the business, with allocations, cash and boring stuff like that all falling under my responsibility. I probably spend around 40 per cent of my time on product design and development, but as we continue to grow this will become higher.

What I actually keep an eye on in the business is *quality* and *cash*, and what my team is up to. I ask the type of questions which are vital, but tough to answer, such as are we providing the stores with the shoes that are selling well, and in the right quantities? And, are we up-to-date with our work?

A retail business is nothing without stock on the floor so this is my big focus. I probably drive everyone in the office crazy with my absolute obsession to get stock out to the stores, but my philosophy is 'we can't sell it if it is in a warehouse, or sitting at the supplier'.

Having already cracked the retail market why did you choose to move into wholesale distribution?

I chose to move into wholesale distribution because it was a natural progression for our business that wouldn't incur too many additional costs. There are many parts of Australia where we are unlikely to ever open our own retail store, perhaps due to distance or because our concept may not be relevant to the particular market. For example some country and regional areas would not be suitable for a Joanne Mercer store because our range is quite 'dressy' and corporate. So it makes sense for us to wholesale to stores where the retailer understands their market and their customers' needs. They can then choose from our range in order to be appropriate for *their* customers. We'd prefer to sell through these stores rather than try and have 250 stores of our own across the country.

Why do you say that the shoe business is one of the toughest to be in?

Footwear is highly competitive and largely driven by price in Australia. The department stores have led an aggressive price war by constantly discounting and eroding profit margins. And there are many other competitors; anyone can open a shoe shop, even boutiques and clothing stores are now moving into the footwear market. Profit margins are slight to begin with because Australian consumers are generally not prepared to spend a lot on their shoes, they're typically more concerned about spending money on their homes or lifestyles. Plus with a population of only twenty million we are not a very big country and we have an enormous amount of choice when it comes to spending our disposable income.

Have there ever been times when you wanted to give up, and if so, what got you through?

Yes, there have been many times when I wanted to give up. For example, I once got someone whom I did not trust involved with the business. If someone can't be trusted, don't go near them, even if you think they may add value. Unfortunately, I learnt the hard way and found myself in a situation where this person nearly succeeded in sacking my business partner and taking over the running of the company.

What has pulled me through times like this is personal pride and a fear of failure. It also helped that my business partners were strong pillars of support. John and Colin were always more positive than me, believing that we would make it in the end, John in particular always believed that we would survive. I was the more doubting, anxious person as we went through our very tough times. I knew that life would be easier and that we could earn more money with less stress working for someone else. Instead, we took salary cuts just to survive, we had to downsize and keep our confidence up in front of our staff and investors – if we didn't believe in the concept then how were they expected to? It has paid off, but certainly there were times when I really didn't feel confident that we were going to make it.

Another thing that got me through was saying to myself, 'Life wasn't meant to be easy'. There are many people in the world who have *real* problems, mine were just business, and they weren't anywhere near as important. Keeping that in mind gave me the determination to keep plugging away.

Who are the mentors that have inspired you and what important lessons have you learnt from them?

I have had a few significant mentors in my life, including:

My dad, he is highly intelligent and a very high achiever within the corporate world, and he always expected his kids to do well too, although both

> 66 I was the more doubting, anxious person as we went through our very tough times. 99

my brother and I have ended up in our own businesses rather than in a big company!

Cathie Molloy, who was my first boss when I became an assistant buyer at Myer, was an inspiration to me in every way. She was one of the most professional people I have ever had the pleasure of working with. She had an incredible work ethic, and always had the time and patience to teach. I will always remember my first day in the buying office; I was really nervous and had absolutely no idea of where to start. Cathie was flying out to Italy the next day and was clearly extremely busy, but she still managed to sit down with me, run me through her expectations, show me how to cost orders and give me some interesting work to do. Cathie inspired me to be more thoughtful and patient, and whatever stress I was under, to give the appearance of calm to the outside world.

Michael Carr, my ex-husband, gave me the encouragement and financial support I needed to give my business idea a go. He taught me that it is okay to take a risk, that it's not something to be feared, and that in life you have to give things a go and believe in yourself.

My current business partner and the Managing Director of Joanne Mercer, John Naccarella, is continually a great inspiration to me. John is a highly motivated person with an energy level that I have never previously encountered – I don't think he ever sleeps! John has a passion for business and an absolute belief in his ability to deliver results against all odds. He always makes me have faith in myself, which helps in the critical times. He has inspired me, even during the low times, over the last ten years.

My daughter Samantha has challenged me more than anyone in my life. Her determination to get things done, her generosity and her sensitivity have really brought a balance into my life that is very much needed.

And then there are my two closest friends, Amber Moore and Debbie Brown. Amber has herself proven that through hard work and determination you can do anything. And Debbie (my running buddy) who is much smarter, more logical and less emotional than me has continually provided me with sensible, positive advice throughout this journey.

What do you think are some of the essential characteristics of a successful entrepreneur?

- Be prepared to take risks based on research, and take the plunge when it is necessary.
- Be focused about achieving your goals.
- Be prepared to sacrifice parts of your life (leisure time, holidays, etc.) in order to reap the benefits later.
- Love what you do.
- You need drive – it could be to make money, to be successful, to become famous – it doesn't matter as long as you have something that keeps you motivated.

If anyone can succeed in business no matter what their background or circumstances, what do you think holds people back from becoming successful entrepreneurs?

I believe that people run out of energy and belief easily. The first few years are often the toughest and I think sometimes people lack the ability to see things through. Starting a business can destroy your personal life, be a huge impost on your family, can be all-consuming, and it will take a toll that leaves many people questioning whether it really is all worth it.

Many good ideas just don't get enough time because people run out of money and confidence. It's hard to keep pursuing something that isn't making money. However, you need to maintain faith in your business and know that if you have a good business plan then there should be nothing stopping you. It's also really important to source enough capital to provide for your business.

You also need to evaluate your staff. Don't put blind faith in people whom you don't know. And although it may be cheaper to go for people of lower quality, in the end it can cost you loads more and be extremely damaging to your business.

What are the key characteristics you look for when employing store managers?

At Joanne Mercer, we employ by looking for attitude first and then for experience. Of course, we do want highly experienced individuals who have been successful in managing a footwear business in the past, but the right person must have the right attitude. Self-starters, who have the passion and will to make a business successful are the most likely candidates. One of our best store managers in Adelaide, Naomi, had never worked in a footwear store before, but her work ethic, her willingness to learn and her passion for the job resulted in her being promoted to the position of state manager for South Australia. We want people who will treat this business like it is their own. I am always saying to my team, 'Treat it like it's your business and your money. If you had to make a decision, what would you do then?'

In order to maintain this calibre of staff, we put all of our area managers through leadership workshops to assist them in their roles. We also regularly send people off for specific workshops and training sessions to keep their minds active and to keep enhancing their performance at work. All of our staff have regular training sessions with their area managers as well as in-store coaching to ensure that customer service standards are consistent and maintained across the company.

We have a very family approach to our business. John and I are both very visible and accessible to our staff. We have had many staff leave only to come back saying they enjoyed their time working with us and that they missed the company. We can't afford to pay more but we try to compensate by creating enjoyment for people in their work. Retailing is fun and should be enjoyed.

Do you have any weaknesses when it comes to business?

Of course, I have many of them! One weakness would be my intolerance. I am impatient and get frustrated with people too quickly. At times, I can be moody and snappy when I am under pressure and when things are not going according to plan. I can also let myself get a bit chaotic – I take on too much and then find myself running around like an idiot and end up tired, run down and inevitably sick. Over the last few years I seem to have had a number of health issues, some of which I have no doubt are related to stress and exhaustion, which I have brought upon myself by trying to cram too much into my life.

I don't always handle criticism well – it seems to depend on my mood. In retail you need to be able to handle criticism because there's plenty forthcoming: the range is never quite right, we never have enough stock of our best-sellers and classic styles, we always have too many poor performing shoes. It's important to possess a very thick skin, and some days it needs to be thicker than others.

I am also not always a great networker or socialiser, I don't enjoy this aspect of the business. While I am a very social individual, I often feel I don't give enough time to friends and family, so I tend to resent having to be out at work functions at night, unless it is for our stores and will have a direct impact on our business.

> 66 It's important to possess a very thick skin, and some days it needs to be thicker than others. 99

If you weren't buying and selling shoes, what other type of business would you be involved in?

I have a passion for retail, so I can't really see myself in any other industry. After shoes and clothing, my next love is cosmetics. To me, this industry knows how to market better than any other. They are experts in selling their customers a dream, controlling and managing their distribution and selling space, and delivering service to the consumer. It is an industry we could all learn from in terms of branding and one I can easily imagine myself getting involved in. Who knows, perhaps Joanne Mercer will one day have a cosmetics range!

What are some of your personal and business goals for the next five to ten years?

- To see our business grow to a sales turnover of between $150 and $200 million per year.
- To be the first choice destination for women in our target market – they need to forget about those department stores where they can never get any service!
- To have more quality time with my friends and family, as they have been somewhat neglected over the past few years, and I would like to see them back up in terms of my priorities.
- To get a dog.
- Recently I hiked through the Himalayas with the most amazing group of people, it was one of the best holidays of my life. Next, I'm looking forward to going skiing in Northern Italy where I spent many a great holiday as a kid growing up.
- To improve my game of tennis, so that I am good enough to have a match with my daughter.
- To grow both the wholesale and retail business overseas. We have an ambition to one day have stores in China and be wholesaling our shoes in England.

Travelling the world buying shoes would have to be almost every woman's dream come true. Do you still get a buzz out of it, or is it all just in a day's work?

Of course, I still get a buzz! Sometimes I resent all the travel I do, because it can be exhausting and I am a bit of a homebody. I also miss my family so much when I'm away, especially my daughter Samantha who means everything to me. But I love it, I love my job, I love our business and I love shoes.

It is hard work though – don't be under the illusion that I pop around the world looking at shoe designs! A large part of my time is spent working in factories, in fairly grim environments, detailing shoes. Some days I leave the hotel at 6.00am and don't return until 10.00pm, having driven for eight hours and spent the other eight hours working in factories. Going to China regularly can be hard work, it's not as though I get the chance to visit the Great Wall while I am away. Time is of the essence, so I fly overnight and am on a tight schedule at the factory. It's sad to say that in seven years of business travel, I don't think I've managed more than three days as a tourist.

Bringing overseas markets to domestic shores is a great opportunity, and as much as I might complain about the travel, I know it's a fundamental part of our business and one that has contributed to its success.

What are your favourite shoes to wear and (be honest now) how many pairs do you own?

My favourites are a pair of diamante evening shoes in pink, which are part of our Joanne Mercer Italian Collection. I love their elegance and classic beauty. I am a big fan of boots, and have about ten pairs of long boots, which I know is ridiculous, but I can't bring myself to throw my beloved old boots out. I probably have around 100 pairs of shoes, which may sound outrageous, but many women have a passion for shoes and while 100 pairs would be on the high side, it's certainly not way out of the ordinary. But even with all those shoes, I will often go to my cupboard and feel that I don't have just the right pair to wear for the occasion!

FREE BONUS GIFT

Sandy Forster (featured later in this book) has kindly offered a FREE BONUS GIFT valued at $47.00 to all readers of this book....

Secrets to MEGA Business Success – Having struggled in small business for many years, Sandy finally discovered the secrets to success and went on to create a number of businesses, generating millions of dollars without spending a cent on advertising! In this special transcript from one of Sandy's LIVE events, she shares her complete uncensored story and how you can explode the success of your business. Certainly a must read!

Simply visit the website below and follow the direction to download direct to your Notebook or PC.

www.SecretsExposed.com.au/female_entrepreneurs

SUE ISMIEL

> ❝ I love sitting around the boardroom table with my talented staff throwing ideas around, and then seeing the fruits of those ideas sitting on supermarket shelves and being used by families around the world. ❞

SUE ISMIEL

Sue Ismiel was born in Syria in 1958 and migrated to Sydney with her family in the 1970s. When she arrived Sue did not speak English, but she quickly learnt and completed her higher school certificate. By the time she was in her early thirties, she was married with three young daughters, and working as a medical records keeper in a hospital.

It was at this time that Sue created a product that would change her life – Nad's Natural Hair Removal Gel. It was originally designed to help her youngest daughter avoid the embarrassment she suffered due to having dark hair on her arms. For more than a year Sue experimented with formulations in her kitchen until she had a product that worked.

With no business skills or experience, but plenty of determination, Sue marketed her new product, first at local markets and shopping centres, and then on television. By 1997, Nad's had won the Woolworths Best New Product award and within a decade, Sue had created a multimillion-dollar business, with Nad's Natural Hair Removal Gel becoming the market leader both in Australia and the United States.

Sue has built on the enormous success of Nad's, launching brand extensions and marketing other personal care products and brands. She employs a small but dedicated team of people, including her husband Sam and daughters Natalie and Nadine.

As a Christian, Sue believes that with success comes obligation, and she supports numerous charities and community organisations. She also thrives on empowering, motivating and encouraging her three young daughters' and the younger generation of women.

Sue is committed to keeping physically and mentally fit and enjoys yoga and meditation.

Why did your family choose to migrate from Syria to Sydney?

We originally came to Australia because my mother's sister (her only living relative) had moved here a few years earlier and my mother wanted to be close to her. Coming to Australia was a dream for my entire family and we arrived here with visions of a better life. But it wasn't as easy as I thought it would be. I hadn't realised that the language barrier would be such a problem. As a teenager I had to go back to basics and relearn my ABCs, and I struggled in my first years at school here as a result. I also encountered racism and taunts from some of the girls at my school who teased me for not being able to speak English. That experience made me determined to not be a victim. I learnt English as quickly as possible and worked hard to achieve success. In hindsight, the difficulties I faced in those first years in Australia were far outweighed by many happy memories and successes.

You were working as a medical records keeper, so where did the inspiration to create a hair removal product come from?

My daughter, Natalie, was my inspiration for creating a natural hair removal product. As a young child she was self-conscious about the dark hair on her arms, which is typical of so many girls from Middle Eastern backgrounds. She was so self-conscious that she always wore long sleeve tops, even in the summer. When she was eight years old she was asked to be a flower girl at my cousin's wedding, and although she looked beautiful, her discomfort about showing her arms made me determined to do something to solve her problem.

We started with bleaching, but that didn't have a lasting effect and only made the hair thicker and stronger. Waxing was too harsh on her delicate skin, so we tried the mechanical hair removal machines, but again we were unsuccessful. One day I thought to myself, 'Enough is enough. I have to stop complaining about the problem and do something about it. There is nothing out there for her, so I'll just have to create it'.

66 I quickly realised that this was something I was going to have to do by myself... **99**

I researched, and through trial and error in my own kitchen, I combined ingredients such as sugar, honey, glucose, water and lemon juice to create a product that worked in the same way as traditional waxes, but without heating or chemicals. I used my very patient husband and colleagues at the hospital as 'guinea pigs' for my experiments. In fact, it was the hospital matron who insisted that this strange green goo that I had concocted for my young daughter should be sold to the wider public, and I gradually began to see the sense in that; after all, if my daughter could benefit, maybe I could help others as well.

Once you had the perfect formula how did you find a manufacturer?

The Inventors' Association of Australia was the first place I went when I wanted to take the product public. They directed me to many people who saw its potential and promised me the world, but in the end no one would take the risk on a new product because the economy was in recession. I quickly realised that this was something I was going to have to do by myself, so I had machinery designed and built to produce the product at a rate of about 150 jars per batch. I was still working at Minchinbury Hospital at that stage, so I took it all one step at a time.

In 1993, following the success of our *Good Morning Australia* (GMA) infomercial, we built a new plant with the capacity to produce 1,500 jars per batch, which was more than enough to meet demand at the time with additional capacity for when we went retail. But little did we know what was around the corner! When we launched in the massive United States market in 2000, our plant was stretched beyond its limits – we had the production lines working 24 hours a day, seven days a week. Trucks loaded with huge pallets of Nad's gel were constantly driving in and out, loading up the shipment to America. It was more than our plant could keep up with.

At that point we had to make a strategic decision – did we want to be a manufacturer or marketer of personal care products? We decided that marketing was our key strength and opted to outsource our production to a large Australian facility. This has allowed us to concentrate on developing other products and brands, rather than just being a manufacturer of a single product. I think it is important in business to concentrate on the areas where your strengths are because ultimately that is what you probably have the most passion for and it will also give you the greatest benefit.

Why did you choose the name Nad's?

Nad's was named after my eldest daughter Nadine, despite the fact that Natalie was the inspiration for it. I originally called the product 'Nadine's', but I found that it was already trademarked, so I just removed a few letters and called it Nad's.

It wasn't until a few years later that I became aware of the *other* meaning of the word. When we launched in America, people used to be intrigued and ask, 'Do you know what that means over here?' And I'd have to say, 'Yes, it means the same thing in Australia'. But why be concerned? We've turned what could have been a slightly embarrassing name into a virtue, and we have fun with it in a tongue-in-cheek way. For instance when we sponsored a surfboat crew we had t-shirts printed with the words 'Go Nad's'. It's a good way of attracting attention, and Australians have such a wonderful, cheeky sense of humour that the name has actually worked very well for us. It's certainly extremely memorable.

What did you think when people told you that you were crazy and that your idea would never work?

I loved it when people told me I was crazy because it put a fire in my belly. It made me think, 'Just you watch me'. The more people told me I couldn't do it, the more determined I became to prove them wrong. Negativity is a very destructive force, but I was determined not to give up. I'm a firm believer in the saying, 'If at first you don't succeed, try, try again'. People find it too easy to say, 'It can't be done', and not give it a go. That's why I find it very important to surround myself with positive people.

With no real business experience how did you influence people to buy Nad's?

Before Nad's I had never sold anything in my life. Even when the girls brought raffle tickets home from school for fundraising, I would buy them all myself because I didn't know how to sell a thing.

My first experience in selling to the public came when my sister and I set up a stall at the Flemington Markets. The first day we went it was obvious that we had no idea what we were doing. We had a display table covered with a colourful cloth, we had jars of the product and signs that we'd made ourselves – and we stood there ready and waiting, but people just walked by because they didn't recognise the product. Standing there with nothing to lose, I decided to start demonstrating Nad's on my sister's arm. A few people stopped to watch, then a few more, and within just a couple of hours we had sold *all* of our jars, and I had learnt a very important lesson about marketing my unique product.

The key to being able to sell the product once we got people's attention was being confident, and because we knew everything there was to know about it, we were confident. We told them how the product worked, what it did, how we came to make it and asked them if they'd like to try it. It was easy, and straightaway they would buy a jar. I replicated this basic demonstration on a *Good Morning Australia* infomercial, risking what was a huge amount of money to me at the time, but it was a risk that paid off. The phones rang hot and we sold 3,000 units in just four minutes.

Ultimately, I think if you have a good product that you believe in, and you are able to convey that passion and enthusiasm with confidence, then you will win people over.

Why did you choose to make the jump to selling on television and how did you finance such an expensive marketing strategy?

One day in 1993 I was watching TV and I saw someone demonstrating a food processor in a direct marketing segment on the Network TEN program, *Good Morning Australia*. I said to myself, 'Hang on, I have a better product than that! I could be doing that too!' So I picked up the phone and rang the program. The producer was so impressed with Nad's and the story behind it that she gave me the segment at a reduced rate, and allowed me to hold off payment until after it had gone to air. The response was absolutely incredible! I had organised a toll free number and a telemarketing company to take the calls, and we had about fifty girls but they couldn't keep up, the lines were jammed. We sold so many units that we more than paid for the infomercial.

Television turned out to be the key to success for Nad's because of its visual impact. The basic idea is to tell a story within a very short space of time – I introduced myself and the product, explained the reason for creating it and gave a demonstration. I believe people really connected with the story of a mother creating something out of love and concern for her daughter, and they could clearly see that the product worked. Over the years we have refined and developed our marketing campaigns, but television has always been a very powerful tool.

66 The phones rang hot and we sold 3,000 units in just four minutes. 99

How did you break into selling Nad's through supermarkets and chemists?

After four years of direct selling and receiving regular letters from my customers asking when they were going to see the product on the shelves, I entered into the retail market in 1997. I didn't know what to expect, but it was what the customers wanted, and I knew that I could sell the product for less by going retail instead of charging postage and handling on each individual order.

I wanted to take a calculated risk, so I began in just one State. We were getting the best results through our direct sales out of Queensland because of the climate, so I went to a broker and asked him to help me get the product into Woolworths in Queensland. The broker was very happy with the level of awareness of the product, as everyone he spoke to knew about Nad's. The Woolworths buyer was a little hesitant because the price positioned it at the premium end of the market, but I assured him that would not be a problem for my customers.

A week later we were given the go-ahead and the product went on the shelves. It was a huge investment but the response was incredible and we sold out everywhere. The number of units sold per store was unusually high for this product category, and within days the Woolworths buyer reported on the phenomenal success of Nad's to all of the other State buyers. That year, despite being the most expensive product in its category, Nad's was awarded Woolworths' Best New Product.

Once you started making money how did you go about growing your business?

Once we were established in the Australian market, I turned my attention to the huge US market. I negotiated a deal with a distributor and we duplicated the winning marketing strategy that we had used in Australia with phenomenal success. Women embraced the product. They loved our half-hour infomercials, which told the Nad's story and my personal journey set against scenic Australian backdrops. We became the highest rotation infomercial for weeks that year, and I became a minor celebrity.

I remember one day touring Disneyland with my daughters and an American man rushed up to us proclaiming, 'It's the Nad's lady!' Another time, I was visiting the Moulin Rouge in Paris with one of my daughters and I could see some people staring and nudging each other. Finally, one of them approached me – they were Americans and they wanted to know if I was the 'Nad's lady'.

With huge brand awareness and success, it wasn't long before US retailers came knocking on our door and we moved onto supermarket and pharmacy shelves, becoming number one in our category in just four years. We also became established in England, being sold in Harrods and Boots, and New Zealand.

After Nad's, what was your next major product launch?

The success of Nad's provided a solid base for the expansion of our product range. In 1999, we ventured into the growing supplements category with the new brand, WYLD. These herbal supplements have become enormously successful. In 2002, continuing our commitment to market naturally based products that solve the everyday problems of women and their families, we launched a range of natural head lice products. We had identified a gap in the market and the desire from women to not use chemically based products on their young children's heads. Again, we've had solid success with the Nad's Natural Head Lice products being leaders in the market.

We've also continued to expand our depilatory range – launching a hair removal range for men with Olympic swimmer Geoff Huegill as the 'face' of the products. And we've moved ahead in leaps and bounds with our women's range. One of our most outstanding successes was the brainchild of my talented elder daughter Nadine, who is the research and development chemist for our company. She identified an opportunity to invent a

> 66...having a network of trustworthy people to work with is very important. 99

device that makes it easier for women to remove unwanted facial hair, and in particular to sculpt their eyebrows, using the Nad's gel. Nadine came up with the concept of a 'facial wand' – a slimline, twist-action tube filled with the gel that enables women to easily get just the right amount to carefully sculpt their brows. The Nad's Facial Wand has been an outstanding success, winning awards and selling almost two million units since its launch in 2002. I couldn't be more proud of my clever daughter.

What's it like working with your husband and two of your three daughters?

My family has been involved with the business right from the start. There is nothing like working with family. If a company is to be successful then it obviously has to have a network of people who support it. In the past I have had bad experiences with people whom I trusted but didn't know very well, so having a network of trustworthy people to work with is very important. I have learnt over the years that the people who care most about you are your immediate family and your close friends, and they're the ones you can trust and rely on.

My husband Sam has always been my greatest support. He gave up his own work in 1993 as soon as I started advertising on TV. He was already working in the business part-time, as well as working in his own job, but the response to the TV campaign was so huge that I needed help, so soon we were working together full-time. Today he is a director of the company. His patience, more than anything, has been a great help to me. Like everyone, we do have our differences, but Sam has a great sense of humour and that tends to diffuse things really well.

In 2000 we renamed our company from Nad's Pty Ltd to Sue Ismiel and Daughters Enterprises Pty Ltd, to reflect the involvement of my daughters. Nadine is head of research and development, as well as being a member of the executive team. She has a very strong personality and often reminds me of myself. Quite often we disagree on things because we are so much alike. Natalie is currently our marketing coordinator, and as a model, she is also the face of Nad's print and television advertising campaigns. My youngest, Naomi, is a graphic designer. It is one of the great pleasures and rewards that I can continue to work and spend every day with my daughters even now that they have grown and left school.

Sue with her daughters, Natalie, Naomi and Nadine.

From your experience, do you believe that you should keep business and family life separate or are they 'one and the same'?

I believe the two go hand-in-hand. I approach the running of the business on the principal that what is best for my business is ultimately best for my family. If running the business presented an obstacle in some way to a happy family life I would review this philosophy, but to date we have worked very well alongside each other. We enjoy each other's company both at work and in our leisure time, and we all share a pride in the success of the business and a regard for each other as family and as professional colleagues.

What can we expect from Sue Ismiel and Daughters in the future?

The future holds endless possibilities for our business. I don't believe it will necessarily be restricted to any one field, but I am particularly interested in products or ventures that help people in some way to improve the quality of their lives. I am a very creative person and am constantly thinking about new opportunities and new ventures. This is a very important quality for an entrepreneur – I think if you can combine ideas, passion, creativity and hard work, you can achieve anything.

As a committed Christian how has the spiritual side of your life helped you in business?

My faith is integral to how I live my life. I believe it's important to live a good, kind and caring life and I try to do this in all aspects of my personal and business worlds. Through my business success I have gained considerable financial rewards, and I certainly enjoy the material pleasures this provides, but I couldn't enjoy them if I didn't also know that I was using my success to help others.

As a Christian I believe that with success comes an obligation to assist those less fortunate than ourselves, and I have financially assisted a number of people and organisations over the years. In 2002, I donated $600,000 to the prestigious Jean Hailes Foundation in Melbourne to fund a world-first study into women's health and hormones. This important research provides vital clues into women's wellbeing, and I hope and trust that it will help to unlock some of the clues to depression in women, and lead to a solution. I also support 100 children in Africa, women's refuges in Western Sydney, and disabled children in New South Wales.

Perhaps one of the most personally rewarding examples of the joy and pleasure of giving came through my being able to help a little Assyrian boy to hear for the first time in his life. His family contacted me about their son's plight and I tried to encourage a large number of people to each donate a small amount of money to help him have the necessary operation. But disappointingly, there was little response. I had already donated tens of thousands of dollars, but they still needed much more. For whatever reason, people didn't come forward to help, but I couldn't abandon him, so I paid the entire cost of the operation. The happiness and joy that was brought to this little boy and his family brought tears to my eyes. His family were so grateful and I feel so very honoured that I was able to help change their lives.

What do you think are some of the essential characteristics of a successful entrepreneur?

Possibly the most vital quality is the courage to have a go. There are many people with good ideas, who are very smart, or who are armed with business degrees but the big difference between those who do and those who don't is the courage and energy to take a risk and put those ideas into action.

A successful entrepreneur has to be single-minded about their success. Obviously you have to work hard, but it's important to have a vision of success in your mind and to relentlessly pursue that goal. You have to have a faith and belief in yourself, and not be dragged down by people who say, 'It can't be done'.

What is the biggest mistake you've ever made in business and what did you learn from it?

Sadly, my biggest business mistake was to invest too much trust in some people who

> 66 I also support 100 children in Africa, women's refuges in Western Sydney, and disabled children... 99

ultimately let me down. I wanted them to share in my success and I felt I was generous, but ultimately they wanted more than I felt was fair and reasonable. I felt exploited and let down, and it soured what had been positive relationships. Today, I have to be firmer in all business relationships and I am very careful to ensure that the I's are dotted and the T's are crossed. I have firm contracts in place that clearly outline what is due to each party, so there can be no risk of difficulties down the track.

What do you love most about business?

What I love most about business is the thrill of seeing ideas turned into reality. I love sitting around the boardroom table with my talented staff throwing ideas around, and then seeing the fruits of those ideas sitting on supermarket shelves and being used by families around the world. There is something magical about seeing a product materialise from abstract concepts, it's like a dream come true! It's a wonderfully creative and dynamic process. I love the buzz of success and I also love meeting new people and becoming aware of the opportunities out there.

If anyone can succeed in business no matter what their background or circumstances, what do you think holds people back from becoming successful entrepreneurs?

I think it can be summed up in one word: confidence. If you don't have the confidence to try and turn your dreams into reality you won't succeed. You have to be willing to get out there and put yourself on the line. Sometimes it can be humiliating and intimidating as there is always the risk of a very public failure and of falling flat on your face. So you really have to have the confidence to take all of that on and to stand up for yourself and what you believe in, even in the face of criticism and negativity.

What do you say to people who think it is too late to get into business and fear they've 'missed the boat'?

I'd say it's never too late. I was a mother in my thirties when I started my business. I had no business background or skills and I'm sure that I would have seemed to many people a very unlikely entrepreneur. But what I brought to my business was life experience and I wouldn't have had that if I'd started in my early twenties. I also had organisational skills, acquired through being a working mother, and an inner confidence that developed over the years, which I would have had less of in my twenties. And I had the invaluable support of a loving husband and family – my own personal cheer squad – whom I know I could not have become successful without. I think opportunities keep opening up throughout life, and you should never let age be a barrier to success.

What advice would you give to an aspiring entrepreneur who wants to get started in a business of their own?

I'd advise someone starting out to ask questions of as many people as they know in business. Find out about their experiences, their successes, their failures, what they would have done differently and so on. There's nothing like the knowledge that comes from the first-hand experiences of others who've been down that path.

I'd also strongly advise getting as much professional legal and financial advice as necessary. It can save a lot of time and grief down the track. Make sure you've worked on all the necessary regulatory issues involved with your business. Ignorance is no excuse. Ensure you have firm, unambiguous contracts in place with your staff and suppliers so there is no room for dispute down the track over who owns what and what the obligations are from both parties.

Have a vision of where you would like your business to be in the future and work hard to achieve it. This doesn't mean that you can't change your ambitions or your path, but you should be clear about the success you anticipate so you can learn to be flexible in your choices. Finally, I'd say believe in yourself and your capacity to achieve business success, and don't be put off or put down by negative people.

What are some of the ways people can go about deciding what type of business to get involved in?

There are a variety of reasons people go into different businesses, such as skills, interests and opportunities. My business was born from a combination of all three, but it occurred almost by chance.

If you have a particular skill-set it makes sense to centre your business on that. However, nothing beats an intrinsic interest in something as a foundation for a successful business. If you're passionate about what you do, you're going to love your work. I genuinely believe it's much easier to be successful if you're having fun doing what you do.

My passion is natural therapies and solutions for everyday problems. My business began because of my love for my young daughter, and I have grown the business around the things that I feel strongly about. I think it's important for people to consider natural alternatives before they start putting chemicals and drugs into their bodies. Of course, I wouldn't have a business if I were the only person who thought that. So opportunity obviously plays a large part in deciding what type of business people pursue; it's a happy coincidence for me that there is a worldwide trend toward natural products.

KIRSTY DUNPHEY

" Outside of work I'm a young looking 27-year-old in jeans and a t-shirt with messy hair and odd socks. In my head I know what a businesswoman 'should' look like...they're polished, glamorous, sharp and professional, but I'm rarely any of those things! **"**

KIRSTY DUNPHEY

Kirsty Dunphey was born in Darwin in 1979 to a very entrepreneurial family. In fact her parents both retired in their thirties after successfully running small businesses and having investment properties. Disaster then struck a few years later with both her parents ending up bankrupt and their marriage in tatters. Kirsty chose to use the examples, both good and bad, to inspire her to pursue her own entrepreneurial goals and as such she became a self-made millionaire by age 23.

Kirsty's business experience started early – at the age of just fifteen, she set up her first two small businesses. In 2001, at just 21 years of age Kirsty became the owner and managing director of M&M Real Estate – a brand new agency, in Launceston, Tasmania. It has recently joined forces with Harcourts with Kirsty and partner Tony Morrison leading this joint venture. Since its inception, M&M Harcourts has smashed many local records and now has the highest grossing sales team per person.

Kirsty is an active member of her local Launceston community and is fast becoming well-known in national real estate and business circles. She has been featured on the *Today* show, *Today Tonight*, and in *Cosmopolitan*, *Ocean Drive*, *BRW* and *Marie Claire* magazines, as well as in the *Herald Sun* and *The Age* newspapers. In 2002, Kirsty was named the national winner of the Telstra Young Business Woman of the Year Award – the youngest person to have ever received this honour.

Combining her passions for real estate, customer service, property investment, building wealth, youth potential, business practices and enhancing the public's perception of real estate agents, Kirsty now delivers around 30 keynote speeches a year to various business audiences. Her first book, *Advance to Go – Collect $1 Million*, was released in 2005.

Today, Kirsty has other business interests, loves to invest in property and was recently married.

When did you and your family first realise that you had an entrepreneurial flair?

Even from a very young age, I never wanted to be a fire fighter, a doctor or a ballerina like most of my friends, I wanted to have my own company, to be rich and to rule the world. When I was six years old I started my first entrepreneurial endeavour. I wanted what every six-year-old wants – toys, lollies and cake – so I set about developing my first business plan to enable me to have those things. The concept was simple really – to have a birthday party and thus receive lots of toys, lollies and cake. I sent invitations to everyone in my class, and even expanded the guest list to other grades in the school. But on the day of my party, my parents were not impressed – it was October and my birthday is in March. Children were sent home unhappy and we actually moved house shortly thereafter…I'm not sure if the two events were related!

What was your first significant business venture and what did you learn from it?

My first significant business venture was at the age of fifteen. While I was staying with my grandparents in Melbourne, I came across a fabulous jewellery shop. It was fabulous not only because their stock was cool, funky and appealing to me, but it was also at a price point that I could actually afford! I plucked up all my courage and put my car deposit on the line to purchase a wholesale order of around $1,000 worth. I didn't even really understand the term 'wholesale' and I was terrified that I was making the biggest mistake of my life. In fact, I was so terrified that I just held the jewellery for weeks not doing anything with it. Eventually I got over my fear, set up a market stall and had a very successful little business selling at markets and to shops, eventually bringing in wholesale orders from Thailand. In doing this, I learnt to trust my instincts, to not let fear control my life, and that once you've already taken the big leap to not stop mid-air but to keep going with it – it's definitely the hardest step you have to take.

> 66 I show my team the respect they deserve, and strive at all times to set an example that defies my age... 99

How old were you when you started M&M Real Estate (now M&M Harcourts) and what made you decide to get into such a highly competitive business?

I was 21 when we first opened our doors. I knew I wasn't the typical real estate agency principal, that is, I wasn't male and in my mid-fifties, but I had vision, drive and I was desperately looking for something to get my teeth stuck into. I wanted to make my mark and to make the transition from being someone who had ideas but thought there were no opportunities to make them a reality, to being someone who scrambled, clawed and grabbed at life until I created my own opportunities. I left a safe, dependable job because I wanted to prove to myself that I was the person I thought I was.

Why real estate? Why such a competitive industry? I've worked in the industry since I was fifteen, and done most jobs you can do in an agency – from being the filing slave, to a sales consultant. At first, real estate was in no way shape or form ever going to be my passion or what I would call a career! It was a stopgap, something familiar that I could do well until I found that elusive 'passion'. It wasn't until I began to sell that I discovered real estate actually fulfilled my career aspirations and that took me by surprise. I found it was fun and exciting, and that we had the opportunity to dramatically impact our clients' lives. The only thing that stood between me and my perfect career was that I was unable to advance to a higher level in the agency that I worked for. So I opened my own. As for the competition, I've always loved competition because it means choice for the consumer. What's more rewarding, winning a deal or listing where you know you've gone up against and beaten the best, or a 'walk in the park' deal? I know which one I would choose any day.

In the beginning was it difficult to manage staff, some of whom were twice your age?

I won't lie, there have been issues, at the end of the day though I believe that if I show my team the respect they deserve, and strive at all times to set an example that defies my age, then I will win their respect.

Where did you get the initial capital to start the business?

The initial capital for the business, $20,000, was funded by two $10,000 car loans; a 21-year-old wanting money to start a real estate agency was laughable, but that same 21-year-old wanting money for a car was apparently quite alright. We set a goal to pay back all of our debts within twelve months and actually ended up paying them back within three, and we've operated virtually debt-free since then.

What were some of the core values that you built your company upon?

My core values rest upon my desire to provide excellent customer service and to build clients for life, ones who are raving fans and the best advocates for our business. I've always been a firm believer that a spoken word from someone you trust is going to convince you of something twenty times more than any other form of marketing. Our aim on a day-to-day basis is to give our clients such exceptional service that they feel the need to spread the word and serve as our best and most powerful form of marketing.

Building a team of exceptional people is also of vital importance. I'm proud of the team we've created and we constantly make sure that this fabulous team are appropriately challenged, motivated and rewarded.

Innovation is another value, but probably the most difficult. We're in a market where it's only possible to be the 'first and only' for a short time before one of your competitors joins you. For example, if you have an active television marketing campaign it will only be a matter of time before your competitors do the same, so we're constantly revising and updating our ideas. Some work marvellously well (for example we have bought the cover of every Yellow Pages in Tasmania, which gives us amazing exposure), while other marketing campaigns do just so-so. At the end of the day we'd rather try something than kick ourselves because our competitors got to it first and made it a huge success.

What is the most important thing you have learnt about succeeding in business?

The power of leverage. Watching my parents in small business throughout my childhood was incredibly inspiring, but I always saw that there was little leverage in their endeavours, which placed a ceiling on how high they could go and how much they could achieve. As hard as they worked, their business was limited by the simple fact that we all have just 24 hours in a day. Ray Kroc didn't become the business mogul he was by flipping burgers; he used leverage in the form of trained teenagers. This leverage was so widespread that in 1992 it was estimated that seven per cent of the American workforce had their first jobs at McDonald's. Janine Allis, founder of Boost Juice, uses the power of a huge workforce and franchising in much the same way. As hard as it has been for me in my business to learn to delegate authority, it's been the best move I've made and has generated so much growth. I promise my staff every day that soon I'll stop being such a control freak!

What do you love most about business?

I love the variety and seeing the fruits of my achievements – the financial and emotional rewards that come from growing a business. However, what I love the most are the challenges that pop up regardless of how well your organisation operates, and the ways that I grow as a person when trying to adapt and overcome them. Something takes over when I'm challenged and pushed out of my comfort zone. That's when I'm most tested as a businessperson and as a leader. I can usually rate the highlights of my week as the times when I've been most thrown by a problem and have managed to make the best of the situation.

I teach my sales team that we need to love objections in the form of prospective home sellers saying, 'I don't want to list with you because....' The reason we learn to love objections is because once you've been given the objection you have a golden opportunity to fix that problem, to resolve that issue and to get the deal. And I've learnt to translate this concept of *loving objections* into my business as well. For example, if a staff member comes to me and lets me know that they're not happy, what they're really saying is, 'I have an objection that I want to get resolved', likewise, if a client has a complaint what I hear them saying is, 'I have an objection, fix it so fabulously that I'll remain a loyal client'. If the staff member or client is saying nothing, then you can guarantee two things: one, they're already looking elsewhere for employment or for another business to service their needs; and two, they're probably bad-mouthing you or your company to anyone who will listen. I love objections, I love challenges, and I especially love the opportunity to fix problems.

What is a typical day in the life of Kirsty Dunphey?

5:50am	I wake up (most days!), bearing in mind that I'm not a natural early riser, this is something I've had to learn because I wasn't finding time to exercise after work.
6:15am	Go to the gym with some girls from work, again not something that's natural to me – I used to think that people who went to gyms were strange, but now I'm a convert.
7:00am	At work, I plan my day. Planning is the most important part of my day. I'm a punctuality freak and a concisely planned day is really important to me. I even plan time for the unexpected interruptions!

7:30am	Read and reply to emails – I get around 150 emails a day so making time to read and answer them is vital.
8:00am	Early staff conferences.
8:30-10:00am	Staff/weekly meetings most days. Each of our departments (administration, property management, sales, and management) meets weekly and we have a monthly team meeting.
11:00-1:00pm	Training sessions. Ongoing training and education is of vital importance.
1:00-6:00pm	Meetings, appointments, media-related issues.
6:00pm	Plan tomorrow.
6:30pm to Whenever	Work on long-term initiatives and make sure I'm on track. If I think I'm getting off track I'll brainstorm ways in which I can fix it.

I'm usually home by 8.00pm at the latest and I now also try not to work on Sundays for more than two or three hours. I also find time to sit on the Beacon Foundation Board, which is a charitable foundation dealing with youth unemployment across the country; the Tasmania Together board; and the Auctioneers and Real Estate Agents Trust. Plus I do a number of keynote speaking and training engagements, and a lot of other fun stuff!

As society becomes ever more sales-resistant, what are some techniques that you and your team use to lower resistance and increase trust?

The community does have a high resistance to salespeople and I believe it has an even higher resistance to real estate agents. I almost feel like it's my personal crusade to prove to people that yes, like in any industry, there have been those not-so-savoury types in real estate, but the industry is also full of hard-working, ethics-driven people.

Our sales team works by getting a high proportion of business through personal contacts and referrals. We cultivate a strong culture of continual client and database contact, so that we're not just strangers trying to sell people a service, but instead we become the trusted real estate advisers to these families. Our mission statement reflects this, it is 'Clients for life through the finest service'.

The team at the Harcourts Australian Awards Night. That's Kirsty with her tongue sticking out!

What makes a good closing for a sale?

The best tip I can give is to actually get up the guts to ask for the business *every* time. It sounds silly, and far too trivial, but it's the most overlooked component of many presentations. Just the other morning our sales team conducted a training session purely on closing – it's a vital component of our business. We spoke first about the initial resistance most people have to closing; all of our lives we're conditioned to believe that asking for things is bad or rude and that rejection is the absolute worst! You really have to break that conditioning within your own head if you want to be a good closer.

At the end of the day closing is an art form and if you want to be good at it, research. Read some books by Zig Ziglar and others that are good at closing sales, and find a terrific closer in your area and ask them when, how soon

66 I'm a firm believer in the saying, 'If you risk nothing, you gain nothing'. 99

and how often they start closing – the answers might surprise you! You'll hear that some people start closing as soon as they get to the presentation, while others start even sooner!

What do you think are some of the essential characteristics of a successful entrepreneur?

One of the most essential qualities is to not be risk averse. Risks can be calculated and well thought-out, but I'm a firm believer in the saying, 'If you risk nothing, you gain nothing'.

You also cannot focus on what you don't have, or who you aren't. If I wanted to I could focus on the fact that I'm a university dropout from a broken and bankrupt family. Instead, I choose to see only those aspects about myself that enable me to be confident and to feel as though I'm the very best person to be doing what I do with our business and with our team of staff.

Most of the successful entrepreneurs that I know don't shy away from hard work and have been brought up with a good work ethic. And many have shown a creative flair or spirit from an early age.

What are some of the ways people can go about deciding what type of business to get involved in?

There's a quote I love that says, 'Choose a job you love and you will never have to work a day in your life'. I believe that being passionate about your job definitely makes it easier to go the hard and long miles that you have to in small business. Conversely, you may simply be passionate about running a business, meeting and exceeding budgets and managing staff, and if that's the case, you're lucky because you could find happiness and success in any almost any business you choose, from a Subway franchise to a Laundromat.

What do you say to people who think it is too late to get into business and fear they've 'missed the boat'?

People have always said that, and they'll continue to say it, there are two things that these people lack – ideas and/or drive. Imagine if in the seventies Bill Gates thought that he'd already missed the computer boat, or if in the nineties Brin and Page, the men behind Google, thought they had missed the boat because Yahoo!, AltaVista and the like were already dominating the market. If you've identified something that's missing in people's lives and have the opportunity to fill that void, then you've never missed the boat. I could have said the same thing when it came time to open our business, after all Launceston didn't *need* another real estate agency, there were already plenty! But I saw a void, something missing in terms of service and innovation, and aspired to fill that void.

If anyone can succeed in business no matter what their background or circumstances, what do you think holds people back from becoming successful entrepreneurs?

A lack of confidence in themselves, and the vision and drive to purse their dreams. Having had strong entrepreneurial desires from such a young age, I only recently came to the realisation that not everyone is like that! And that was difficult for me to accept, but I've realised that you have to want it badly to make it as an entrepreneur. Some will dream about it, some will do it and some will be perfectly happy and content to work for those entrepreneurs, rather than trying to become one themselves.

Where did your motivation and passion to achieve the things you've done come from?

My parents have always involved me in their lives like I was an adult. From an early age I was in awe of them. I watched them build their businesses, invest in property and work toward early retirement and freedom. But disaster struck, and after having achieved their financial goals and retiring, my parents went through some bad times financially. I've seen what went wrong and how it decimated our family, and that's been a strong motivator. I've been doubly blessed because I've had the best financial education anyone could possibly have by seeing both what success is like and what a downfall is like. My passion comes from wanting to make sure that my family never struggles again. I use the lessons my parents taught me on a day-to-day basis to work toward this.

Who are the mentors that have inspired you and what important lessons have you learnt from them?

I only discovered the concept of mentors in the past few years when another real estate principal approached me and offered to be my mentor. He gives me advice and assistance based on his own considerable experience and the relationship has worked fabulously well. I now have a public speaking coach/mentor and many wonderful businesswomen whom I consider mentors. I've been surprised by the generosity and openness of the people whom I've approached or who have approached me.

If you feel like you need a mentor, ask someone whom you respect, and if you're someone who is experienced in your field, please go out and find a young or less experienced person who could benefit from your assistance and mentoring. If all else fails, find books (just like this one) that can give you all the information and advice you need until you get a real-life mentor. I always say that a mentor is only as far away as your local library and it's free, so no one has an excuse not to get inspired.

What habits have you formed in order to create a life of success?

I'm a spontaneous person by nature and yet I realise the need to form habits, routines and patterns to shape my business days. My daily routines include:

- Exercise on a daily basis. Now that I've been doing this for a few months I really notice the difference on the days I miss out – I'm not as relaxed and I don't feel as healthy.

- Make someone else feel amazing. Whether it is a staff member, a client or my partner, it's a daily goal to make someone go home with a smile because of something I've recognised about him or her.
- Learn something new each day. This could be anything from a new word from dictionary.com's word of the day or a new business technique.
- Get inspired. I usually do this by finding quotes that inspire me, these are a few of my favourites:
  - *Success is getting what you want; happiness is wanting what you get.* Ingrid Bergman
  - *Focus always precedes success.* Denis Waitley
  - *Your attitude is either the lock on, or key to your door of success.* Denis Waitley
  - *It's not what you are that holds you back, it's what you think you're not.* Denis Waitley
  - *People often say that motivation doesn't last. Well, neither does bathing – that's why we recommend it daily.* Zig Ziglar
  - *If you don't risk anything, you risk even more.* Erica Jong
  - *Effective communication is 20% what you know and 80% how you feel about what you know.* Jim Rohn

Apart from business, are there any other asset classes that you invest in and why?

The most obvious choice for me is real estate and over the past few years I've build up a good-sized portfolio of properties in Tasmania and Melbourne. I'll also happily invest in other businesses; it's just a matter of finding ones that take my fancy.

I was recently challenged by some girl-friends to find a hobby. My involvement in the business can sometimes mean a lack of time and balance, and I can be fairly lopsided in my interests. I often try to

> 66...a mentor is only as far away as your local library and it's free, so no one has an excuse not to get inspired. 99

convince people that work counts as an interest…right? I decided to take up their challenge and learn about the stock market. I'm in the middle of doing some online classes and recently created a small portfolio of leveraged shares that are doing quite well. It's my aim to build up my financial literacy in this area and then expand my investments further in the next few months.

You recently wrote your first book, tell us a bit about it.

My book, which came out in 2005, is called *Advance to Go – Collect $1 Million*. The title comes from my childhood love of playing Monopoly, and symbolises how my life has changed from playing with little green houses, to owning lots of real houses.

There are two main sections in the book. The first is the story of my life so far – but I'll be the first to say this is *not* an autobiography! My aim was just to show that financial achievement is possible no matter what background you come from. I'd like to think of teenagers (as well as adults) reading it and getting inspired to start working toward their own financial futures, believing that they have no boundaries and no limitations regardless of their current situation. The second part of the book is tips and lessons I've learnt so far in my real estate and small business careers. It's my aim for the book to be relevant not only to people in real estate or running their own businesses, but to anyone who is just starting out in any industry – especially those where superb customer service is a must.

You are now an accomplished public speaker. Were you always good at speaking or is it a skill that you've had to develop?

I'm a terrified public speaker! After winning the 2002 Telstra Young Business Women's Award a lot of doors started to open for me with the media and speaking. The only problem was, I'm not a public speaker. I'd never been interested in it. I had never so much as done a debate, been on stage or in a play and I was petrified at the idea of talking to a group larger than about ten people – in fact, even speaking to ten strangers would send me into a tailspin! However, I do thrive on a challenge and I hate the thought that I can't do something or that I'd let my emotions hold me back from a positive experience. So I bit the bullet and decided to accept a small speaking gig. I started with school groups so that I could speak to young people and now I speak around three or four times a month at different types of seminars. Ironically, the ones I now find the most fun are those in front of more than 1,500 people because I find that people lose their inhibitions more in a large group and I can get them excited and involved. I'm still very much learning the craft of speaking, I have a coach who is fabulous and I always get as much feedback as I possibly can after speaking.

Still being so young, do you find the time to let your hair down and just have fun?

At 27 I am still young and of course I still have fun! Perhaps it's condensed into smaller timeframes, but I'm concentrating a lot more effort right now on making sure that I have more balance in my life, even if that means I need to pencil 'fun' into my schedule. I make sure I get to the gym often with some girls from work, I'm a huge movie fan and television is my total relaxation so I make sure I get to the movies and relax in front of the TV often. Apart from that, like anyone I just make sure I'm allowing time for friends and family.

What sets you apart from the other women in this book?

I'm usually intimidated at first, despite my confidence, when I meet other female entrepreneurs. Many of the other women in this book, without them even knowing it, are mentors and role models to me. What makes me different to them? I would suggest that I don't necessarily always look the part.

Outside of work I'm a young looking 27-year-old in jeans and a t-shirt with messy hair and odd socks (which I somehow manage to wear to work as well). In my head I know what a businesswoman 'should' look like, after all I've been reading about them for so many years. They're polished, glamorous, sharp and professional, but I'm rarely any of those things! In the beginning, this self-imposed stereotype certainly did hold me back somewhat in terms of my own confidence about what type of businesswoman I was! But now I've come to grips with the fact that short of hiring a professional stylist 24/7 I'm not always going to be polished – and I'll just have to live with that!

If you had your time over again what would you do differently?

I wouldn't change a thing. All the mistakes, all the rough times, everything I've gone through has led me to where I am today and I'm delighted with the result. The journey, regardless of its many twists and turns, ups and downs, highs and lows, has made me the person I am today and I feel like it's a person that I can be proud of, that my family can be proud of and that my team can be proud of. I'm continually growing, learning and striving to be better.

 FREE BONUS GIFT

Kirsty Dunphey has generously offered a FREE BONUS GIFT valued at $29.95 to all readers of this book...

Kirsty's Tips to Business Success – Having become a self-made millionaire at the tender age of 23, in this eBook Kirsty shares 21 powerful tips to maximise your business success and create a happy life. Learn how to turn obstacles into opportunities, how to find your life's purpose, how to become financially savvy, and how to create long-lasting relationships.

Simply visit the website below and follow the directions to download direct to your Notebook or PC.

www.SecretsExposed.com.au/female_entrepreneurs

SANDY FORSTER

66 Only a few years ago I was throwing my hands up in despair, wondering what the heck was wrong with me, and what I had ever done wrong in my life to deserve such bad luck. Today, just a few short years later, I'm living my dreams – and if I can do it, any woman can. 99

SANDY FORSTER

Sandy Forster was born in Melbourne in 1959, and grew up spending her summers camping along the Victorian coast. When she was fifteen, her parents took the family travelling around the world for almost a year, before returning to Australia and settling on the Sunshine Coast.

Sandy left school in Year 11, and soon decided that teaching aerobics was much more fun than working nine-to-five. When she found it difficult to buy suitable leotards, Sandy began designing and manufacturing her own.

After ten years and a divorce, Sandy found herself $100,000 in debt, with two small children to support on a $15,000 a year government benefit. When she increased her income to over $150,000 she thought her money worries were over, but a lack of money management skills and the right mindset meant that she once again lost everything. This led Sandy on a tireless search to understand money, prosperity and abundance, and how to make it flow, grow and multiply.

Sandy co-founded Wildly Wealthy Women to share what she had learnt about attracting wealth through the power of the subconscious mind. This was followed by WildlyWealthy.com, which currently has tens of thousands of people from over 88 countries learning her success strategies through live tele-classes, workshops, seminars and her international best-selling book *How to Be Wildly Wealthy FAST*.

Sandy has written or contributed to four books, shared the stage with such giants of personal development as Mark Victor Hansen (*Chicken Soup for the Soul*), been featured in a number of Dr Wayne Dyer's books and audio programs, appeared on national television, and speaks to audiences around the world.

Sandy lives on Queensland's Sunshine Coast where she loves watching sunrises, early morning walks, relaxing with her children and having fun with friends.

When did you and your family first realise that you had an entrepreneurial flair?

When I was 22, I quit my first full-time job at the local library to start my own business teaching aerobics classes, which were the latest craze to hit Australia. My parents were stunned that I would throw in a perfectly good job to do something with no certain future, but money was never a deciding factor for me (which was lucky because it took me nearly fifteen years to find a business in which I could make a profit), it was the freedom of being my own boss that most appealed – and it still does.

With aerobics being so new to Australia it was a real challenge to buy leotards in anything other than basic black. I used to sew on weekends and bought some lycra to make my own gym wear. Then, a friend asked me if I could make her a copy of a bikini that she loved and the next thing I knew I had started designing and manufacturing swim and gym wear. It was fun at the start, I was married and it was more of a hobby business that gave me extra spending money. But it turned into a nightmare after I divorced and was trying to raise a six-month-old baby and three-year-old toddler while running a business that wasn't making enough money to live on.

While I had the creative side of the business down pat, the financial and administrative side of things was a disaster. After ten years, $100,000 in debt, I closed the doors and walked away.

How did you come to develop what you call the 'Millionaire Mindset'?

I'd been living on a $15,000 a year sole parents benefit and trying to pay off the $100,000 I owed – to say that I was totally stressed out about money would be an understatement! After I closed my swim and gym wear business, I started working with a company marketing personal development courses. I thoroughly enjoyed it and I was good at it, it wasn't long before I'd increased my income to $150,000 – but I was still struggling with

> 66 I continued to ride a financial roller coaster; even though I knew what to do... 99

money. I couldn't believe that I could go from having a $15,000 income to a $150,000 income and still be having the same problems with money.

That's when I realised that I needed to do something. It clearly wasn't the amount of money I was earning that was the problem, it was my mindset about money that kept me struggling even when I should have had more than enough. This experience led me to begin a journey that will probably never end – to learn about and understand how our minds, beliefs and attitudes affect our ability to create and keep money, and it led me to develop what I call the Millionaire Mindset.

I began to really understand that prosperity isn't only determined by the amount of money you have and what you do with it – but also by your mindset about money. If you have a 'poverty mindset', then no matter how much money you earn, you'll continue to have struggles with money. I found that the lessons I learnt about managing my money mindset really worked, and I was eager to share that information with others.

I began teaching these principles and seeing how they worked in anyone's life. I was always receiving emails from my students telling me the amazing difference I had made in their lives. They wrote to me about the prosperity that had begun to flow, the cheques that appeared in the mail, the unexpected pay rises and huge increases in their business. But although I had proven to myself that these techniques worked, and was seeing the results in my students' lives, I continued to ride a financial roller coaster; even though I knew what to do, I was slow to truly accept the lesson myself. I think that's because everyone has a natural 'default mindset' that is conditioned in them from the time they are young – some people have a true and easy belief in their ability to attract money into their lives, while others (like me) really have to work on changing their conditioned poverty consciousness before lasting changes can take place. I felt like a complete fraud – a so-called 'prosperity mentor' who couldn't even pay her own bills – what a joke!

I knew with certainty that the principles I taught absolutely worked, and I understood that the real challenge was to permanently change my conditioned money mindset, so little by little, I began to apply everything I was teaching to my own situation, and my circumstances changed. Before I knew it, I was a prosperous prosperity mentor!

In hindsight, I'm glad that it was initially a struggle for me to change my financial situation, because now if I have clients that say, 'This will never work for me, I'm doing everything you say but it's just not working', I can come from a place of integrity having had that very experience myself, and push them even harder.

Where did the inspiration for WildlyWealthyWomen.com come from?

I met Dymphna Boholt (who would become my business partner) at a wealth creation seminar that I was speaking at, and we initially joined forces to promote a real estate education package that we had huge success with.

I'm the type of person who likes to know the 'why' behind everything, and needs to ask dozens of questions before moving forward. As I started investing in real estate myself, I was very fortunate to have Dymphna there to answer all of my questions (Dymphna is an accountant, asset protection and taxation expert, economist and highly successful property investor, and she has a wealth of knowledge). I began to think about how many other women were in the same situation as me – women who were intelligent enough, had read all the books, listened to all the tapes, knew all the practical steps to take, but because they didn't have a husband or partner to bounce their ideas off, never actually moved forward with their investing.

I decided we should find some of those women who were ready to create their own financial freedom, and were just looking for a supportive, like-minded network to assist them in achieving their goals. I wanted to create a program that approached the topic of money and wealth from a holistic point of view, to encourage women to look at money as the means through which they could achieve the freedom to do whatever is most important to them – whether it's to own their own home, to be able to spend more time with the kids, to be financially independent. I wanted to create something that would be built around a supportive community of women all helping and encouraging each other, not just a one-off book or seminar, but something that would coach and mentor women every step of the way, and that they could remain a part of after they had completed the program. I wanted to create a program designed for women, by women. I thought that with Dymphna teaching the practical steps to creating wealth and me teaching the mindset techniques, we would be a winning combination – and from the success stories we've had from thousands of WildlyWealthy-Women.com members I was absolutely right!

Once you had the initial idea, how did you get the business up and running?

First, I registered the website name, then I waited about a month before telling Dymphna about my idea – we were due to go to the US to attend a seminar and my plan was to tell her about it then. She almost pulled out of the trip at the last minute because of another business venture, but I enticed her to come along with promises of lying beside the pool, sipping juice and brainstorming about a great idea that I'd had.

As soon as we began discussing WildlyWealthyWomen.com we knew it would be successful. There was nothing else like it in the wealth creation industry – nothing that was targeted directly at women, presented by women, for women, in a way that women like to learn.

We decided that we had to begin by getting the word out. We didn't want to only help women on the Sunshine Coast (where we both lived), we wanted women from all around Australia to be able to tap into this amazing program and create the life of their dreams.

Without much funding to get the program off the ground, I approached a friend who was doing some marketing and told her that we were looking for national publicity to kick-start registrations. Our plan was to promote the opportunity for women who signed up for the program to go into the running to have their fees refunded, in exchange for us being able to follow their stories and successes for a book. And instead of offering a fee for the project, I offered my friend a percentage of every registration we received.

Sometimes ignorance is bliss, my friend hadn't had a great deal of experience in working with the media and PR, so when I told her that it would be easy to get on national television she believed me – and when you believe something, it's easy to make it happen. Within a month we were on the front page of newspapers and on television all around Australia. Hundreds of women signed up for the program, and my friend, together with a couple of assistants, made close to $100,000 for just a few weeks work!

What was it like when you started presenting the seminars? Had you always been a confident public speaker?

I vividly remember the first time I spoke in front of a large crowd. I was actually attending a seminar, and after one of the sessions they asked the audience for feedback. I was sitting in the front row and when they gave me the microphone and asked me to stand up I started shaking like a leaf, I could feel my knees beginning to buckle. I said what I had to say and quickly sat down again. The whole experience lasted less than a minute, but it shook me so much that it took almost the entire next session (45 minutes) for my heart rate to slow down, my body to stop shaking and that sick feeling in my stomach to disappear. If you had told me at that moment that I would become a public speaker within the next three years I would have thought you were completely deranged!

> 66 I started shaking like a leaf, I could feel my knees beginning to buckle. 99

When I was working for the personal development company they held training sessions via conference calls, and that was the beginning of my speaking career. I found it was far easier to speak to a crowd at the end of the phone where I couldn't see anyone, than in front of a live audience.

Within a year or so, I began holding my own teleconferences, teaching a program that I had developed called 'Creating Your Millionaire Mindset'. Because it was held over the phone I was able to read from my notes, which stopped me from being too nervous. After doing that for a year or so I knew my material inside out, and decided that I was ready for a real live audience – *and I loved it*. I loved the interaction and the fact that I could see them smile and laugh and nod their heads in agreement with me. Now I thrive on it, once I start talking to an audience I don't want to stop.

In your opinion, what is financial freedom?

To me, financial freedom is about being able to make choices based on your desires, rather than on your bank balance. Having financial freedom can also give you time freedom, which for me means being able to do what I want, when I want. For example, I love to learn and I love to travel. This year I went to Los Angeles with a friend to meet up with Mark Victor Hansen (best-selling author of *Chicken Soup for the Soul*) at one of his events, and we did a bit of sightseeing while we were there. Last month I took my kids to Disneyland and then to Peru for a month to trek the Inca Trail, which was such a wonderful adventure. Next, I'm off to Hawaii for a Mastermind weekend with some of the world's most dynamic innovators, and then I'm going on safari across the Serengeti Plains in Tanzania and climbing Mt Kilimanjaro. I'm also looking forward to going on a yoga retreat that includes a dolphin swim in Hawaii.

The best part of all this is that even while I'm away, my businesses will continue to make money for me because I have set them up so that I earn a passive income, which is the best type of income! I'm not telling you this to show off, I just want to share what is possible for you too. Only a few years ago I was throwing my hands up in despair, wondering what the heck was wrong with me, and what I had ever done wrong in my life to deserve such bad luck. Today, just a few short years later, I'm living my dreams – and if I can do it, any woman can.

Sandy and her daughter Danielle – proud as punch at the Gateway of the Sun at Machu Picchu in the Andes Mountains, Peru.

Why do you believe that it is so important for women to take control of their finances?

I believe it is important for *everyone* to take control of their finances – not just women. We live in a society that seems to think we should have everything we want, right now, without having to wait. We have our credit cards maxed-out, we are in debt up to our eyeballs, and we are creating an enormous amount of stress that we just don't need.

What are some practical things that people can do to improve their 'attraction' for wealth and prosperity?

My approach to wealth is twofold: create a Millionaire Mindset, so you begin attracting prosperity into your life, and implement practical strategies for keeping and multiplying your money.

> **❝ I use the power of my mind to attract what I desire into my life, rather than mapping out my goals... ❞**

A Millionaire Mindset is about knowing that the words you say, the thoughts you think, and what you focus on consistently become the seeds you plant for your future. So if you focus on lack, money challenges and everything that is going wrong, those are the seeds that you will sow in your future. On the other hand, if you focus your attention on everything that is wonderful in your life, then you begin to plant the seeds for wonderful things to happen.

Although it sounds simplistic, it's very powerful – change your thoughts and the images in your mind to those of prosperity and abundance and the Universe *must* deliver.

Some people tap into the abundance stream as soon as they learn the secrets while others, including me, take a little longer – but it absolutely without a doubt works for everyone – guaranteed. I wrote *How to Be Wildly Wealthy FAST* because I wanted to share dozens of different ways people can attract prosperity and abundance, all of which are derived from the Millionaire Mindset principles.

We know you are a big believer in setting goals, but how do you actually do that?

My goal setting process is a little different to the more traditional methods. I use the power of my mind to attract what I desire into my life, rather than mapping out my goals and devising a step-by-step plan to achieve them.

I do this by taking the time to think about what it is that I want – what makes my heart sing. Then, I write down the desired result as if it had already happened. Every day, I take the time to close my eyes and visualise the end result as if it's already happened. At the same time, I flood my body with the feelings I would feel if it had already happened. This process allows me to become a magnet for the things I want and to draw them into my life rather than having to run after them. Visualisation is a very powerful tool that many people completely underestimate.

What are the most important things you have learnt about succeeding in business?

Don't be afraid to make mistakes, don't listen to negative comments, and if it makes your heart sing – never give up.

What do you love most about business?

First and foremost, I love my businesses for the freedom they give me. I work from home, so I'm able to be there with my children and I'm doing something that I'd be doing even if I weren't getting paid for it. I love to learn, I love metaphysics, I love prosperity principles, I love personal empowerment, I love creating success and I love sharing what I know. I would be immersing myself in these things every day anyway and telling anyone who would listen, so to have a business where I get to share all that I learn with others is truly a blessing.

What was the reaction from your two children as they saw their mum grow and develop?

I felt like such a bad parent in the beginning. I was stressed to the eyeballs and so scared about my financial situation, and that had a huge impact on every area of my life. I seemed to spend all of my time shouting at my kids. It was not a fun time in my life, but once things began to change and the prosperity started to flow, I regained freedom in my life – and financial freedom allowed me personal freedom, so I soon became a more relaxed, more tolerant and better mum.

My kids are very proud of what I have achieved and even though it was a huge struggle, I'm glad that we experienced those hard times. You should never take your success for granted. I live on the beautiful river at Mooloolaba, and now and then when my son and I are lying on the jetty with our pillows and blankets, staring up at the stars, I say to him, 'Do you know how lucky we are? Remember when we couldn't even afford to rent a video? Or when you couldn't have tuckshop? Remember how yucky it was? We are so lucky, so blessed'.

My kids have seen where we were, and they see where we are now. I try to instil in them the belief that they can change their whole world when they change the way they think. I want them to know that anything is possible if they just put their minds to it.

What is the biggest mistake you've ever made in business and what did you learn from it?

Two of my mentors, Mike Litman and Jason Oman, authors of *Conversations with Millionaires,* told me that many entrepreneurs today suffer from 'The Idea Avalanche' – meaning that they come up with a brilliant idea, get all excited, take steps toward turning it from an idea into reality and before they get anywhere, they come up with another brilliant idea, so they drop the first and move on to the next. They do the same thing over and over again and wonder why they never achieve the success they desire. Looking back, that was my biggest mistake. I'm very creative, so I'm constantly coming up with new ideas and I spent years starting and stopping so many ventures, I never stuck with anything long enough to make it successful.

Now, instead of following up every new idea, I write them all down, choose one or two to focus on and forget about the rest for the time being. I think that's why WildlyWealthyWomen.com has been such a success – when I came up with the idea, I threw all my other ideas aside and just focused on making it happen.

Have there ever been times when you wanted to give up, and if so, what got you through?

I've wanted to give up many times, but I didn't throw in the towel because part of me felt I was destined for so much more than I was experiencing. Inside I knew that I was born to be rich, it was only a matter of time until it happened. I also believe that the bigger the challenge, the bigger the gift – so I felt I must have a whole warehouse of gifts coming to me one day!

I remember one of my business ventures involved these great little slippers that used magnet therapy and reflexology to help you lose weight. My idea was to import them from China to sell. I used the power of my mind (and plenty of phone calls) to get a TV station to do a story on them. They told me that stories on either making money or losing weight generated the most interest and to expect hundreds, if not thousands, of enquiries. This was going to pull me out of my financial hole. I was going to sell Slim-Slippers all around Australia, pay off all my debts and live the life of my dreams. It was all about to happen for me and I was ready!

The story was scheduled to air on a Monday night, I was so excited. Then, over the weekend, tragedy struck for the first time in Bali. My story did go to air on the Monday, but with a story about the Bali bombing immediately before it and a special about the bombing straight after it. Who in their right mind would be focusing on silly SlimSlippers with all that tragedy going on? At least twelve people I guess, because that's how many orders I received after the show.

At first I was shattered. Things couldn't have looked any worse for me at that point, I was so far down the financial gurgler that I couldn't see any way to get back up again. But in hindsight, I am so glad that my story flopped because it sent my life in a whole new direction. You see, the Universe knows what's going on. I had my sights set on a SlimSlippers empire and if my plan had

> **❝ I never stuck with anything long enough to make it successful. ❞**

tully

worked, I would be selling little slippers, posting parcels all over Australia. Instead, here I am living my life's purpose. I'm living my dream, teaching people around the world how to create a life filled with prosperity and success, and showing them that anything is possible. That wouldn't have happened if my SlimSlippers business had gone as planned. The Universe had to mess it up so that I wouldn't miss the opportunity that ultimately led me to my destiny. So don't get down when things don't go according to your plan, it usually means that the Universe has something bigger and better in store for you.

What is the most common mistake that new business owners make?

Spending money that they don't have, particularly on things like advertising. There are so many other ways to tap into the media and get publicity that won't cost you a cent. You can invite them to do a story on your business, the success of your clients, a fantastic new product that you have, or a new direction that your business is taking.

Also, businesses sometimes become very focused on one thing, which can be good, although it's important to diversify at the same time. For example,

I was teaching a program called Millionaire Mindset for a number of years and my students loved it, but it wasn't going to make me a millionaire as fast as I wanted, so I decided to branch out and add additional products and services. I recorded some coaching sessions and made audio CDs from them, I wrote a book, offered one-hour group coaching sessions, created affirmation and visualisation CDs, and I expanded the coaching into a nine-month mentoring program. In other words, I stayed within my area of expertise but added a whole range of new products for my clients to purchase. Most business owners could do the same thing. There is so much out there for your clients and customers to spend their money on – why not increase your own bottom line by giving them more options to purchase from you?

What advice would you give to an aspiring entrepreneur who wants to get started in a business of their own?

Find a mentor or network of like-minded people – it will cut your learning curve and you'll take a quantum leap toward success. Why spend time making mistakes and wasting valuable hours and money when you can utilise someone else's knowledge to catapult you forward? I've had dozens of mentors and have tapped into mastermind groups that have allowed me to create a level of success that I would never have achieved through trial and error on my own.

Tell us about your international expansion.

WildlyWealthyWomen.com has already expanded into New Zealand and is currently in negotiations with Dr Dolf de Roos (real estate adviser to world renowned author of the *Rich Dad, Poor Dad* series of books, Robert Kiyosaki) into the US. We're planning on starting in Arizona, as that's where Dolf's company is located, and we'll branch out from there.

My other business, WildlyWealthy.com (which is for both men and women and provides resources, seminars and short programs), has been international from day one. My website attracts people from Australia, New

> 66 It'll be a haven for stressed-out businesspeople to relax, unwind and learn a new way of thinking. 99

Zealand, The Netherlands, France, Germany, Nigeria, Sweden, Ireland, the UK, Spain – in fact currently over 23,000 people from 88 countries. It's extremely exciting when people from around the world discover your business, that's why I'm a big fan of internet businesses – the possibilities and opportunities are endless.

What are some of your personal and business goals for the next five to ten years?

My goal last year was for my book, *How to Be Wildly Wealthy FAST,* to become an international bestseller – which it did. Next, I want Oprah to discover my book, to love it and to invite me onto her show. Then I'll have a much larger world presence and will continue to create CDs, home-study courses, seminars and workshops that empower women to energise their bodies, expand their minds, uplift their spirits and tap into the unlimited supply of abundance that is there for everyone – I'm on course for all of that so far.

My long-term goal is to build a prosperity retreat on Queensland's Sunshine Coast. It'll be a haven for stressed-out businesspeople to relax, unwind and learn a new way of thinking. They can fill their days with yoga, meditation, massage and other alternative health therapies that balance the body, mind and spirit. They'll also have access to an amazing array of self-empowerment sessions so that they leave not only feeling refreshed, but with a whole new mindset and the skills to transform their futures. I also want to open the retreat up to underprivileged families who would otherwise never be able to afford such a holiday. They can come and stay for free, and while they're enjoying themselves, can begin to learn strategies and skills to create a brighter future, rather than just letting life happen to them.

You have been studying self-help literature and attending personal development seminars for many years. What are some of the most important 'life-lessons' you've learnt from those studies?

The most important lesson I've learnt is to *apply* all that you learn. I spent years reading books, buying tapes, attending seminars and workshops, getting so inspired and motivated to go out there and 'make it happen' for myself, but I never achieved the success I desired because I really wasn't applying what I had learnt in my own life. I was so hooked on learning that I didn't stop to evaluate where I was, where I wanted to go, and which strategies and ideas would help me get there.

As a self-confessed learning junkie, I still read, listen and travel the world attending amazing seminars and workshops, but now I always take the time to reflect on what I've learnt and apply it in my life. Even if it's only one small thing, that one thing can make all the difference to your future.

Is there a significant quote or saying by which you live your life?

'Be Realistic – Expect a Miracle' is something that I live my life by and it's what my business is based on. Realistically, we create the situations that occur in our lives, we create our futures and we create our destinies. Day-by-day, we can create the most amazing events and circumstances in our lives. I used to think that if something wonderful happened, it was just a coincidence or luck, now I know that by tapping into the subconscious mind and utilising the Universal Laws, we can make miracles happen on a daily basis.

My other favourite is *'Life is not measured by the number of breaths we take, but by the moments that take our breath away'*. This is the essence of how we should live our lives. It's not about *how long* you live, but *how* you've lived. It's about being grateful on a daily basis for just being here and taking pleasure in all that life has to offer.

What do you see as the major business opportunities over the next ten to twenty years?

Without a doubt, it would be building an internet business. Creating successful online businesses is my specialty and I now teach others how easy (and low cost) it is.

When I first published *How to Be Wildly Wealthy FAST*, I sent an email out to my database letting them know that the book was about to launch. Within weeks, I had orders from all over the world – Australia, New Zealand, Canada, the USA, Germany, Spain, the UK, The Netherlands and even Nigeria! Keep in mind this is a self-published book, I've spent no money on advertising or marketing at all, and yet I've sold tens of thousands of copies to people I would never have reached if I'd placed an ad in my local paper.

At the end of your career if you could be remembered for one thing, what would it be?

I'd like to be remembered for helping millions of people around the planet transform their lives into ones filled with abundance, prosperity, wealth, happiness – and the time to really enjoy it all.

FREE BONUS GIFT

Sandy Forster has kindly offered a FREE BONUS GIFT valued at $47.00 to all readers of this book....

Millionaire Visualisation – In this special 35-minute audio product, Sandy (with music) will guide you step-by-step through a powerful visualisation experience designed to unlock your inner wealth. You'll discover what makes your heart sing and how to see your future with more clarity to attract greater levels of abundance into your life.

Simply visit the website below and follow the direction to download direct to your Notebook or PC.

www.SecretsExposed.com.au/female_entrepreneurs

KRISTINA KARLSSON

66 I also maintained second and third jobs for quite some time to provide additional funds. I would work in a hotel doing breakfast shifts at 5.00am before heading off to work on kikki.K, then waitressing on weekends. It took lots of energy but it just had to be done. 99

KRISTINA KARLSSON

Kristina Karlsson was born in 1973 and raised in the Swedish city of Falkenberg. After finishing school she became infected with the travel bug and worked all over the world. While in the beautiful mountains of Austria she met her Australian partner Paul Lacy and returned home with him to settle in Melbourne.

Soon after Kristina recognised a burning desire to start her own business. In the process of creating an inspiring home office she discovered a total lack of stylish office products available in Australia. Like so many fashion-conscious women Kristina had always loved stationery, and growing up in Sweden she had developed an appreciation for the clean, simple lines and style of Swedish design. Some detailed research proved that many others saw the need for something different too. It was the business opportunity she'd been looking for and the chance to combine two of her greatest passions – stationery and Swedish design; the concept for kikki.K was born.

Within a few short years Kristina's first stationery boutique won an award for being Melbourne's Most Innovative Store, followed by an award from the Nine Network *Small Business Show* for creating Australia's Best Small Business Website and the *My Business* magazine's Young Gun award.

kikki.K now has five gorgeous boutiques in Sydney, Melbourne and Brisbane, is available online at www.kikki-k.com.au, and is sold in more than 120 independent gift and homeware stores. Kristina has also started exporting to the UK and back to her home country of Sweden.

Today Kristina lives in Melbourne and together with partner Paul. Having never forgotten her cultural ties Kristina regularly travels back to Sweden – to gather inspiration, design new ranges and to visit family and friends.

When did you and your family first realise that you had an entrepreneurial flair?

I guess the first indication I had of my entrepreneurial instinct was at the age of ten, when I used to ride my bike around the snow-covered streets in my neighbourhood selling Christmas books door-to-door. I was completely driven by the rewards on offer and had a clear vision of being able to win my own TV. I decided that I would do whatever it took, and finally I did win a TV for my efforts as the region's best saleswoman!

This little venture taught me that it's possible to achieve something when you really want to. It also taught me that you can make money and earn rewards by doing something that you love. I just loved being out in the fresh air, peddling my bike around, being invited into people's homes and getting a chance to see how they lived. It was such simple fun. I'm sure my enthusiasm rubbed off and was a factor in my sales performance!

What made you decide to start your current business?

I arrived in Australia from my native Sweden at the age of 22, and once I had decided that I wanted to stay it quickly led to the question, 'What am I going to do here?' I became quite restless trying to work out what 'my thing' was, and in the end it was my partner who helped me bring some clarity to it all. One morning, at about 4.00am, I was tossing and turning as I struggled with ideas of what I could turn my hand to when Paul turned on the light, took out a pen and paper, and encouraged me to at least write down some parameters that could help guide my decision making. This led to what I call my '4.00am List', which went something like this:

- I wanted to do something that I would be passionate about. Something that would excite me as I drove to work on a Monday morning.
- I wanted it to be something that would keep me in touch with Sweden, and my family and friends.

- I wanted the freedom of running my own business – although I'd had no formal business training and little experience, starting my own business had always been a dream.
- I wanted it to be something to do with Swedish design, which I'd always had a passion for.
- And I wanted to make about $500 per week!

The simple act of creating that list was really powerful in moving me from a state of restlessness to a place where I could take clear action and it brought definition to my search. Then, my own desire to create an orderly and stylish home office uncovered a simple opportunity and the concept for kikki.K was born. I just couldn't find a collection of stationery products anywhere to turn my home office into the orderly and inspiring space I wanted to create. I didn't want it to look like 'just another boring office', I wanted it to be an extension of my home, my personality and my ideas on fashion and design. And after speaking with friends, I found plenty of others with the same need.

When I looked into it further, I found a trend toward people working from home, both part-time and full-time, and often with uninspiring stationery products 'borrowed' from work which just didn't fit with the style of the contemporary home. I also found a swing back to city apartment living, where the effective use of space and stylish storage solutions are really impor-tant. My research revealed that the Australian stationery industry was being driven by price – with very little in the way of value being added via product innovation, creativity, design or branding.

To me, these findings were really exciting and I knew I'd found the oppor-tunity I was looking for. I soon had a vision of having my own group of beautiful retail stores with fashionable collections of products that addressed the needs I'd identified. So I picked up the Yellow Pages, and not knowing much about how I'd actually put a product range together, I started by looking under 'S' for 'Stationery Manufacturers', and began working toward my vision of kikki.K having a presence in every fashionable working life.

What previous business experience did you have before starting kikki.K?

I had very little business experience and no experience running a business of my own. I'd worked in a broad variety of jobs including being a tour bus guide in Europe, working in an Austrian ski resort, hosting tourists at a winery in Germany and being a nanny in Beverly Hills. I'd also spent a year working in the travel industry when I first came to Australia. I thought it was a career that I could become passionate about, so I offered to work for a month without pay to get a job at what was then one of Australia's most innovative travel groups. Luckily they started paying me after a couple of weeks and promoted me to account manager quite quickly. But I soon realised that it wasn't for me.

In the beginning, what were some of the business skills you were lacking and what did you do about it?

With no formal business training, there was an endless list of skills I lacked. With English as my second language, I didn't even know what the word 'invoice' meant. I thought it was something to do with talking, as in, 'in-voice'! I had almost no skills in the areas of finance, accounting or bookkeeping, no idea about marketing, no idea how to run a retail store, no idea how to recruit employees and no idea what performance management was. I'd never even heard of logistics or operations and had no idea how to put together a product development schedule, run a trade show, negotiate a lease, make a sales presentation, build a website or write a position description. Having said all that, I had a great idea, a clear vision, boundless enthusiasm and I knew that I could always find a way to overcome challenges.

> 66 I didn't even know what the word 'invoice' meant. I thought it was something to do with talking... 99

Looking back, I knew there was so much that I had to learn to make my vision a reality, but that excited me. I just loved the mission that I was on and there was no way I was going to give up. In some ways I was really ignorant and that was a bonus – I didn't know that I couldn't do it!

Having a clear vision and being passionate about it was key to overcoming my lack of skills, as was continually asking questions, not being scared to look silly and having an attitude that it's okay to make mistakes and that making mistakes creates great learning opportunities. In the words of a mentor of mine, 'It's about progress not perfection'.

I've also always read as much as I could about the things I need to learn, attended training courses and sought out inspiring speakers. One of the books I've read recently is John McGrath's *You Inc*. It's a must read. Networking and having mentors has also helped me to bridge the skills gap, as has understanding that I couldn't do it all myself and building a team of competent and motivated people to work with.

What seminars or courses did you attend to fill in some of the gaps in your business knowledge?

For someone who started a business with very little in the way of business knowledge I think it's important to remember that common sense can get you a long way, and not being scared to ask questions will get you even further. I've never been scared to ask the questions that lots of people might think are stupid. In fact, I don't think a question is ever too stupid, because what I've learnt from asking those questions has been a huge contributor to filling the gaps in my business knowledge.

I did do a simple Starting Your Own Business TAFE course, which was some help, but it was certainly no substitute for just getting into it and learning as you go. I'd recommend to anyone considering starting a business to just do it or at least try a business of some type – anything will do – a garage sale or a lemonade stand – whatever will expose you to business experiences like buying, budgeting, merchandising, promotion, pricing, selling, and so on. There's no way like just doing it to learn how to do it.

I am conscious that as my business grows I need to grow myself and my abilities. Adding better people to my team helps fill my knowledge gaps, but a business never outpaces its leader. So now I take courses at places like the Australian Institute of Management to fill any gaps I see as important.

What made you believe that fashionable stationery and storage would be a viable business venture?

It was quite simple, really. I felt the need and when I spoke to friends they felt the need too.

It was obvious to me that a gap existed in the market. One day I stood on Chapel Street in Melbourne and stopped people to show them sketches of what a kikki.K store might look like and asked them what they thought of the concept. The ones who didn't think I was mad gave me very positive feedback. Soon after that I borrowed a few thousand dollars to create a sample range, and ran about 40 focus groups of ten or more people each – explaining my concept to them and showing the sample products. The response was overwhelmingly positive and I got loads of orders.

So I guess it was a combination of what I felt in my gut and the positive research results that assured me I was on the right track.

Why do you believe it is important to have a clean, well thought-out workspace?

Having a well organised, stylish and enlivening workspace is really about quality of life. People spend so much time working these days and the environment in which

> 66 I guess it was a combination of what I felt in my gut and the positive research results... 99

we work, and how well it supports our workflow, really impacts on our productivity and creativity. At a functional level it saves you time, energy and money because you'll find things quickly when you need them, which avoids stress, late fees and unnecessarily having to repeat work you've already done because you can't find it. But more than that, at an emotional level, it provides a satisfying sense of wellbeing, control and confidence.

Creating a workspace that reflects their own ideas and style is also a way that people can create the type of impression they'd like to make on colleagues, customers and even managers. And for the many people who work from home, it's even more important to create a workspace that blends with the style of their home and becomes an enlivening and stylish work environment.

Why do you believe that colours are important in someone's working environment?

There are numerous studies into the effects of colour on the state of mind. The key thing colour can do in a work environment is help to create a sense of order. For example, simply changing a shelf of old multi-coloured folders to a single colour can have a huge positive impact on the sense of order a workspace projects, and subsequently the state of mind of people who enter that space.

What are your tips for turning chaos into clarity in the average workstation?

1. Treat your workspace as an important part of your life. Give it a sense of style and fashion, so that it reflects your personal taste. Keep in mind that it can easily be transformed into a sanctuary, a place where you feel inspired by your surroundings, in control and able to get on with productive work.

2. Good organisation is vital, and it's easy. Keep your workspace tidy, a messy environment disturbs your ability to concentrate and think clearly. Remember: cluttered office, cluttered mind. Think hard about

what is really needed in your office and on your desk, and remove unnecessary piles of papers, magazines, CDs and computer discs, and store them in easily accessible storage nearby.

3. Use clearly labelled colour coordinated magazine holders, folders and storage boxes to control the clutter and add a touch of style. This is really important to free up your feelings of energy and to help you avoid feeling overwhelmed.

4. Colour coordinate other desk accessories such as pens, rulers, scissors, tape dispenser – everything. That way they match your theme and create an inspiring feel.

5. Avoid covering your desk with scrawled notes on paper scraps or sticky notes. They're too easy to lose and just create more clutter. Instead use a stylish and durable spiral notebook to jot down thoughts and ideas as you have them, so you can free up your mind and you'll know exactly where to find them. Keep an A4 or A5 notebook by the phone, and always carry a conveniently sized A6 notebook in your bag or pocket for catching important thoughts.

6. Take five minutes at the end of each working day or session to clear up your desk and office. Put away any clutter into your clearly marked storage boxes and give yourself (or whoever you share the office with) a fresh clear start to the next work session. To have a mass of clutter as the last image when you walk out, and the first when you walk back in is a major cause of stress and it affects how you feel about yourself and the world.

Why was getting a website together a vital part of your strategy?

When we first thought about a website, the brand was very much in its infancy. I found myself talking to people about the brand and the kikki.K concept, and going over the story again and again. After dozens of conversations I felt it was necessary that the brand had a 'home', a place I could point people to so they could check it out in their own time and discover the brand for themselves. That's really where it started.

> 66 We've proven to ourselves that you don't have to spend a lot of money to create an effective website... 99

We also realised very quickly that consumers wanted the convenience of being able to buy kikki.K products online, so we developed an easy-to-use online sales process that provides a great service for people who want to shop from home. It works really well to support our retail stores.

We were very fortunate to have won an award from the Nine Network *Small Business Show* (from among 670 other sites) for having Australia's Best Small Business Website. This gave the business a big boost and became a major element in the promotion of our brand on a national scale.

Do you believe that you have to spend a lot of money to have an effective website?

When we first looked at creating an e-commerce enabled kikki.K website, we developed a brief for agencies to quote on. I nearly fell over when the quotes came back. As a small start-up company they were way beyond our means so we found a friend who was a self-taught web developer and set about doing it ourselves. It made the process quite a lengthy one, but we've been very happy with the result and we found it to be very cost effective, at about a third of the lowest price quoted by agencies. We've proven to ourselves that you don't have to spend a lot of money to create an effective website that moves product.

How important is keeping costs down in a start-up business and how have you been able to do that?

I've never had any option but to keep a very close eye on costs. When you sell your house to back yourself in starting a business, I can assure you that you become quite careful about getting a return on every dollar you spend, and I think that's the real issue. Incurring costs is just part of doing business. Getting as much value as possible from the cash you have at your disposal is the important management challenge – particularly in the early days when cash is limited. There are many ways you can get results without much money, for example, I've found that networking has been a very good way. I'm often able to get valuable advice or assistance at no cost, and in return I will do something of value for another person. It's a nice way to connect with people and a good way to keep costs down.

When anyone starts their own business they carry a certain emotional attachment to it. Why do you say it is important for an owner to let go of certain parts of the business to ensure its growth?

Growing a business involves investing so much of your effort and energy, you sacrifice so much and go through many ups and downs – so it's hardly surprising that you grow a very close emotional and intuitive attachment. It's probably a little like nurturing and bringing-up a child!

From my own experience though the answer is very simple – you just can't do it all yourself. At some point if you want to grow your business and have a life – no matter what your level of emotional attachment is – you need to hire other people, let go and clearly delegate responsibility to them. Then you have to give them whatever support they need to get their jobs done.

I'm still closely emotionally attached to kikki.K. However, even though I started by doing everything myself, I quickly realised that I needed to get help from others, so after a short while, letting go of many of my functional tasks and responsibilities has been very easy so I can focus my time on leading and working on the business. I've found it's very important though to provide clear guidelines and systems for others to follow.

What are some of the core values that you built your company upon?

Identifying our core values and taking what I've always done intuitively and putting it into a form in which it can be shared with all new members of the kikki.K team is something that we've done a lot of work on recently. Our six core values are:

Customer Focus

I've always had a total focus on understanding and meeting the needs of my customers, trying to inspire them with gorgeous products and 'wow' them with fantastic service, while being natural and fun to deal with.

Creativity and Innovation

Embracing contemporary design and being willing to go beyond the boundaries of conventional thinking was what drove kikki.K in the beginning and what will continue to drive it in the future. Leading and not following is important to us and always will be.

Enthusiasm and Fun

A desire to follow a passion and create an enjoyable and fun career was my reason for starting kikki.K. It's an approach that's helped overcome many barriers and has inspired those around me. Fun is an integral part of the kikki.K approach and it flows through all levels of the business. Life's too short to not have lots of fun at work!

Committed Team

Everyone at kikki.K sharing in the team vision and enthusiastically working toward its achievement is another core value. This means we strive to provide an environment where our people are stimulated, where personal and professional growth is encouraged, and where everyone enjoys coming to work.

Honesty and Integrity

There is no other way.

Community and Environment

I've always wanted to do whatever I could to contribute to the community I live in and to take a proactive approach to operating my business in ways that don't harm the environment. Our aim is to leave the world a better place.

What are the most important characteristics you look for when hiring a new team member?

It totally depends on the role I'm hiring for. I start by thinking through what the role needs, what type of person will be best suited to it, and what the most important characteristics of that person might be. The characteristics of a good finance person will obviously be very different to the important characteristics of a good designer or a great store manager. But I must say that it's a big plus to be a stationery addict, and an enthusiastic and energetic contributor if you want a job at kikki.K.

I've found that the best way to find good staff is just by being passionate and having fun in what we do. As a result, our best staff have been the ones that have been attracted by what we do and the way we do it, and they have come to us.

One of Kristina's stylish retail stores – kikki.K Bondi Junction, NSW.

Obstacles are common when starting a business, especially a unique one like yours. What were some of your toughest experiences and how did you overcome them?

Having limited financial resources to start and grow my business was probably the hardest challenge I faced in getting kikki.K off the ground. However, I overcame that by being creative, working hard and with 'do it yourself' as my mantra in the early days. I also switched-on to the power of networking – exchanging favours with other people as a way of getting things done without having to find cash.

The banks certainly weren't too supportive in our early years, they needed high levels of security which we couldn't give, so I sold the house to fund business development. That being the case, I really had to do my home-work and develop a comprehensive business plan.

I also maintained second and third jobs for quite some time to provide additional funds. I would work in a hotel doing breakfast shifts at 5.00am before heading off to work on kikki.K, then waitressing on weekends. It took lots of energy but it just had to be done.

Another obstacle I found initially was decision making. I used to find it hard to choose from restaurant menus, let alone to make the hundreds of decisions that you have to make each week when you run your own busi-ness! I soon learnt that unless you make decisions your business stands still.

With such a unique business concept it was also a little difficult at times to convince others that it would be viable. I could clearly see it and what it could become, but I found that I had to slow down a little to explain it to others. So many people want to tell you why it might not work, or that you should be really careful. Just days before we sold our house to open our very first store, planes flew into the World Trade Centre and turned the world upside down. Friends advised us not to sell the house as it was too risky. It certainly caused me to think through my plans a little more carefully, but I was so confident in my vision that I chose not to make that issue an obstacle, so we sold the house and opened the doors of our first kikki.K concept store. A few months later, we won an award for Melbourne's Most Innovative Store – and sales boomed!

It has been said that people don't want to be sold, they want to be educated. How has kikki.K adopted this philosophy and what are some of the practical things that you do to educate your clients?

I'm not so sure about educating people versus selling them, but our focus is definitely on providing solutions to people's needs rather than just trying to sell them things. Often people who purchase things from our stores are unaware of other complementary products they may need, so it's part of our service to let them know what else is available.

As a result of having so many customers ask us for advice, we also run workshops which are very popular. They aim to help people learn how to create organised workspaces and to set-up systems that work for them to maintain order and a sense of clarity and control. It's such a fun way to interact with customers and to pass on some of the knowledge we've learnt along the way.

What is the most important thing you have learnt about succeeding in business?

Have you heard the one about ten per cent inspiration and 90 per cent perspiration? It's so true.

If anyone can succeed in business no matter what their background or circumstances, what do you think holds people back from becoming successful entrepreneurs?

It sounds so cliché but it really is bloody tough building something from nothing, which is what entrepreneurs do. You have to have a very clear vision and a very strong desire to achieve it. I believe it's desire and tenacity that get people through and those things come from having a really good reason for doing it. History shows that with the right reason, people achieve the most remarkable things. In my experience, one of the key factors that stops people from becoming successful entrepreneurs is a lack of really strong desire. Obviously having a good idea is vital too.

What are your top tips for becoming a successful entrepreneur?

1. Do something you're really passionate about. You're going to need to invest considerable energy and time into it, so make it something you really enjoy. In other words, have fun!
2. Create a crystal clear vision of what you want to achieve and let that guide your decision-making and your team. When times get tough (and they will), your vision has to be strong enough to pull you and everyone else through.
3. Write a business plan that becomes your road map for achieving your vision. Going through the process of putting it on paper is a must, and a great discipline that forces you to face reality. Review it regularly and don't be afraid to refine it.
4. You can't do it all yourself. Network, find some mentors and build a team.
5. Welcome decision making and decide that there is no such thing as a bad decision. All decisions bring their own new learnings.

What do you love most about business?

I get so excited and inspired when developing new products. It's such a rewarding process to start with a blank page and create beautiful objects that people use every day and come to love. Then to work in one of my stores and see people's reactions to them is just so much fun. On a personal level that gives me masses of enjoyment. But I also just love to see the people that work with me growing and evolving via their work with kikki.K. It's become so much more than my business now. I share it with all the people that work in the kikki.K team and I love seeing people achieve their own personal goals through their experience of working in a stimulating and fun young business.

Who are the mentors that have inspired you and what important lessons have you learnt from them?

Gillian Franklin who founded The Heat Group and was recently named by *The Age* as one of Australia's most powerful businesswomen, has been a wonderful mentor and inspiration to me. She has taught me so many things. Perhaps the most important has been the value of having a mentor. My partner Paul has also been a total inspiration and a very supportive mentor – guiding me to one of my most important learnings – to find something I was passionate about and make it a career.

What do you love most about living in Australia and what do you miss most about your native country Sweden?

I just love the Australian outdoor lifestyle, the optimism of Australian people, the multiculturalism, the huge range of wonderful fresh food and great restaurants. I also love the way Australia is embracing simple contemporary design in so many areas. Having said that, there are so many things I miss about Sweden – my mum and dad and family, my friends, being surrounded by Scandinavian design and the wonderful energy as Sweden comes alive in summer.

SHELLEY BARRETT

66 We never want to become a mass brand, our appeal will always be niche and our brand will always speak to a savvy beauty and trend-focused consumer who is looking for premium quick-fix, multipurpose beauty products. 99

SHELLEY BARRETT

Shelley Barrett was born in Sydney in 1973. As a teenager, Shelley was very gregarious and had a love of tennis. She led a fulfilling and busy social life and always had an entrepreneurial spirit and a certain determination to succeed.

At just 21 years of age, Shelley started her own boutique modelling agency. Over the next ten years it grew into Shelly's Management Group, comprising FACE Models, Lollipops Children Model Management and Commercial Faces Actors, and was recognised as one of the most highly respected management groups in Australia. The group managed a talent pool of 1,200 people across Australia and its models graced the pages of international fashion magazines and worldwide advertising campaigns.

By 2002 Shelly was looking for a new challenge, and based on her first-hand experience working behind the scenes in the fashion world with models and hair and makeup artists, she identified a niche opportunity for innovative, quick-fix and multipurpose beauty solutions. Her first product innovation, the Lash Wand heated eyelash curler was launched with resounding worldwide results. Within just a few months it had sold out around the world and was featured in beauty editorials across the globe.

In its first two years Shelley led ModelCo to an impressive $5 million in turnover and an astonishing 200 per cent growth in turnover. ModelCo is currently distributed throughout Australia, New Zealand, Europe, Asia, the United States and the Middle East.

Today, Shelley enjoys working with her fabulous team creating world-renowed quick-fix beauty tricks, travelling the globe. Shelley and husband Damien had their first child in September 2005, a beautiful baby girl, and Shelley is loving being a mother. Weekends are spent with her family, close friends, and doing the Bondi to Bronte costal walk.

When did you and your family first realise that you had an entrepreneurial flair?

Owning my own business had always been a goal from a young age. However, I discovered my entrepreneurial talent at the age of eighteen with my first business venture, Elite Productions. With Elite Productions, I coordinated fashion shows and model search competitions, and managed events such as weddings, 21st birthdays and parties. The money I earned and saved from this business enabled me to set up and fund my modelling agency.

At the time, my godfather, Ian Elliot, who is a former CEO of advertising agency George Paterson Bates, was such an inspiration to me. He taught me so much, but the main lessons I learnt from him were to trust your gut instincts; keep your team 'in the loop'; believe in yourself and your vision; and know when you're steering off course and get back on track. Ian taught me that in business it's all about focus.

In the beginning, what were some of the business skills you were lacking and what did you do about it?

I wanted to know more about business management in the beginning so I invested in a management course, which taught me how to better deal with people, how to empower employees and how to delegate effectively. I also completed a Diploma in Psychology, which has been invaluable in developing my people skills and learning how to communicate effectively.

You started your career as a receptionist in a modelling agency, what made you decide to go out on your own at just 21 years of age?

While coordinating fashion shows and national model search competitions, I saw so many young hopefuls with great potential but a lack of support,

> **"**...my turnover had gone from zero to $1.5 million per year and we were ranked in the top ten agencies...**"**

and I felt that there was a gap in the market for an agency that offered great service. At the time, the industry was dominated by five major players, so I conducted some research to find out if there was room for another agency. To my surprise, there was a definite niche for a new style of agency that offered impeccable service and great models. I started Shelley's Model Management offering the models personalised service and to this day, we are the only agency that provides complimentary nutrition, deportment, fitness and health advice. Over the years, we've gained a reputation as being one of Australia's leading boutique agencies.

Within six months of opening, 30-40 of the models on my books were gracing the covers of national and international fashion magazines, and featuring in TV commercials, advertising campaigns and fashion shows. After one year, I started a new acting agency, Commercial Faces. Six months later, Lollipops Children Model Management opened. And at the end of our second year we added a fourth arm to the management business, FACE models, which specialises in bringing international models to Australia and sending our talent off shore. By that time, under the corporate umbrella of Shelley's Management Group Pty Ltd, I had the only agency in Australia that offered models, actors and child models in the one company. I had four staff looking after 800 talent Australia-wide, my turnover had gone from zero to $1.5 million per year and we were ranked in the top ten agencies in Australia.

What made you decide to start your current business?

As demanding and challenging as Shelley's Management Group was, I craved something new. Having worked behind the scenes in the fashion world with models and hair and makeup artists, I identified a niche for innovative, quick-fix, multipurpose beauty solutions, which is how my beauty product company, ModelCo, was born in 2002. ModelCo creates premium beauty products that combine cutting-edge creativity and technical innovation. I formed a team of five people focusing on research and development, PR and marketing, importing and exporting and brand management. We developed a five-year strategic plan and brand architecture with an essence of *'wow'*. We defined our target market as 'innovation insatiates': those who are always scouring magazines for the next new thing.

What was your first product and how did it come about?

ModelCo's Lash Wand heated eyelash curler was the first product launched, and within just a few months it had sold out worldwide. It was featured in beauty editorials across the globe in publications such as *Vogue, Harper's Bazaar, Marie Claire* and *InStyle*, and it had created a cult-like following among the fashion industry and beauty-savvy celebrities alike.

The idea came about when I was having my makeup done for a TV appearance, and my eyelashes were being squeezed into a painful eyelash curler. I thought, 'If only every woman could have a heated curler that curled your lashes without all the pain!' Within two weeks I was on a plane overseas to search for manufacturers who could develop the concept; three months later the wheels were in motion with a manufacturer in Asia. I had already approached Myer and David Jones and convinced them that Lash Wand was going to change women's eyelashes forever.

In May 2002, Lash Wand was launched in Australia and I released it to the beauty media at Australian Fashion Week in conjunction with *Harper's Bazaar* and guest editor, Elle Macpherson. Within one month it became a best-seller in Myer throughout Australia. I then presented it to major international beauty buyers and received enormous orders from top-end beauty department stores around the world such as Space NK in the UK, Lane Crawford in Hong Kong and The Bay in Canada.

What products followed the launch of Lash Wand and how did you ensure their success?

In 2003, we launched TAN Airbrush in a Can, which transcended convention and the way women self-tanned forever. TAN is a revolutionary self-tanner that sold out within a week in David Jones and Myer in Australia. It became a best-seller in department stores over Christmas

2004 and outsold all luxury beauty brands over the eight-week Christmas period. By May 2004 we had sold 100,000 cans of TAN at an average retail price of $32.00. Since November 2003, we have launched another 40 products.

ModelCo's range of unique products have made the company a global success, and it has been recognised as an Australian beauty company that is 'wowing' the international beauty world with its 'never before seen' beauty innovations.

The beauty industry is highly competitive, how have you been able to stand out from the crowd?

Much of our success is due to the fact that we consistently produce premium beauty products that are innovative in either their packaging or formulation – or both. Another important factor in ModelCo's ongoing success is being able to maintain our speed to market. This is something that larger beauty brands can't always achieve, but being able to respond quickly to rapidly changing markets and increasing customer expectations is crucial. In addition, because my background is in fashion, rather than beauty, it allows me to look into the world of fashion and anticipate beauty trends.

ModelCo's products also stand out from the crowd because they are loved and endorsed by celebrities, stylists and models. A growing group of devoted ModelCo celebrity users includes Elle Macpherson, Kylie Minogue, Lily Cole and Sophie Dahl. We have also leveraged our relationships with models and the fashion and beauty media for endorsements and promotion.

What are the most important things you have learnt about succeeding in business?

The most important thing I've learnt is that you must work hard. You need to be committed and passionate, and prepared to put in the hard yards. You must also be prepared to take risks. The way to deal with risk is by researching your product. It also helps to have a good support network around you. Surround yourself with a talented team of people who share your vision. Another thing I've learnt is the need to be persistent. I never take *no* for an answer – or at least not 99 per cent of the time. I know the saying is so cliché but it's absolutely true – where there is a will there is a way!

The final thing I have learnt is to do things differently and creatively. This can be seen in the process I used to pitch my initial product idea to David Jones and Myer. I had an interactive presentation that had the buyer using the product so they could experience it first-hand. Boring diagrams and paper do not have impact, and buyers see so many presentations – so make yours exciting and creative!

What do you think are some of the essential characteristics of a successful entrepreneur?

A successful entrepreneur needs to be, above all things, a leader. This requires skills such as the ability to communicate effectively, and to have a flexible plan that is constantly revised. I have a detailed business plan and I make sure that I revisit it regularly.

❝ I never take *no* for an answer – or at least not 99 per cent of the time. ❞

A successful entrepreneur also needs to have a good positive, 'can-do' attitude. This encompasses passion for the business and an ability to accept constructive criticism that will improve the business. But be careful not to accept everyone's criticisms and know who is trying to help you and who may be jealous. One of the biggest mistakes I made was believing what everyone told me. I learnt that I needed to develop a thick skin pretty quickly and that sometimes people don't have the company's best interests at heart, even if they say they do.

What advice would you give to an aspiring entrepreneur who wants to get started in a business of their own?

Make sure you have a real passion for the industry you wish to break into; ensure that you have a good business plan; surround yourself with a great team of people who share your vision; and most importantly, *set goals*! A goal is not just something that you aim for, it is a powerful contributor to successful business growth in several ways. To begin with, the process of setting goals forces you to think through what you want from your business and how growth may or may not provide that. This helps to suggest directions for pursuing that growth, which can greatly improve your chances of achieving your goals in the first place.

Goals also give you a framework within which to work, which focuses your efforts and helps you to rule out actions that won't contribute to their achievement. A very important part of that framework is a timetable. A good timetable will influence your actions profoundly. For example, if your goal is to retire by age 40, you'll know that any growth plan with a payoff that won't occur until your 51st birthday is not one that you'll consider, no matter how attractive it might seem.

Write your goals down and put them somewhere you'll see them every day, such as on your bulletin board, by your desk, on your bathroom mirror, even on your refrigerator. You may think you'll remember your goals five months or five years down the road, but a visual reminder will do wonders to help you stay focused on the goals you've set and on the tasks you need to complete on a daily basis to achieve them. Create targets worth reaching but be realistic and set goals that can be achieved. If you set a goal to earn $100,000 per month when you've never even earned that much in a year, that goal is unrealistic. Begin with small steps, such as increasing your monthly income by 25 per cent, and when you achieve that goal, you can reach for larger ones.

What are some of the ways people can go about deciding what type of business to get involved in?

First, you need to have a genuine passion and interest in the business or industry you choose. Then, you need determination and hard work. You have to have done lots of homework and research on the market – you have to know who your competitors are, how your business will differ from theirs, where the opportunities are, and all about pricing, service, quality, etc. After researching thoroughly, if you still feel passionate and believe in your business plan, then go forth and conquer!

What are your top tips for becoming a successful entrepreneur?

1. Plan for success, set goals and review them every few months.
2. Develop great time management skills.
3. Have a good work/life balance.
4. Know who you are marketing to.
5. Protect your business and its assets.
6. Get a grip on your finances from the beginning.
7. Have a sound knowledge of the business you intend to create.
8. Be technologically savvy and ensure that you have the best systems in place for your business.

When it comes to branding, they say you can't be all things to all people. How have you been able to adapt this philosophy to ModelCo?

ModelCo has a brand essence of '*wow*' and ten clearly defined brand values that must be evident in everything we produce. In addition, we have identified our core target market and we know what makes them tick. We make a conscious effort to stay true to our market. We never want to become a mass brand, our appeal will always be niche and our brand will always speak to a savvy beauty and trend-focused consumer who is looking for premium quick-fix, multipurpose beauty products.

What is a typical day in the life of Shelley Barrett?

I start my day at about 6.30-7.00am with brisk walk. After applying a few of my favourite ModelCo products I dash out the door via my local coffee shop to the office. My first call of the day is usually to the USA, as this is their afternoon, and I then spend the day working on new product development, new business, liaising with manufacturers and the day-to-day running of ModelCo in the Australian market. At 5.00pm Europe opens, so I brush up on my French and go into overdrive for the next few hours talking to our European distributors. I try to leave the office by 8.00-9.00pm, and go home to catch up with my husband and recap on the day's events.

How important is it to expand business ideas overseas?

To compete on an international level it is crucial. However, it can be difficult to understand each country's regulations so make sure you are up-to-date on the law or you could end up losing money or breaking the law, which is never good.

We have been fortunate enough to have companies from different countries come to us. In a little over two years we've gone from 35 stores in Myer Australia to over 500 worldwide. And I am now inundated with

requests from buyers all over the world who would like to stock ModelCo products. If you do need to find yourself a distributor though, make sure they have close relationships with the buyers in the markets you want to go into, that they understand the power of public relations and marketing, and that they share the same vision and passion for your brand that you have.

What do you love most about business?

I love the ability to create innovative beauty products and being able to follow my passion and vision. I also love the sense of satisfaction that comes when our products outperform our predictions and truly make women feel happy and positive about themselves and the way they look.

> 66 You may have a big vision and goals but you can't think that they will just fall into your lap. 99

If anyone can succeed in business no matter what their background or circumstances, what do you think holds people back from becoming successful entrepreneurs?

I think that what usually holds people back is a negative attitude. They don't believe in themselves or they aren't willing to put in the hard yards necessary to succeed. This can be the result of many things such as not setting clear goals or a lack of sheer determination. You need to be prepared to start at the bottom and work your way up. You may have a big vision and goals but you can't think that they will just fall into your lap and that you won't have to get your hands dirty to achieve the end result. I've learnt you can't skip the steps. In the end, going through all the hard work gives you a better understanding of all aspects of your business and the industry around you, and that helps to ensure success in the long run.

The prospect of failure also holds people back. Never give up on your vision, even when you may have had rejections and/or setbacks. There have certainly been testing times that have left me feeling deflated, but I have never wanted to give up. It's just not in my mindset. Plus, I'm surrounded by my family and friends who give me strength, love and encouragement.

What are some of your personal and business goals for the next five to ten years?

My overall goal is to ensure that ModelCo is an international beauty brand that is recognised for its innovative, leading-edge products. In the next five years for me, competing against the biggest and the best in the world is a goal and challenge that I will relish. I see it as a huge opportunity. As markets become more globalised, with fewer geographical and trade barriers, it pays to be ambitious and to actively seize new opportunities. I've set myself huge goals for the next five years and have the best team to help me achieve them.

ModelCo will also continue to strengthen and widen its worldwide distribution and increase sales, as well as continue to focus on innovation and reinvention. I have plans to launch a colour cosmetic range very soon, and in addition to new product launches and continued line extensions, I am currently researching key products that will continue to be revolutionary, scientifically sound, highly desirable and chic.

In ten years, my goal is to have sold the company to a multinational conglomerate and remain on the board. This would be after a couple of years with a turnover of several million dollars.

Personally, in the next five years I'm very much looking forward to success-fully combining the role of motherhood with remaining actively involved in my business.

Margaret Lomas

MARGARET LOMAS

66 I want others to see that you *can* be successful and remain 100 per cent honest, ethical and genuine. I want people to know that hard work and commitment do pay off and that integrity brings success. Helping others really does help you. 99

MARGARET LOMAS

Margaret Lomas was born in Sydney in 1960, one of five children. At the age of eighteen she was selected as a Rotary Exchange Student and spent twelve months living in Indonesia.

After many years working in a variety of industries such as banking, training and community services, Margaret, together with her husband Reuben, began to explore opportunities to assist people with their financial circumstances. They began Destiny Financial Solutions to help people work toward financial independence.

Margaret's unique ability to make complex concepts simple led to the release of her first book, *How to Make Your Money Last as Long as You Do*, in 2001. This book was quickly embraced by the property-investing public which helped Destiny Financial Solutions to expand Australia-wide. Margaret has since written five more books: *How to Create an Income for Life*; *How to Invest in Managed Funds*; *How to Maximise Your Property Portfolio*; *Pocket Guide to Investing in Positive Cash Flow Property*; and *The Truth about Positive Cash Flow Property*.

Today, Margaret is an in-demand public speaker and financial adviser. She has been a co-host and regular commentator on a number of real estate radio shows, and is a regular contributor to investing magazines across Australia.

In 2003, Margaret was appointed to the Board of Business Central Coast, and in 2004, to the Small Business Development Corporation of NSW – an advisory body whose role it is to advise the government on emerging trends in the small business sector. Margaret was also a state finalist in the 2004 Telstra Business Woman of the Year Awards.

Margaret lives on the New South Wales Central Coast with her husband Reuben and their five children.

When did you and your family first realise that you had an entrepreneurial flair?

My father always encouraged us to be the best we could be. He has been the greatest influence in my life. I learnt a very powerful work ethic from him: to work very hard as well as very smart – and he demonstrated this by example in how he ran his own business. This had a profound influence on me as a child and I was always creating or making something. I remember publishing a small family 'newspaper' when I was about nine years old, which I sold for five cents to anyone who would buy it.

At one stage you were a single mother with three small children. How did you get through that tough experience?

It was hard, hard work. I lived 4,000km away from any kind of family support and there were days when I wondered how I was ever going to pull myself through.

When I married my first husband, most people thought it was a bad idea; the mismatch was abundantly clear to everyone except us. While I have a million ideas a day, a one-year plan, a five-year plan and a ten-year plan, he preferred to set himself up in a good job and take each day as it came. After two years we separated, only to get back together and go on to have three children in four years.

I worked the whole time I was having children, but like many mothers, I worked at whatever I could that would have the least impact on my family. I had a part-time job in a chemist and did some training consultancy work on the side. In 1987, after the birth of our second child, we moved to Perth in search of a better and less expensive life. Within two weeks of arriving I was bored and decided to use my creative and sewing skills to make and sell baby clothes and accessories. I walked the streets showing a sample of my work to a range of baby shops, many of which placed orders on the spot for far more than I could handle on my own, so I employed a 'piece

> **He was my perfect man, and he had goals and dreams just like mine.**

worker' (another mum needing some extra cash) and away we went. I soon opened my own shop and promptly fell pregnant again. I sold the shop four months later for no profit. Not long after this I fell into a bit of a rut. I was doing some work running baby massage and Kindy Gym classes, but in between I was being a housewife. Rather than dwell on the very ordinary future I appeared to be heading for, I did what I still do best – and refused to think about it. Of course, under these circumstances the relationship between my husband and I completely floundered and we separated again. I found myself wondering every day how I had ended up in this life, with all the dramas of a soap opera.

I decided that I was not going to be single mum on a sole parent's pension, in a rut whose walls would grow ever higher until I could no longer get out, so I applied for a job as the manager of a community-based service that helped unemployed people to find work. All of the people in my life told me that I had no hope of getting a job like that, so I did two things: first, I got the job, and second, I stopped associating with such negative people. From that day on things started to turn around. I went shopping in second-hand stores for a new business wardrobe and formulated some new goals for my life. Then I met Reuben. He was my perfect man, and he had goals and dreams just like mine. The fact that he was almost ten years younger than me was a small drawback and we did face much opposition, but in the end we worked it out for ourselves, threw caution to the wind and decided to be together forever.

When Reuben and I first met, we had nothing. I'd bought my house from my ex-husband with a special low-income earners' loan that resulted in the loan being more than the value of the house. Reuben had $1,000 in savings, and when I sold the house, my final proceeds were minus $1,000. So we literally had *nothing*. We could have lamented this fact or felt angry at the injustice of it all and sat around with our friends at barbecues blaming the government or our upbringing, but we didn't. Instead we dreamed, and we dreamed really big. Not the kind of impossible daydreaming that many people do, but real, goal setting dreaming where we'd set a goal and look at how we could possibly achieve it.

We did very well in those early years, building our dream home in Perth and paying off our debts more quickly than most. However, it was still just an above-average existence and we wanted more. We knew that there would be more opportunities on the other side of the country, so in 1996 we moved to the Central Coast of New South Wales.

Where did the idea for the company 'Destiny Financial Solutions' come about and how did you get it off the ground?

I had started the Australian National Training Company and it was doing quite well, but the company was really only just me and it would only ever make money through my own personal exertion. I knew it wasn't the thing that was going to make me a success; it was just an in-between activity that paid the bills. As a sideline, I started to prepare résumés and job application letters for people in the evenings. I had just had my fifth child and although I was still getting training work, the additional income was helping us to pay off our mortgage faster, which was our burning ambition at the time.

One day a man named Brenton Bandy came to me for a résumé. He rushed off saying, 'I have someone coming to tell me how to pay off my mortgage more quickly' and I asked him for the person's name so I too could have a consultation. The next week this person showed me a remarkable new system for debt repayment and asked me to pay him $3,000 to implement it. If he had offered me some real service and support for the $3,000 I would have agreed, but it seemed to me that he wanted me to pay him just for the idea. I told him that I could implement such an idea on my own, but that I appreciated there were others who might need a helping hand, and that I wanted to work for him as a consultant. I knew I could use my skills and knowledge to add value and provide a real service to people. And of course he saw the money making potential of sending me out to recruit new clients, so we started a business relationship. It wasn't long though before I began to feel that very little was being delivered to clients for the fees they were paying – and of course I also thought I could do it all so much better!

Reuben was a policeman at that time and in his spare time he taught himself computer programming. He felt that he could write the software necessary to deliver the financial reports that we would need to service clients with this type of system, and I knew we could supply a far greater and more professional level of after-sales support than the company I was working for, so we made the decision to give it a go on our own.

How did you get your business to grow so phenomenally?

When we moved from Perth to the Central Coast, we sold our house for less than it was worth and just moved. We had a business idea which we knew could work and we were prepared to pretty much risk everything on that idea. But after about six months the business was not doing well, we hadn't been able to get noticed, and by then we only had around $20,000 left. I remember coming home one day and saying to Reuben, 'One of us has to get a job', and we both looked at each other with horror!

Instead, he called the radio station to discuss advertising and they came back to us with a campaign proposal that would cost almost all of our remaining $20,000 – we decided to risk it.

The radio people told us that an ad takes about a week to begin seeing results, but ours worked instantly. We received so many phone calls that we were booked for three months solid – and we've never really looked back.

What do you love most about educating people?

I love showing them how to build a secure future. I love the look in people's eyes when I speak to them, the way they smile so you can just see their excitement brimming. I love the people who stay back after a presentation to hear more, or to tell me of their own successes. I love the way people take the time to email and tell me how much they got from my books.

Most of all, I love the thought that when I die, my place in this world will have been justified because I did more than just take up space. If I can change the destiny of just one person, then it has all been worthwhile.

What are some of the practical things you do to increase referrals?

We make sure that when people are happy with what we do, we ask for referrals. We reward happy clients for sending us to their friends, but you cannot ask for a referral until you are very sure that your client is happy – too many businesses ask for referrals too early in the relationship and people don't like that.

Our VIP newsletter is free and we have around 15,000 people on our database. We're careful not to exploit this opportunity by over-selling our services, rather we provide really good, free information. This way people get to know us first and I believe that when the time comes for them to need help they will feel comfortable with us.

66 We received so many phone calls that we were booked for three months solid... 99

How important is it to have a supportive and encouraging spouse when setting up your own business?

In my case, Destiny Financial Solutions would not be here without Reuben. We have always been a team.

Reuben understands the person I am. We've always shared everything from the housework to the care of the children, but we have had to learn how to work together in the workplace and that hasn't been easy. We have made it work, often because of the compromises Reuben is prepared to make. Recently we have defined our roles within the business so that we are not treading on each other's toes. I am an extrovert and good at communication, so being the 'face of the business' is right for me. I am also pretty good at conflict resolution, so I handle the complaints which, I hate to admit, you do get once you begin to expand and lose a bit of control.

Reuben is the managing director and takes care of the daily running and development of the business and the software. He has broad shoulders and bears the responsibility of liaising with the franchisees so he is in the line of fire much more than I am. I get to waltz in and waltz out and keep every one happy while he catches the fallout!

So I think you need much more than just a supportive and encouraging spouse – you need a life partner and a soul mate!

Being in the financial planning industry you must have seen many unethical practices. How does someone determine whether a particular investment is ethically sound?

When I first began as a financial adviser it was like wading into shark-infested waters! There were too many people trying to do too many things, and it appeared to me that most of them had their own interests at heart! That was when we decided to specialise only in direct property investment – no other financial adviser seems to do this, yet it is the investment of choice for so many people.

I don't advise on potential investments and when it comes to property I don't tell people where to buy either. We teach people strategic financial management and property investing rather than providing advice on what or where to invest. I teach them how to recognise viable investment opportunities for themselves, that way they're not reliant on anything I tell them and they can decide whether a particular property is right for them. Just as in the old proverb, we believe that you can give a man a fish and he will eat for a day, or teach him to fish and he eats for life!

What are the most important things you have learnt about succeeding in business?

I've learnt that what people want from you is to simply deliver on your promises; to always provide more than your client expects; to own up to your mistakes; to ensure that you handle complaints immediately and with great care and consideration for the person making them. I've learnt that people only complain if they're not happy, and if they're not happy it's because you gave them an expectation of service which you did not deliver.

I have also learnt that the three most important attributes everyone in business needs to have are compassion, honesty and integrity. People pay lip service to these qualities all the time, but few really deliver.

What were some of the challenges you had to overcome on the journey to achieving your personal and business goals?

The challenge of balancing work and family was the biggest one. I would continually beat myself up about my choice to work rather than be a stay-at-home mother. It's only now that I can see what a terrible stay-at-home mum I would have been! My children are all flourishing as independent young adults, which is largely a result of having to fend for themselves so

> **❝ I had to learn how to step back and allow him to make decisions and implement strategies...❞**

often! I now appreciate that we must choose the path from which we can derive the most personal satisfaction, and through this we apply ourselves to all areas of our lives far more effectively and successfully.

In business the challenge was learning how to work with my husband and to appreciate his input. My biggest weakness is thinking that I know everything! My husband has enormous talents without which there would be no business. I am really mostly the figurehead – the 'front person' of the business, while Reuben handles the back end. I had to learn how to step back and allow him to make decisions and implement strategies without insisting that he run everything past me. We had to work out what we each did best and then assign respective roles, allowing each other the autonomy and freedom to make decisions. Of course, I now realise how great this is and what a huge relief it can be to have someone else carrying so much of the load!

Have there ever been times when you wanted to give up, and if so, what got you through?

When it was just Reuben, myself and two employees, we used to hold 'staff' meetings all the time to work out how we would get enough money to pay the bills the following week. We would brainstorm all of the things we could possibly do, and sure enough something would come off for us and we would live another month! At these times I just wanted to have a normal job and not have to feel the pressure of those two employees' needs as well as the needs of my own five children.

Now that we have expanded and are franchising, there are still the odd days when I think that it would be easier if we were back when it was that simple!

Our franchisees do an amazing job helping us to assist investors all over Australia, but once your business begins to grow nationally in the way ours has, there will be challenges every day. It's easy for onlookers to think that Reuben and I sit at the top of our network and do little to earn our money, while it's difficult for others to appreciate the blood, sweat and tears that went into the years before you became successful. On these days, I really do want to give it all up, but then I usually get an email from a reader that makes me feel good again.

What made you decide to get into the business of writing books?

When we first began Destiny Financial Solutions, we were about helping people to get out of debt faster. Since we have always practised what we preach, Reuben and I were doing really well with our own mortgage, and soon we started to invest in property. I was stunned at how little good information there was and how many people were simply waiting to take advantage of the unsuspecting. So I made a point of collecting as much information as I could and disseminating it as easy-to-understand concepts.

Pretty soon my clients began to hear about our property investing, and as they were also doing well paying off their mortgages, it was natural that they wanted us to guide them with their next steps, so I would teach them how to invest and help them along the way. I don't think I had a single client who didn't say to me at some time, 'You explain things so well, you should write a book!'

I have a great love of writing. As a teenager I penned pages and pages of pained tomes expressing the trauma of young unrequited love! So writing has always been 'my thing', far more than financial planning is. It was wonderful to be able to combine my writing skills with my career and a book was such a natural progression for me.

How have you been able to successfully juggle being a full-time mum (with five children) and a full-time businesswoman?

The most important thing is to understand yourself and don't ever feel guilty for the choices you make. The longest I've ever stayed at home after having my children was four months with my first. By the time I got to the third I was taking a week off for the birth and then going back to work part-time at first and full-time after three or four months. I used to think this was a money issue, but I now realise it's just who I am. I like to work, I like to be busy and I like to be stimulated. Staying at home just doesn't do that for me. After I had my last child I thought I would give it a try. I would get up, do the housework by 10.00am and then go shopping for something to do. After three weeks I realised I was better off working and earning money than not working and spending it, so I went back to work.

Had I stayed at home, I would not have been a very good mother. My patience is not that great and I'm sure I would have gone mad. The most important thing in a child's life is to be with people who can love and nurture them, and that doesn't always have to be the mother. I made sure my children were in good quality day care centres where there was low staff turnover, and that I spent quality time with them when I could. I am not a full-time mum, but we are definitely a full-time family.

What are some of the things parents can do to give their children a better financial start in life?

There is only one thing you can do – lead by example. We have lost the art of delayed gratification and as adults we send the wrong messages to our children. It's not only giving too much to our children that can cause problems, it's having too much for yourself. By this I mean using credit to get things you just cannot afford simply because you can't wait.

You must look at the example you are setting today. Are you everything you can be? Are you happy with your life, rather than just accepting of where you are? If not, then you cannot expect your children to succeed where you have failed. Understand the truly great impact that every action you take has on your children's lives, and commit to being the best person you can be.

What are some of the most important values you have tried to instil in your children?

You never get anything in life unless you are prepared to work for it – We have never given our children a lot of 'things', nor do we buy them lots of toys at Christmas. They have to work for everything they get and this has always been the case.

You must remember those less fortunate – We have always taught the children to give ten per cent of everything they earn to charity. You must have compassion for those who do not have the same advantages as you, and understand that people have things in their lives that may make them unhappy or even unfriendly, so *you* have to take responsibility for being the happy, friendly one.

You will only get ahead if you learn about money – And, you must start a savings plan as soon as you can. Sadly, once they turn sixteen they seem to temporarily forget this rule and spend everything they earn. I'm still waiting for them to get old enough to remember this again and to start paying more attention to their own financial futures.

You have to take time to smell the roses – Appreciate your achievements along the way and don't get so committed to the future that you forget about today. Take some time out to reflect on where you are, every day.

Tell those you love that you love them as often as you can – One day they will be gone. My father passed away very suddenly three years ago and I still cry when I think about him. He knew I loved him, but I still

66 My patience is not that great and I'm sure I would have gone mad. 99

don't feel that I took the opportunity to tell him often enough. I was too caught up in my own daily life and worries. My mum lives with us now and although some days I don't feel like it, I try to look in on her just to say hello.

Margaret and Reuben with their five children after renewing their vows.

What do you love most about business?

Everything! I get up every day and *want* to come to work. I don't even have to be here anymore as the business is self-sufficient, but I still come in.

I love being able to come up with an idea and then see it come to fruition. Business allows me to have an impact on people's lives – from the staff throughout the network of Destiny branches, to the clients who use our services. I love getting emails telling me about how people have managed to change their lives and seeing people at expos and shows who are so thankful for what we have done for them.

More recently, I love the freedom of choice that being successful in business has given me. I enjoy being able to decide on a whim to go away for the weekend, or to take the day off to play golf, and not worry about the budget. This has been a long time coming, and because we spent so many years being frugal, I have an even greater appreciation of this opportunity.

If you had your time over again what would you do differently?

I would take more risks, seek out successful people with money and convince them that they need to invest that money with me. Mark Bouris from Wizard took the opportunity to use his personal networks to form a relationship with the Packer family, which resulted in a hefty investment in his idea. This huge kickstart paid off for him. I have always been too scared to take such a leap and have tried to build my business with no debt, which has its upside and downside – we have no business debt and we're still growing very well, but I always wonder how big we would be today if I had been able to convince someone to give me $20 million or so when we first had the idea!

If anyone can succeed in business no matter what their background or circumstances, what do you think holds people back from becoming successful entrepreneurs?

To be brutally honest, I don't agree with this statement. I think that your background and circumstances do play a large part in what you do and where you go. You only have to look to third world countries to see an abundance of very clever people starving every day due to their circumstances. Even a huge positive mental attitude cannot produce food and water for these poor people.

I feel that I have had advantages that others may not have had, such as an encouraging family environment, willpower and determination. Having said this, there are many, many people in this world who do have the wherewithal to achieve great things, but never do. Usually it is because they have a barrier in their minds which is being inadvertently used as an excuse. We hear all kinds of excuses from clients every day – 'I can't do that because of…my wife, my job, my back, the kids, my childhood…' and so the list goes on.

> **❝** ...before I make a decision, take a risk, or do something new, I remind myself that it won't kill me...**❞**

Life has taught me many things: when one door closes another always opens. Perhaps not right away, but every time something bad happens to me, I just know it's because down the track there is a good thing that could not have occurred without the bad thing happening! But the main lesson I have learnt is that the worst thing that could happen to me is that I could die. So, before I make a decision, take a risk, or do something new, I remind myself that it won't kill me, and that anything else that happens will be manageable. This is a good way of removing all the excuses and just giving most things a go.

What advice would you give to an aspiring entrepreneur who wants to get started in a business of their own?

Research your business first and be very sure that you are not just buying yourself a job. I have so many clients who want to start their own businesses, often a franchise, because they 'want to be their own boss'. What they don't realise is that often all they are really doing is buying themselves another job, with more hours, far more responsibility and less pay, and that staying with the boss they don't like may be a better option.

When you start a business of your own, your first goal should be to get out of it! There is a huge difference between being 'self-employed' and being 'in business'. Someone in business should be able to leave their business, for months at a time, and have no impact on its success. If your business is all about you, then you do not have a business at all. So, make your first goal to become replaceable and then deliver. Look at what others do and do more. Go an extra step and when you think you have done enough, ask yourself what else you can do to make it even better. Understand the importance of value-adding – you do not need to discount to be successful. Keep your prices the same, but add value in ways that don't add a huge cost to your bottom line. In Australia, people are so tired of being let down in terms of service delivery that if you can over-deliver, you will have happy clients.

What are your top tips for becoming a successful entrepreneur?

1. Choose something you love to do.
2. Do it better than anyone else does it.
3. Know your competition.
4. Value-add.
5. Start today.

You have now written a total of five books on wealth creation. What advice can you give to someone who is thinking about writing a book?

Write as if you are in the room speaking to someone. When people meet me for the first time, they usually tell me how pleased they are that the impressions they have of me from my books are right! I'm exactly as they expected me to be! This is because I write as I would speak, in pure and simple terms without trying to make people feel stupid. I'm always being told that people feel a real truth and honesty in what I write, and this is because I write from my heart. I am passionate about my subject, I know what I am talking about and I want everyone else to know it too!

Why is it important to never compromise your integrity and reputation?

I simply don't know how people can live with the knowledge that they've been anything other than ethical, and bad behaviour certainly gets emulated throughout the generations by our offspring. In this day and age there are so many opportunists with no ethics taking advantage of the unsuspecting, relieving them of their money and proposing all sorts of wild strategies which do little more than line the pockets of these charlatans. Little wonder people have lost their ability to trust.

I want others to see that you *can* be successful and remain 100 per cent honest, ethical and genuine. I want people to know that hard work and commitment do pay off and that integrity brings success. Helping others really does help you. If people choose me as the person to derive some inspiration from, then I have an important job to do in living up to that task. I will spend every day living my life according to the principles that I hold dear in my heart, and if I cannot be successful after all that, then perhaps it's not success that I really want.

FREE BONUS GIFT

Margaret Lomas has generously offered a FREE BONUS GIFT valued at $30.00 to all readers of this book...

Live Interviews with Margaret – This transcript of several live radio interviews takes you up-close and personal with businesswoman, wealth strategist and best-selling author Margaret Lomas. Packed with practical information on investing and purchasing positive cash flow properties, you'll also learn the '20 Must-Ask Questions' before acquiring any piece of real estate.

Simply visit the website below and follow the directions to download direct to your Notebook or PC.

www.SecretsExposed.com.au/female_entrepreneurs

AMY LYDEN

66 Success brings power and money, two things
that are highly valued in our society. By
attaining success through business, a woman's
voice becomes louder, and she is able to create
change more effectively. 99

AMY LYDEN

Amy Lyden was born in the US in 1966. She grew up in Las Vegas and studied marketing at the University of Nevada. Amy spent ten years in the travel and hospitality industries in the US, Canada and Australia.

In 1995, Amy got two kittens but was unable to find just the right identification tags for them – she wanted something with more style and personality than was currently available. She had a hunch that other pet lovers would want something different for their beloved pets too – and she was right. Shortly after starting Bow Wow Meow, it was awarded Best New Product at the Annual Pet Industry Trade Show, and today it is a leading producer of fun and functional pet tags. Its products are distributed through more than 1,500 pet shops and veterinary clinics around Australia, New Zealand and Singapore, and sold throughout the world via www.pet-tags.com, an innovative and interactive website designed to help pet owners match their pet's nametags to their colour and collar.

Bow Wow Meow has won numerous business awards including the 2002 National Telstra Small Business Award and the 2000 NSW Micro Business of the Year Award. Amy was also selected as the 2004 winner of the Leading Women Entrepreneurs of the World™ grant, an international organisation that helps female entrepreneurs grow their businesses.

Amy is passionate about helping other women in business and is the Chairperson for the Australian Businesswomen's Network, and is a regular mentor for the Women in Business Mentor Program run by the NSW Department of State and Regional Development.

Today Amy lives in Sydney with her husband Mark and their two gorgeous cats, Rajah and Champers.

When did you and your family first realise that you had an entrepreneurial flair?

I was always interested in business on some level. When I was about eight years old, I used to 'play business', pretending that I owned a large organisation. I'd set up pretend cheque accounts to manage the money, and have my cats as employees.

When I was a little older, about twelve years old, I used to sell candy for a profit at school. This was largely driven by my own candy habit and the desire to find a way to fund it! I would stock up at the 7-Eleven on my way to school and sell it for a premium price. I discovered that people will pay a premium for things they want immediately, it's just a matter of finding out what they want. From then on I knew I was destined to be in business, it was just a matter of which one and when.

What was your first significant business venture and what did you learn from it?

When I was 22, I moved from Las Vegas to San Francisco to manage a branch office for a wholesale travel company that I was working for at the time. They were ready to close it down because it was so unprofitable, so I practically had to start from scratch. I hired staff, did budgets, sales and marketing, and set up sustainable systems. I also learnt about the importance of building relationships and networking. Because I was new to the Bay Area, I joined a number of associations where I met potential customers and other key people in my industry, and these relationships contributed greatly to the success of my office, which went on to become one of the highest performing branches in the group. This was an excellent learning experience and a perfect training ground for starting my own business.

My current business, Bow Wow Meow, makes pet tags with personality and distributes them through shops and veterinary clinics around Australia and New Zealand, as well as via the internet. I started it because I came across

66 ...it wasn't easy and there were many tearful days along the way when things didn't go to plan. 99

an opportunity and had a go. Several years ago, I got two kittens and was really disappointed with the identification products available. I thought there would surely be other pet owners out there who loved their animals as much as I loved mine, and who wanted a good quality tag. That was the initial thinking behind it.

Did you have a lot of critics and how did you overcome their negativity?

It was more that people underestimated me, but I find it's good to be underestimated – it actually gives you an advantage, the quiet achiever emerges and surprises everyone. I like that. It's important to have your supporters around you – your personal cheerleading squad. When you have one it's harder for the critics and their negativity to get through to you. I can't emphasise enough how essential it is to have a support team. Whether it's your own goals-group, a leadership circle, or just other people in business that you can call on when you need a hit of energy, they all help to combat any negativity you may encounter.

What is your company's mission statement and why should all businesses have one?

Our mission statement is:

Bow Wow Meow exists to provide high quality, unique pet products to keep pets safe, healthy and handsome.

Our contribution to the global community is to ensure the existence and longevity of animals and their environments on Earth.

It is important to have a mission statement to remind us of what our bigger goal is; it's ultimately what drives us as an organisation. Businesses should be wholly inspired by their mission because that will be what keeps you going on those really bad days. Without a mission it can be too easy to get caught up in the day-to-day, which is quite often not inspiring. I think there must be a higher purpose to a business, and it's important to be able to connect to that when you need to.

A mission also keeps you on track so that you can really enjoy what you have achieved. When I look back and see the growth and the impact that my company has had on the market – when it didn't even exist ten years ago – I am extremely proud.

In the beginning, what were some of the business skills you were lacking and what did you do about it?

Although I had experience setting up offices for a large organisation, there were a lot of gaps in my skill-set. I knew nothing about the pet industry and nothing about manufacturing. I joined the Pet Industry Association and volunteered time to the State Committee. Even though I had very little time to develop my own business I knew it was important that I get to know what issues were affecting my industry, and who the major players were. I met so many people through this connection and it was crucial to my success.

When it came to manufacturing, I simply persisted. I had no experience with this, I just knew what I wanted the finished product to look like. The Yellow Pages became my bible. I just started ringing different companies and if they couldn't help me, I asked them if they knew anyone who could. Learning how to manufacture came down to sheer determination and persistence. I didn't give up until I had my final product, but it wasn't easy and there were many tearful days along the way when things didn't go to plan.

Education is one of my core values. If there is an area where I feel I am lacking, I sign myself up for a course, buy a book or hire an expert to coach me. One can never know everything and I believe in continually learning. Part of my yearly planning includes taking stock of my skills, identifying which areas are the most in need of help and putting a plan into action around this. For example, a few years ago I was doing a lot of presentations and speaking so I did a couple of courses and read some books on the subject to better equip myself. Another area in which I needed to develop some skills was with the media. I was doing a lot of interviews and wanted to be able to handle them easily. At the time, the thought of a live radio interview scared the pants off me, but after some training and lots of practice I now feel confident handling these.

When did you first discover that the internet was a powerful tool for selling your products internationally?

When we first started, we built an extensive library of names that we made available to help pet owners find a name for their new pet. It was hugely successful. Our first site, www.bowwow.com.au was launched in 1998 and we had over two million unique visitors in the first year alone.

We kept adding content to the site, but didn't actively sell any product until we launched our e-commerce site, www.pet-tags.com, in 2000. I didn't want to just put up a catalogue of pet tags that people could choose from, I wanted to keep with the spirit of our original site and make it interactive, fun and helpful. With this in mind we created an interactive colour-matching site whereby people can see what colours best suit their pets. The site also helps people to choose the correct size, based on the size of their pet. Again, this site was a huge hit and we have now sold pet tags to more than 50 different countries, from India to Chile. Our philosophy is to create value on our sites for our customers, to offer free relevant information, make them fun and easy to use, and completely automate the back-end processes.

It blows me away knowing that dogs in Iceland and Fiji wear our tags thanks to the internet! It's something that I couldn't have imagined when I started the business. This excites me greatly. Opportunities emerge that you can never predict and it's a matter of moving with them. You need to stay on top of what's possible because the business environment is a moving, changing thing.

What is the biggest mistake you've ever made in business and what did you learn from it?

The biggest mistake I made was trying to do everything myself, but I learnt to get help. Having a great team, both internal and external, is critical to growth and success. It's important to have a team from the beginning, but that doesn't just mean employees. It can be anyone you work with to build your business – your programmers, designers, accountants or lawyers. Think of them as team members, rather than people you pay to provide a service to you. Include them in your planning sessions, share your dreams and vision for the business and get them excited about being part of your 'team'.

66 It blows me away knowing that dogs in Iceland and Fiji wear our tags thanks to the internet! 99

What were some of the challenges you had to overcome on the journey to achieving your personal and business goals?

In the early days of building my business the biggest challenge was having to sacrifice everything for it. I rarely saw my friends and family, my health suffered and my marriage ultimately failed. I worked twelve to eighteen hours a day, seven days a week, and it was very difficult.

There was a point at which I had to start separating Bow Wow Meow 'the business' from Amy Lyden 'the person'. The two had collapsed into one and I lost myself for a while! This was hard to go through, but an important lesson. It can be difficult in the beginning, because whenever you are trying to start and grow a business it takes time, but it's important to take care of yourself as well – whether it's building in time with friends and family, exercising, eating well or relaxing. A long holiday may not be possible, but it's critical to take care of your health. Also, having a good support team around you is essential. At around this time I would meet once a week with four other women in business. We helped to support each other in our businesses and in our lives, and it totally helped me through this difficult period.

These challenges almost made me give up, but I persevered. When I was young and my mum or I had a bad day, she always repeated the famous quote by Scarlet O'Hara in *Gone With the Wind*, 'After all…tomorrow is another day', and it is!

These days I don't work such ridiculous hours because I have a good team around me and I don't have to take everything on myself. And I've learnt not to make major life-decisions in times of turmoil. There are times when everything seems wrong and bad and it's important to just accept that and move through it – light will eventually come.

Who are the mentors that have inspired you and what important lessons have you learnt from them?

My mum is my greatest mentor. She is a very strong, independent, self-motivated and highly artistic woman. I have learnt from her that with determination one can accomplish anything in life. She went through some tough times in her life and many days lived with the motto 'This too shall pass'. She just gets on with things and doesn't let an upset get her down for long. I learnt my optimism and strength from her example at a very early age. She inspires me every day.

One of my first mentors in the workplace was a manager I worked for named Kathy Catlin. She was all about customer service and our customers *loved* Kathy. I had never seen such loyal customers. She made them feel special, and was a true master at turning customers into advocates. I learnt most of what I know about customer service from watching Kathy. Without happy customers, there is no business, period. Customer service is simple – make people feel special – but as easy as that sounds, it's not always easy to do. Our entire service policy at Bow Wow Meow stems from this. If you always start with the customer in mind you can't go wrong.

In terms of business mentors, I would say that Anita Roddick, founder of The Body Shop, is one of the top mentors around. Anita incorporates her core values into her business and really makes a difference to the world (not just her own pocket) through what she does. She truly makes business more about the power of helping others – she is a true humanitarian. I am inspired by this and try to incorporate a sense of 'contribution' into my daily business. We donate a percentage of sales to the World Wide Fund for Nature and I also donate my time to the Australian Businesswomen's Network (ABN), of which I am the Chairperson.

The male equivalent for me would be David Bussau, the founder of Opportunity International, a leading global aid organisation. Through his generosity and amazing leadership he has built an organisation that is

> **"" Without happy customers, there is no business, period. ""**

helping to empower people and end poverty. David is such a powerful person, yet is so humble and completely driven by the need to help others. He spoke at an ABN event in 2004 and the quote that sticks in my mind is, 'It's not about success, it's about significance'. That really got to me. David has inspired me to be generous with my spirit and to take on huge challenges. If his organisation can make an impact on poverty, what am I able to do? Certainly much more than I think I can! It's important to me to have business mean more than just 'making money', it's also about making a difference.

Is there a significant quote or saying by which you live your life?

I have a few favourites that inspire me.

- *You must do the thing you think you cannot do.* – Eleanor Roosevelt
- *It is so important to stretch yourself. We are all much bigger than we think, and can achieve huge things. We won't ever know it if we don't try it!*
- *Our greatest glory is not in never failing, but in rising up every time we fail.* – Ralph Waldo Emerson
- *Failing is part of success. Most very successful people have 'failed' their way to success!*
- *Attitude determines altitude.* – Anon
- *Good attracts good. Bad attracts bad. Expect the best, get the best. Simple as that.* (This is also about knowing yourself, and how to manage your emotions. It's about taking care of yourself physically, mentally and emotionally so that you do feel good, positive and healthy.)
- *There is nothing either good or bad, but thinking makes it so.* – William Shakespeare
- *Whether you think you can or think you can't, you're right.* – Henry Ford

These last two quotes are very similar but probably the most important. It comes back to your beliefs, attitudes and expectations. The outside world merely reflects your own projection of these things.

- *It's not about success it's about significance.* – David Bussau, Founder, Opportunity International
- *Life must have meaning. Growing a business is not just about money – it's about the difference one can make to the world.*

What do you think are some of the essential characteristics of a successful entrepreneur?

I think the most essential qualities are determination, the ability to visualise, dream big and have eternal optimism. Entrepreneurs tend to see how things *can* get done and what *is* possible. They don't see obstacles as stopping points and they aren't afraid to fail, in fact, they believe that failure is compulsory for success. They are passionate about building their business. I think they are also fiercely independent. They like to do things their own way and are prepared to put in the hard work necessary for success. So many people want success but they aren't ready to make sacrifices to achieve it – you can't have your cake and eat it too.

If anyone can succeed in business no matter what their background or circumstances, what do you think holds people back from becoming successful entrepreneurs?

What holds people back is themselves. People are brilliant at blocking themselves from their true potential. It's easy to blame external things or to play the victim, that doesn't take any work at all. What is confronting is realising that *you* and *only you* are 100 per cent responsible for your own failure or success. That is a scary proposition, and one that we need to be reminded of constantly.

> 66 It's easy to blame external things or to play the victim, that doesn't take any work at all. 99

What advice would you give to an aspiring entrepreneur who wants to get started in a business of their own?

First things first, put together a great support team of other people in business that you meet with regularly and help each other out. Surround yourself with people whom you admire or can learn from. Create your own personal cheerleading squad – people who only want the best for you and who are prepared to help you shine and be the best you can be.

Next, consider what you are going to do. Try to think of things that make people's lives easier. Life is getting more and more complicated, how can you make it easier? Also, as a consumer, what are some of the products and services that you want that others might too? This is how I got the idea for my business.

Then, start researching. One of the key areas that I find people need to do extra research in is understanding the financials. This is absolutely essential. Often, new business owners underestimate or don't understand cash flow. I highly recommend a course called 'Beyond Survival'. It's a two-day course put on by the Westpac bank. It is a highly practical, hands-on course designed to help business owners understand a profit and loss statement, balance sheet and the key ratios that determine the health of a business. Numbers do not lie, and if one doesn't understand what they mean it can be a serious disadvantage. Many people block themselves in this area by saying, 'Numbers aren't my thing' or 'I was never good at maths'. This is very damaging talk. It is critical to understand the financial aspects of your business – this is one area that should *not* be abdicated to the bookkeeper or accountant. The bottom line is that no one knows your business better than you, even a CPA. I'm not suggesting that you micro-manage the financials, but you should at least understand the financial statements and cash flow of your business.

What are your top tips for becoming a successful entrepreneur?

1. *Create a support network* – Get to know other people in business and form relationships with them. Form a goals-group or leadership circle where you all support and help one another.

2. *Create alliances* – Network within your industry. Form alliances with other companies that have the same customers as you and be open to ways of working together that could benefit everyone.

3. *Sell yourself and your business* – Make yourself known. Don't be afraid to tell everyone about your business. Get out there and promote.

4. *Create a board of advisers* – If you don't have a board of directors, set up a board of advisers. I have four people on my board, including myself. We meet quarterly to discuss my company's performance, to go over the financials, and to look at potential opportunities. Make sure that the people involved have complementary skill-sets with expertise in different areas such as marketing, operations/systems, general management and finance. Another thing to consider is the direction of your business, make sure you have someone on your board that can help you go where you want to go. For example, if you plan to start exporting you may want someone on your board that has experience with this. And make sure they have a balance of personalities. It's also important to have each of the following on your board:
   - A Clarifier – someone who asks how things will get done and thoroughly assesses the risks involved.
   - A Challenger – someone who helps you act boldly and really go for it!
   - A Wise Elder – someone who has been there, done that, and provides invaluable wisdom.
   Recruit these people from outside of your organisation, family and friends if possible. This will create an objective board.

5. *Contribute* – Donate ten per cent of your sales to a charity and volunteer time with an industry association. Spend time mentoring others who

need it if you are in a position to do so, and give talks and presentations to share information.

6. *Develop great systems* – Build long-term sustainable systems in your business. If you do something twice, create a system for it!

In your opinion why do so many small businesses fail?

Many small businesses fail because of two reasons:

1. *Poor cash flow* – Many business owners underestimate the time it will take to break even. It's better to be conservative about this and have enough in the coffers to keep you going in the meantime.

2. *Owner burnout* (not enough support) – It's so important to have good support structures in place and a network of other business owners whom you can talk to for support.

What do you see as the major business opportunities over the next ten to twenty years?

Over the next couple of decades I believe the major opportunities in business will be in:

- *Anti-ageing Products and Services* – As the baby boomers get older, there will be a lot of opportunities for anti-ageing products and services, such as teeth-whitening and non-surgical processes like micro dermabrasion and Botox treatments. Pretty much anything to make people look or feel younger will become a focus.

- *Health Centres and Retreats* – With the pace of life as it is these days, health is a major opportunity. Day spas, retreats, detoxing centres, and any type of place that people can go to recharge and revitalise their health will be very popular. Alternative treatments and therapies will also grow in popularity.

- *Natural Foods* – Opportunities have emerged in natural, healthy or organic food. With our increasingly busy lifestyles, people are looking for fresh and natural fast foods. We've already started to see this in Australia with the huge popularity of juice bars, which first started in the USA in the mid-nineties, and this will expand into food as well.

- *Time Savers* – The other major opportunity will be in anything that saves people time, or makes life easier. Time compression is a 21st century phenomenon. We are constantly in a hurry, trying to do too much with too little time. If a business can help save our most valuable commodity, it is bound to succeed. Some examples are home services – cleaning, cooking, child carers, pet carers – as well as innovative ways to offer your product such as pick-up and drop-off car servicing, dry cleaning and pet care.

As a mentor to other women, what are the most important messages that you want to impart to aspiring female entrepreneurs?

The most important thing I say is to have a go. Don't be a wallflower – get out there and promote yourself and your business. I think many women have trouble with this and they need to learn to put themselves out there in order to succeed.

Also, get the help that you need. Put together a goals-group, a board of advisers, or simply ask people for help in the areas in which you need it. Women have so much to offer in the realm of business. It's about standing up and creating a company that you are proud of, one that can help you to become a leader in your community and create change on the planet. Think like Anita Roddick.

What are your top five favourite books on business and life?

1. *The Prophet* by Kahlil Gibram – Beautifully written in 1923, this book truly touches my soul. My mum recommended this one to me a few

years ago as her mum had recommended it to her. So it's a personal thing as well.

2. *Das Energi* by Paul Williams – This was written in the early 1970s. I first read it when I was only fifteen years old and it changed the way I thought about the world. It's still a major influence on my thought process.
3. *The E-Myth* by Michael Gerber – Without a doubt, this is the best business book I've ever read. It transformed the way I do business. I think it's compulsory reading for anyone who wants to get into business.
4. *Rich Dad, Poor Dad* by Robert Kiyosaki – This changed the way I think about wealth creation.
5. *Understanding Life* by Lawrence West – This teaches you how to become a powerful person.

What are the wider opportunities for women in business?

I see business as an opportunity for women to empower themselves. It is a forum in which a woman can create what she likes, how she likes it, without any glass ceilings or politics obstructing her. It's completely up to her to be successful.

When a woman becomes successful in her own business, she not only contributes to the business world, but she has an opportunity to contribute to her community and society at large. This is a way for women to truly make a difference. Success brings power and money, two things that are highly valued in our society. By attaining success through business, a woman's voice becomes louder, and she is able to create change more effectively. Again, Anita Roddick is a perfect example of this in action.

I believe we need more women in powerful positions. We need women to be the change merchants in the world today and to help truly transform our world. We are facing massive global problems – poverty, illiteracy and environmental sustainability. We need leadership to deal with these effectively, and I think this is where women have so much to contribute. It's just a matter of all of us committing to play a much bigger game.

SUE WHYTE

  66 I thrive on the adrenaline and the

anticipation of what each day may bring. When

you are in business you are never bored. There is

always something to do, somewhere to go,

lessons to be learned, people to meet and

successes to enjoy. **99**

SUE WHYTE

Sue Whyte was born in Melbourne in 1953. Her earliest childhood memories were of her grandmother sewing the family's clothes on her antique Singer sewing machine. It ignited in Sue a love of fabrics, colour and fashion which eventually led her to Flinders Lane in Melbourne, the hub of Australian fashion in the 1970s.

Sue's career spanned all aspects of the fashion industry from design and manufacturing, to licensing and importing. During the 1980s she introduced the children's fashion label, Hangabouts, into Australia. It embraced the style and presentation of an adult fashion brand for the under tens; it was an instant success and instrumental in revolutionising children's fashion. At the same time, Sue was also importing ladies' fashion labels from the US and Norway.

By the mid 1990s, Sue had sold the fashion labels and married her soul mate David – she was ready for a new challenge. She identified an untapped niche in the market for a brand of lingerie in extended sizes that could be purchased in a comfortable setting. She had herself long found it difficult to source fashionable lingerie in larger cup sizes and had heard many horror stories from other women about ill-fitting bras and awkward underwear shopping experiences.

In 1995 Sue launched Intimo with just five staff and a small collection of imported lingerie, available in only two colours. But with a dedication to personalised service, product innovation, exclusivity and the genuine opportunity for women to build a successful Intimo consultancy, the company grew rapidly.

Intimo is today a multimillion-dollar company with 50 staff, more than 1,000 consultants, and one of the most comprehensive ranges of lingerie available under one brand in Australia and New Zealand.

When did you and your family first realise that you had an entrepreneurial flair?

My family had hoped that I would become an academic, but by the age of sixteen I was desperate to leave school and get into business. I got my first Christmas holiday job with a deportment and finishing school in Melbourne, and went on to join as a trainee. I learnt everything from administration to teaching deportment classes, and I was hooked. I knew then that I had to have my own business.

When I was in my early twenties, I went into partnership developing a range of affordable evening wear for younger women. At the time, the only formal wear available was plain, mother-of-the-bride-type ensembles, which did not appeal to the younger generation. I would visit Europe for inspiration and then come back and reinterpret the shapes and designs I'd seen for the local market. The range was sold through department stores and boutiques, and proved to be very successful.

From that experience I learnt that finding and filling a niche in the market is very lucrative and rewarding. Anyone can do the same thing, you just need to keep your eyes and ears open and ask, 'What's missing?' or 'What could be done in a better way?' Business is all about fulfilling people's needs and it's just a matter of listening to find out what they are.

How did you get into the fashion industry and where did you get your business experience?

My first foray into the fashion industry was through family contacts, and I later went on to work with a number of different people who were also introduced by family or friends. I place tremendous value on this type of networking because it's personal and credible, and I think women naturally network very well.

> **❝ I discovered that more than 75 per cent of women wear the wrong sized bra... ❞**

I gained experience from everyone I worked with. I always came into the office with an open mind and prepared to absorb everything around me. I also attended seminars, workshops, conferences, networking groups and read widely, which I continue to do. I place a great deal of importance on learning from different people and places – you can only benefit from being flexible, adaptable and open to new learning experiences.

What made you decide to start Intimo Lingerie?

I have always loved lingerie and adored fashion, but as a larger cup size woman I found it incredibly difficult to find attractive, fashionable and affordable lingerie in my size. At the time, I was in fashion importing and wholesaling so I decided to diversify to fill the obvious gap in the market.

It quickly became apparent that the lingerie business is not only about creating a quality product, it is also about how it is presented and sold. Lingerie is such a tactile, intimate and 'feel-good' product and I wanted to create a complementary buying experience. In addition, I discovered that more than 75 per cent of women wear the wrong sized bra, so a fitting and measuring service was imperative in ensuring that our customers had a supportive and comfortable bra.

That was when I discovered party plan! It was the perfect business model for this type of product – it created an opportunity for fitting and measuring, a chance to feel the product and try it on in a comfortable environment, and it enabled each person to get the individual service that is appropriate for such a personal product.

How important is it to find a niche in the market?

I believe it is a critical feature of business success. Finding and filling a niche, whether by offering a product that no one else has, or a style or level of service that is missing is essential in order to stand out from the crowd.

I did a great deal of research to define my market before I jumped into the business. Because the concept for Intimo straddled two industries – underwear and party plan – I had to consider both markets. I met with lots of people in both industries and I was pleasantly surprised by their generosity in sharing information, and I also looked overseas, in particular at the US and UK markets.

Intimo has set about doing a number of things differently from other lingerie companies. One of these is designing our lingerie in 'stories', or fashion groups, rather than just in sets. This enables customers to mix and match both within and across stories to create the combination that suits them best. We also offer a wide range of sizes, including colourful, fashionable lingerie in larger sizes. We provide a fitting and measuring service to ensure that our customers select the correct bra size and style for their needs. Our product is sold in a comfortable environment with the advice of our trained consultants who recommend shapes and styles for different body types. So, whilst many companies might sell lingerie, we offer a complete experience.

In the beginning, what were some of the business skills you were lacking and what did you do about it?

When I started Intimo, my role was in the background looking after production and administration. But over time, as the company grew and developed, my role became far more high profile and I unintentionally emerged as the 'face of Intimo'. Although I wholeheartedly believed in the company and its goals, I was not confident that I had the sales and public speaking skills required to convey that passion and belief to others. To compensate for this, I attended sessions with a business coach who helped me to clarify my personal vision for the company; I then found that I could convey it more genuinely and convincingly. Ultimately, this helped me to realise that if you believe in something passionately and work hard you can achieve anything.

What research is involved in determining the design for a product?

Lingerie design and production is a deceptively complicated process because of the number of components involved – there's up to 30 in a single bra, not to mention the different sizing options. You also have to factor in the type of fabric that will be used. For example, a rigid lace will behave differently to elastane in terms of its support features, overall comfort and of course how it looks. As a result, lingerie production has long lead times. We do a lot of fashion and colour forecasting as we are often working eighteen months in advance of a release. We look to the European trends and identify the key elements emerging from the industry fairs that are held each year. We also conduct a great deal of internal research. The beauty of the direct selling industry is that you are one-on-one with your customers. Our consultants tell us what customers like, what they want and what they need. And because we are receiving this information first-hand we are able to respond very quickly to the needs of our customer base.

Why did you make the strategic decision to distribute your products through party plan?

Party plan provided all of the elements that I felt were necessary for a positive lingerie purchasing experience. It ensured a comfortable, secure, stress-free environment in which you can touch the products, try them on and be fitted for the correct size. So many women had told me that they hated buying underwear in retail stores, and that they'd never been fitted for their correct size. Lingerie is one of those products that gives women a special boost – no matter what else is going on at work or out in the world, a matching set of gorgeous lingerie can give you an amazing feeling of inner confidence. I wanted to make the purchasing experience pleasurable and uniquely feminine, and with party plan I could do exactly that.

Party plan is convenient, fun and exclusive – it has been haunted by the image of the 1950s housewife in fluffy slippers, but I am pleased to say that it is back in vogue and a fabulous way to do business. It offers people a chance to socialise while they shop and our knowledgeable sales consultants understand the range and offer helpful advice, which is essential for today's smart consumer. It is so simple, convenient and fun and offers a personal touch in a high-tech world.

How did you overcome the perception of lingerie party plan being disreputable?

Lingerie party plan can sometimes be associated with the adult industry. Therefore, when we were entering the market it was imperative that we develop a professional, stylish and sophisticated image. This is something that I have been passionate about and I've spent a great deal of time and resources researching and developing our marketing materials, corporate image and professional identity. And as a result, I am fiercely protective of our brand image. We have strict advertising guidelines to which our consultants must adhere. These apply to any activities associated with the Intimo brand, and we will not tolerate any association that would discredit the brand image.

By incorporating Nicky Buckley as the face of Intimo we have positioned the brand as stylish, professional and contemporary. Nicky's endorsement of our product has provided us with the credibility needed to overcome any suggestion of impropriety. Nowadays, we find that this issue has become almost irrelevant as our product and name continue to gain recognition.

❝ Lingerie design and production is a deceptively complicated process... ❞

Intimo has a network marketing aspect to the business, how does that work?

We like to say that with Intimo you are in business *for* yourself but not *by* yourself. As an Intimo consultant you can sponsor new consultants and develop a sales team up to three tiers deep. This allows you to develop your business across both Australia and New Zealand and move along the Intimo 'management path' (known as the Business Plan), which offers a range of additional incentives and rewards. We are often told that the relationships and friendships that emerge within teams are the most rewarding aspect of an Intimo business, even more so than the income!

What are some of the reasons why women should consider a direct selling business?

It's all about freedom and independence. In this type of business you are your own boss and you can control when you work, how often, what your income will be and how your business is configured. So many people want to start their own businesses in order to gain independence and control over their lives, but they struggle with the start-up costs. With direct selling you enjoy all the benefits of running your own business with a minimal capital outlay.

We offer women the chance to achieve balance in their lives. Women today want a sense of control over their own lives and lifestyles, and we can offer the flexibility that gives women more control over the balance between family life and a career.

The advantages of starting a direct selling business are flexibility, social interaction, the opportunity to develop new skills, recognition for your achievements, a sense of purpose, validation of your abilities, a career path, new friendships and self confidence – just to name a few. This type of business really offers a great opportunity for personal development as well as professional growth in an environment that is nurturing, supportive and encouraging.

We are proud of so much that has been achieved with Intimo, but possibly one of our proudest achievements is our ability to empower women. Most women are not recognised for their efforts and statistics continue to show that women do more of the work, but earn less money and own less assets. It doesn't add up, and we are in a position where we can help to redress this.

What are some of the things you do to ensure that your products are of the highest standard?

Almost all of our products are manufactured in China, which has become the epicentre of global lingerie production. Over the last ten years, the standards and technology have improved dramatically and they keep getting better. That being said, we still have a rigorous quality control process both in China and Australia. We regularly visit the factories in China to ensure that the facilities are maintained in peak condition and that they adhere to our environmental and social standards.

When we're developing a new style, it undergoes a series of sample stages and is washed and worn repeatedly before going into final production. Then, it is re-examined in China and again upon arrival in the warehouse. If we don't believe that a product is up to the Intimo standard it will be returned to the supplier. We don't want anything substandard bearing the Intimo brand as it would corrupt our reputation, we'd much rather recall and return a product.

How much emphasis do you place on training?

We place a great deal of importance on training because we believe that it's a significant part of the Intimo consultancy experience. We offer training programs, workshops, conferences and seminars regularly, as well as resources such as manuals, audio packs and videos. These are designed to foster an environment of constant learning and skill development both professionally and personally. And they also provide many people with the opportunity to pick up new skills and regain the confidence to re-enter

66 She was famously quoted as saying that P&L means not just profit and loss, but also people and love. **99**

the workforce. It can be very intimidating to look for a job when you haven't worked for a few years. An Intimo consultancy not only provides income but free training for people who want to renew their skill levels and regain their confidence at their own pace.

Who are the mentors that have inspired you and what important lessons have you learnt from them?

Susan Johnston, of the self-titled deportment and finishing school in Melbourne, encouraged me to believe in my own abilities and to never give up, even in the face of adversity. She taught me that you only get out of life what you put into it and I attribute my hard work ethic to the foundation I received working with her in my late teens.

More recently, I have found the late Mary Kay Ash has been a great inspiration. She was a pioneer in the party plan industry and showed that hard work and dedication, coupled with a genuine empathy and affection for people can create a very powerful and successful business. She was famously quoted as saying that P&L means not just profit and loss, but also people and love. She built a company in which women had the opportunity to utilise their talents and skills without having to choose between family and career. This is the philosophy that we live by within Intimo.

Of all my mentors, my greatest hero was my grandmother. She was four-foot-eleven and a pocket dynamo. She packed more into one day than anyone else I know and her energy was infectious. She taught me the significant values of life including determination, compassion, strength and integrity. If I achieve half as much in my life as she did in hers, then I will have been successful.

What are the most important things you have learnt about succeeding in business?

I have learnt six key values over the years:

1. *Keep your customers happy* – If you have a happy customer you will have a customer for the long term. The quality of customer service is just as important as the quality of the product. Our customers are happy because they have a beautiful, exclusive product, they receive individual and personalised attention from their consultant, and efficient processing and delivery of their orders. Our product is unique and the service they receive is genuine, caring and professional throughout the entire experience. Our consultants are not only attentive at the time of purchase, they also follow-up to make sure that customers are satisfied and happy with their purchases. I often receive letters from customers who were delighted with their consultant and their purchasing experience. Your customers are the most important part of your business because without them there is no business. Give them reasons to be loyal and satisfied.

2. *Surround yourself with people who share the vision* – You must surround yourself with people who share the same vision and passion as you. I could not have built my dream company without my loyal staff by my side, many of whom have been working for Intimo since the beginning. Good people are a company's greatest asset and it is important to retain the right people. Communicate regularly and get to know your people. Understand their needs and their lives outside the office – get to know their partner's and children's names, and find out what's important to them. Everyone's needs are slightly different so it's important to care about them as individuals, not just as someone doing a job.

3. *Delegation* – Don't be afraid to delegate. Trying to do everything yourself will inhibit the potential of your business. Learning to delegate and become more selective of what I devoted my time to removed what was holding me back – and it also empowered my staff. Delegating demonstrates trust and gives everyone a sense of ownership of the

organisation. It is also a key to managing growth. As a business owner, it can be difficult to let go of 'your baby' and trust others to treat it with the same level of care and understanding. This comes down to making sure that you employ the right people. If you don't let go, the business will never realise its true potential.

4. *Transparency* – Make sure your staff has a very clear understanding of what you are about and what you are trying to achieve. By engaging them and collaborating you are taking them on the journey with you, not for you.

5. *Commitment* – Never lose sight of what you believe in and never give up. Absolute commitment and determination mixed with an ability to always see the positive is vital. Try not to dwell on the negative. If a difficult situation arises, always try to find the light at the end of the tunnel. None of us is perfect and unexpected things do happen. It's okay to make a mistake as long as you don't lose your focus. Deal with it, learn from it and move on.

6. *Treat the business like a marriage* – You need to take as much care when selecting a business partner as you would in choosing a life partner, and you need to constantly work on developing that relationship. Never take it for granted. Nothing can stall an organisation faster than a deteriorating business partnership.

What are your top tips for becoming a successful entrepreneur?

1. Do your research and find out about your market and your product.
2. Establish your goals and clarify your vision.
3. Be proud and passionate.
4. Keep fit and eat well.
5. Recognise your strengths and do something about your weaknesses.
6. Visualise your dream company.

What is one of the best business decisions you've ever made?

The decision to adopt the party plan model was the best business decision I have ever made. Although it was about identifying the best forum for the sale of our product, it created a whole new dimension to the company that is now the core component – people.

Intimo really isn't just a lingerie company. It's an organisation all about people and that presents a number of challenges, but it is overwhelmingly the most rewarding and amazing part.

What do you love most about business?

I love the variety, excitement, the chance to be challenged each day and opportunities to meet lots of different people. I thrive on the adrenaline and the anticipation of what each day may bring. When you are in business you are never bored. There is always something to do, somewhere to go, lessons to be learned, people to meet and successes to enjoy.

What is the biggest mistake you've ever made in business and what did you learn from it?

My biggest mistake was not paying sufficient attention to the financial side of the business. This is a mistake that a lot of start-up business owners make. I learnt the hard way that a lack of financial planning can have dire consequences. Without a sound financial base your vision is severely compromised. You need to have both the financial reality and the company vision in balance.

66 I am proud to report that in 2003 Intimo became a totally debt-free company. 99

You do not have to be a brilliant accountant to be successful but you do need to be getting sound financial advice. I believe that I have a moral obligation to provide the consultants with financial security so they can invest time and effort into their businesses without having to worry about the future of Intimo. With strong financial controls we have reduced our costs and increased productivity, and I am proud to report that in 2003 Intimo became a totally debt-free company.

Another of my greatest challenges revolved around inventory management. Unlike a lot of businesses that produce to order, Intimo must have stock on hand to satisfy demand. When a consultant sees a product at a presentation, she expects that it will be available in our warehouse for delivery to her customers within five days. Product forecasting can be extremely challenging because of the long production lead times. We need to predict colours, sizes, styles, fashions, shapes and quantities twelve months in advance. We also need to factor in expected growth and the correct product mix of bras and briefs. For example, it is no good if we have all of our bras in sizes 18 – 24 and all of our briefs in sizes 8 – 12. The right mix is critical to ensure minimal obsolescence and maximum profit. Moreover, we need it all sitting in our warehouse at the one time, ready to fill every order.

Over the last three years, we have worked hard to consolidate our inventory and maximise the product range. It has been challenging, yet rewarding, and I now feel that we have one of the most comprehensive and universally appealing collections of lingerie in this region.

Have there ever been times when you wanted to give up, and if so, what got you through?

I have never wanted to give up. Intimo is not only my business but a conglomeration of hundreds of individual businesses that I am responsible for, and I take that responsibility seriously. It has not been an easy journey, but it has been an incredibly rewarding one. The belief that I have in Intimo has never wavered. I have always remained positive and true to the vision.

If anyone can succeed in business no matter what their background or circumstances, what do you think holds people back from becoming successful entrepreneurs?

I would assume that it is the fear of the unknown. Launching your own business requires a certain 'leap of faith' and a strong belief in your vision. Moving away from the traditional nine-to-five security of being an employee and becoming your own boss can be quite daunting. And some level of fear is justified – if you are not fearful, perhaps you are not fully prepared. Embrace the fear, acknowledge it but don't let it stop you.

An entrepreneur needs commitment, passion and perseverance to make their business succeed and to be confident that they can face new territories and overcome the unknown. Within Intimo we have seen women of all ages, demographic profiles and educational backgrounds make the commitment and build incredibly successful businesses. Opportunities are there for everyone, you just need to take a chance and not give up.

To be an entrepreneur, you need to always think positively. Make sure you are passionate and love what you do. I firmly believe in Sam Walton's philosophy, commit to your business and believe in it more than anything else. If you love your work, you'll be out there every day trying to do the best you can, and pretty soon everyone around will catch the passion from you.

What are some of the important lessons you have learnt about effective leadership?

Some of the most important lessons I've learnt are:

- *Positive Communication* – Be supportive and encouraging and recognise people's achievements, both large and small.

- *Company Vision* – Be clear about your dream and share it with everyone so you are all working toward the same goal.

- *Care for Staff* – Look after your staff, recognise them as one of your company's major assets. You cannot grow without surrounding yourself with good people. Make yourself accessible to everyone, don't climb into an ivory tower. Always have your door open and be ready to listen.

- *Recognition* – At Intimo we love to use every opportunity we can to highlight people's achievements. We have found that a supportive culture that recognises and thanks people is far more effective than one that does not. You cannot underestimate the power of recognition in someone's life. It helps them maximise their potential and achieve their goals. We have different forms of recognition ranging from a personal letter to an overseas holiday. We recognise consultants in our weekly newsletter, monthly field meetings, bimonthly journal and annual conferences, and offer a range of incentive and reward programs.

Sue Whyte with celebrity and Intimo spokeswoman Nicky Buckley.

If you had to start over again with nothing, what would you do?

Become an Intimo consultant! Intimo offers unlimited growth and income potential so it would be the obvious way to start again. I would also have the opportunity to meet new people, win some fabulous rewards, work the hours I wanted and develop a new range of skills.

What do you see as the major business opportunities over the next ten to twenty years?

I think a major opportunity is providing feel-good experiences to customers. In today's environment, consumers are smart, savvy and knowledgeable. It is a high-tech, fast moving, innovative marketplace and I believe that in this environment the businesses that offer a personal touch and good experience will stand out from the crowd.

I also believe that businesses with ethical, social and environmental practices will be the organisations of choice for both employees and customers. I predict that businesses that consider the triple bottom line, not just profit, will be the ones that rise to the top.

It is said that at the end of the day everyone is ultimately in the 'people business'. What are your top tips for improving people skills?

- *Listen* – We have two ears and one mouth, use them proportionally and listen to what people are saying.

- *Get involved, interact and ask questions* – People generally like to talk about themselves. By displaying a genuine interest you learn how to best meet the needs of the person you are talking to, and the results are win/win.

> 66 I am dedicated to raising awareness about the effects of domestic violence in our society... 99

- *Praise people to success* – Praise is the best way to motivate people, it inspires them to maximise their true potential.

- *Create good working relationships* – Take time to make the other person feel important whether they are a staff member, supplier or customer.

What is your long-term vision for Intimo?

I am dedicated to raising awareness about the effects of domestic violence in our society through the Intimo Aware program. This program is designed to educate, inform and inspire discussion about domestic violence and to assist victims by providing access to resources and support services. One in five Australian women have been affected by domestic violence. This is an issue that we need to recognise and speak about. I would like to see a significant reduction in the stigma suffered by women and the silence surrounding domestic violence.

The other aspect of our vision is to continue to empower and enrich women's lives by providing them with choice – the choice to run a business as they want, to earn an income that provides lifestyle options and to realise their goals and potential.

Our long-term vision is to build Intimo into the most significant distributor of lingerie in this region and then to go global. I believe the Intimo range is unique in the way it is presented as a collection and in the way it is distributed. Taking on the world will be an exciting venture!

SUZY YATES

66 It has never been easier to be successful in business than it is now. There are thousands of business opportunities, interest rates are low, consumer confidence is at an all time high and people want to spend their money. My advice is don't wait for the next big thing, it is here now so grab it... 99

SUZY YATES

Suzy Yates is a media junkie, dog lover, endurance athlete and businesswoman. Born in 1964 she grew up in Strathfield in Sydney, the middle daughter of John and Margaret Yates.

Suzy's media career began at just eighteen years of age, when she landed her first job at radio station 2GN in the southern NSW town of Goulburn. She went on to work in radio advertising sales at Sydney's 2UE where she also presented a weekend talkback show.

While working in radio, Suzy found that many of her advertising clients would seek her opinion on their overall advertising and marketing campaigns, and she soon realised that there was a need for a complete service agency. With no previous experience, she decided to start her own PR company. Today, Bay Street Mediaworks employs thirteen full-time staff and three consultants, and has become part of the Photon Group which listed on the Australian Stock Exchange in 2004.

Suzy is a keen athlete and since beginning a fitness regime in her mid-thirties has competed the Sydney Half Marathon, the Hawkesbury Canoe Classic (a 111km event), numerous long distance swims, the Byron Bay Triathlon and has hiked the Cradle Mountain Overland Track.

In 2003 she accepted voluntary positions on the boards of both Doggie Rescue (which helps save dogs from 'death row') and the Australian Businesswomen's Network (which helps women take the plunge and establish their own businesses).

Whether it is charity work, training for endurance events, spending time with her three dogs, numerous nieces, nephews and godchildren or checking out investment properties, Suzy is constantly setting new business and personal challenges for herself and is an inspiration to everyone she meets.

When did you and your family first realise that you had an entrepreneurial flair?

My father established a business at a young age and after my sisters and I left school Mum worked in the business too, so conversations about business were always around us. Dad is passionate about sales (he sells machinery) and he would entertain us for hours with stories about his sales tactics, the jokes he told clients and the people he met. He made business sound so exciting and his genuine love for what he did was contagious. It wasn't until I had been in my own business for some time that I thought I might have inherited some of his ability.

You worked in radio selling advertising for a number of years, what did you learn from that experience?

Learning to sell is the best skill I've learnt because sales is the key to business. Selling is really just about getting to know people – talking to them and hopefully doing business together. I've attended 'millions' of sales courses and picked up some good tips, but the key to selling is laughter. It sounds simple but it's true. If you can make people laugh and share laughter with them, they'll want to do business with you. That doesn't mean you need to be a stand-up comedian, but have some sense of humour about you when you make a business call or meet someone for the first time.

My friend Susie Christie is one of the best sales people I have ever met and she is a riot. We shared an office for years when both of our businesses were growing, and every day I'd hear her on the phone making sales calls and laughing her head off, really enjoying it whether she made the sale or not. Make them laugh and they'll never forget you, that's the key to sales!

> **❝ I was stranded with another three hours to fill and only a microphone and a phone! ❞**

At the age of 22 you got your big break and were given your own talkback show. Do you think that sometimes being thrown in the deep end is the best way to learn?

Being thrown in at the deep end was the best thing that ever happened to me. Talkback radio is one of the most competitive fields and when I started in the late 1980s there were very few female talkback broadcasters.

The weekend mid-dawn announcer invited me to join him in the studio and have a listen. Throughout the morning he started asking me questions and switching my microphone on, then he started asking listeners to talk to me, and invited them to comment on how they thought I was doing. After the 3.00am news, he packed up his things and left me alone in the studio with the panel operator. I thought he was playing a joke on me, but it was the real thing. I was stranded with another three hours to fill and only a microphone and a phone! There was nothing else to do but chat away and get to know people. Talkback audiences are wonderful. The people are devoted listeners, very loyal and supportive. You do get the occasional 'nutter' but they come with any profession. The audience got me through that night and many other long mid-dawn shows.

Your life took a dramatic turn when you met Robert Kiyosaki. How did he change your outlook and perspective on life?

I met Robert Kiyosaki in the late 1980s when I enrolled in a number of his business and personal growth courses. It was a most exciting time and it helped me to determine the career path that I would take. Robert taught me that the worst thing I could have was a job. What was the point in letting someone else determine my future income? Radio is a particularly fickle industry – you can be the Queen of the ratings one day and the bottom of the pile the next. In effect I was trapped: if the station's ratings fell, then advertising revenue fell, and because I was on a commission, my key income was affected. As a broadcaster, if my ratings fell, then my talent fee was also threatened. Through Robert I realised that the only thing that should affect my income is my ability to create it.

Robert also taught me about investments and the importance of passive income (income you don't have to work for such as rent, royalties and dividends). I chose to become a real estate investor because it is something that I am passionate about and I now have a number of properties, both residential and commercial, throughout Australia.

With a lot of media experience but no real business background, how did you go about starting your own PR agency?

The initial task of setting up the business was quite easy, my thinking was that if you tell people you have a business, they will come! And as I was young, I did get a lot of support from clients and I learnt that most people do want you to succeed. It was as the business grew that the challenges began. I made classic mistakes and set dangerous precedents, things such as taking on too much work and not having enough staff, and trying to do everything myself. I mostly flew by the seat of my pants. Gradually I learnt the importance of having the right people on my team, my leadership skills developed as I watched and learnt from others, and I also learnt to handle disappointment, rejection and setbacks.

I invested $2,000 of my own savings to start the business, and I have never had a bank loan. When things got tight I'd put in some more of my own money to keep the business running. I didn't pay myself a salary for the first two years and I have never paid myself a managing director's fee. Initially, I paid the rent a year in advance as I knew if I had a premises I had a business. All bills were paid on time no matter what, my offices were always comfortable but never flashy and all the office equipment was bought at auction. I'm no master in financial planning but the business has always made a profit, the staff's salaries increase every year and they have benefited from profit sharing. Thinking about it now we probably could have grown faster and bigger with a bank loan, had nice company cars for everyone and interior-decorated offices, but what for? Would we have had a better business? I am not sure, but I do know that I wouldn't have slept at night knowing that I owed money to the bank.

In the beginning, what were some of the business skills you were lacking and what did you do about it?

In the very first days of starting my PR business, the skills I was most lacking were PR skills! It sounds weird that a person with no PR skills would start a PR business but I didn't see it as a barrier. I knew how to sell, how to write and how to pick up the phone, so that was how it started.

The accounting process was the most difficult for me to master. I had no skills in preparing invoices, keeping accounts or even knowing how much to charge. One of my earliest memories was one month when I thought I was going to go broke. No cheques had come in for two months even though we had so much work on – the problem was that I'd been so busy, preparing the monthly invoices just slipped my mind! That was a learning experience. With a bit of investigation I learnt to handle the accounting side of the business and as we grew an accounting software package saved my life!

What are the different forms of publicity and how do they compare to advertising?

Publicity comes in many forms including stories in the newspaper, interviews on radio or TV and magazine pieces. Many people get their information from the internet which has opened up new avenues for PR. Sponsorships are another wonderful method of achieving exposure, as are product associations and branding. Linking your business to a charity or good cause is another effective method of generating publicity, however you must be involved because you want to give something back, not because you want the kudos! These are all very important and form the basis of most PR campaigns, but word of mouth is among the most valuable publicity you can get. Most of our business comes through word of mouth and reputation, and to me that is the most important PR you can have.

Advertising versus public relations is an age-old argument. While PR has been the key area of my business, we also design and place creative campaigns for a number of clients, so I believe that PR and advertising work hand-in-hand. If you have complementary PR and advertising campaigns you'll be ahead of most advertisers.

The advantage that PR offers is credibility. Someone is more likely to be interested in your product if they read an editorial about it rather than just see an advertisement. It can also be more cost effective than advertising because you are not paying for space in a publication or air time on the TV or radio, but don't think of it as coming for free, a PR company charges for its time, contacts, experience and creativity. Getting the media to pick up on a story is not as simple as sending out a media release and then answering the flood of calls from journalists!

Do you believe it is important to have a well thought-out media strategy as opposed to trying to get anything you can?

Media strategies are a good starting point and all clients like to see a plan before they commence their project, but flexibility is the most important thing and you must be prepared to change the plan at any given time.

Never count on the media. Just because there have been stories written about you in the past, don't assume that you are always newsworthy. The media is governed by what happens on a day-to-day basis and while your media strategy may be a wonderful creative document, if you get

> 66 Getting the media to pick up on a story is not as simple as sending out a media release...99

the editor-from-hell who is not interested in your story you have to change tack. Guessing what will be of interest to the media is the daily challenge for every publicist no matter how much experience they have.

Another thing to keep in mind is that you cannot control the news. You may have the most exciting story of the week but if you suddenly find yourself up against a political or celebrity scandal, you can forget it!

What are your top tips for writing successful media releases?

Writing media releases takes practice and the ability to sell your story briefly, most releases are way too long. These are a few things I look for in a well-written release:

- Be controversial (if you can)
- Have a gimmick (something you do that is unique)
- Solve a problem (always a good angle)
- Have a great headline
- Grab attention in the first paragraph
- Use quotes
- Keep it short (maximum of one page)
- Use a 12-point typeface
- Apply one and a half or double spacing
- Put your name, phone number and date on the top of the release
- Check for grammar and spelling mistakes
- Have at least one other person proofread it

What are some practical things people can do to make their story more attractive to the media?

The media is only interested in you if you are newsworthy and if you make their job easier. Providing journalists with information in the way they like it is essential. Sometimes people spend hours putting together pages of information that the editor or journalist will throw straight into the bin. The best strategy is to call first (or email, but I prefer to call) and see if they are interested and what information they would like. It saves so much time and the journalist is expecting your information when you send it. It doesn't guarantee that it will be used, but you'll have a much greater advantage than if you just send a standard media release.

It is also good to have what is called a 'hook'. The hook is the interest factor. Something that makes you or your company stand out from everyone else. What can you do that is different from your competitors and that will spark the interest of the editor or journalist you are sending your story to?

Radio and television producers look for someone who will inspire a reaction from the audience. In radio, it is the person that makes the talkback phones 'light up' because the listeners agree or disagree with the guest. Often they look for someone who can give good advice, whom their listeners will identify with and who they can call for a personal consultation. On TV, the guest must be interesting and able to get their point across in a short space of time.

The media is unforgiving, so if you are boring, have a speech impediment or look scruffy, your chances of being invited back are limited. Get professional help if you are going on TV or radio for the first time and practise before you do an interview. It is a daunting experience and poor media performers are rarely given a second chance.

Remember, there are never any guarantees with the media. Even if a journalist is interested in the story, conducts an interview, schedules a photo shoot and tells you when it will run, it's still not in the bag. Until you see your story in print, watch it on TV or hear it on radio, there's always a chance that it will be canned because something better comes along, or simply because they run out of time – plenty of TV stories and radio interviews get scrapped at the last minute due to a lack of time. This is the one thing that makes dealing with the media incredibly frustrating and many clients simply don't understand that their story is just not newsworthy enough.

> **66** ...but the day I understood the importance of the team was the day my business changed forever. **99**

When is it appropriate to do your own publicity and when is it better to use a professional?

Most people could do their own PR and with some training and writing skills could produce nicely written media releases. But for the best results you need to invest the time to follow up the media, discuss the story ideas and encourage them to conduct an interview. And the question is, do you have the time to do it? In the early stages of a business when money is tight it can be worthwhile doing your own PR, but later it becomes a question of whether that is the best use of your resources.

Another time when it can be valuable to use the services of a PR professional is when you are in trouble and are getting negative publicity. Your business and reputation can be severely damaged in these situations and unless you are skilled in handling the onslaught, you should pick up the phone and get help immediately.

What is the biggest mistake you've ever made in business and what did you learn from it?

The biggest mistake I've made was persisting with the wrong team members for far too long because I was too gutless to let them go! The hardest decision I have ever had to make in business is asking someone to leave, but I now realise that prolonging the inevitable helps no one. I did it too many times in the earlier years and it was very damaging, not only to the person who feels the tension but also to the other team members who can't understand why you persist with the wrong person. I have jeopardised my business on a number of occasions by hanging on to staff, thinking that I'd be hated if I let them go. In reality, it is the good people, who love their jobs that suffer the most. They also question your sanity as you try every way you can to motivate, encourage or make excuses for the wrong team member. I will never make that mistake again. I keep in mind a saying that my mentor Robert Kiyosaki told me – hire slow and fire fast!

What is the most important thing you have learnt about succeeding in business?

There are so many things I have learnt but most importantly I've learnt that you cannot do it alone. Success in business is a shared experience and having a team with you is the highlight. For many people in small businesses building a team seems like an impossible task, and it is challenging to find the right people and create a harmonious environment, but the day I understood the importance of the team was the day my business changed forever. Suddenly you are not alone, you learn to trust and you empower others to take responsibility. Watching the team learn and grow is extremely satisfying. And as individuals come forward for leadership positions and grow in their confidence and knowledge, you realise that you are not the only one who loves the business.

Another thing I've learnt is that successful entrepreneurs always have four great attributes:

*   *Optimism* – They always see the best in any situation and know within their soul that everything will work out. Optimism is essential if you want to be a great entrepreneur. You also need determination and the ability to never give up. 'Quitting' is not a word in an entrepreneur's vocabulary – no matter what challenges arise.

*   *Generosity* – You need to give back and contribute to society. Most of the world's most generous philanthropists are entrepreneurs and they know it is their responsibility to give back. Many of the wealthiest entrepreneurs had nothing when they first started, so they know what that's like.

*   *Thirst for knowledge* – It is also important for entrepreneurs to constantly improve their education. Most are inquisitive and keen to develop new

skills or learn new methods to keep ahead of the competition. They are also keen to pass on their knowledge and happy to mentor someone whom they can see has great potential and enthusiasm.

- *Enthusiasm* – Most entrepreneurs ooze enthusiasm. You can't contain them once they start talking about what they love best, whether it is business, sport, family or charity, they are enthusiastic and that enthusiasm is contagious.

Who are the mentors that have inspired you and what important lessons have you learnt from them?

Having wonderful mentors has been one of the greatest gifts I have enjoyed. My parents were my first mentors as they always encouraged me to 'go for it'. Those early years of talking about business around the dinner table, encouraging me to get a part-time job when I was fourteen years old and the financial discussions we always shared were invaluable. Dad is the ultimate salesman – always enthusiastic, excited, eagerly anticipating the next sale and working to make his clients laugh. Mum is really the brains behind their business! She steers the ship on a steady course and was invaluable in my business as she stepped in and did the accounts, was available to answer the phones and offered really sound advice when needed. They are both real estate investors too and we share a love of property. Mum and Dad guided me through the scary experience of buying my first home at the age of 23.

The world of broadcasting is competitive and cut throat and I was lucky to have a number of mentors to guide me through. The station manager at 2GN Goulburn was a wonderful father figure to me when I was an eighteen-year-old living away from home for the first time. I was also fortunate enough in 1986 to meet the most respected radio programmer in Australia, Mr John Brennan, who is one of life's gentlemen. He saw in me something that he believed could be developed into a talkback broadcaster. Brenno, as he is fondly known, was generous with his time, encouragement and love. You couldn't ask for a better mentor to guide you through the wonderful world of radio.

In 1988, I was fortunate enough to meet Robert Kiyosaki who is now known as the best-selling author of the book *Rich Dad, Poor Dad*. At the time Robert was not writing books but educating people like me about money. My association and friendship with Robert and Kim Kiyosaki has grown over the years and the education I have received has been invaluable. I still receive wonderful advice and when Robert was in Sydney earlier this year, I proudly showed him my first commercial property investment.

If you had your time over again what would you do differently?

If I were to do it all over again I would make some significant changes. For example, having some PR training might have helped rather than making it up along the way. Understanding the finances is a must and right from day one I would have an accounting software package. I used to do it all manually, which was time consuming and highly stressful. Staff issues would be sorted out much quicker and the hiring of staff would be handled very differently. Early on I just took people at their word and didn't call their referees for an opinion. Blindly trusting what the job applicant tells you is not the way to hire staff, it only ends in tears when you realise they can't do the job to your satisfaction.

What do you love most about business?

Business excites me. I love waking up every day knowing that something exciting may happen. You never know when the phone is going to ring with an opportunity, a new client, a fantastic project or an old friend who really needs some help. Plus, there are the rewards that come from doing a great job, being extraordinarily proud of your

> 66 If I were to do it all over again I would make some significant changes. 99

team, or receiving an endorsement from a happy client. You also meet the best people and get invitations to some wonderful places.

What do you think holds people back from becoming successful entrepreneurs?

What holds people back is a lack of belief in themselves. Most often it is a lack of self confidence rather than a lack of ability or education. Some people are just lazy and not willing to do what it takes. Others come up with all sorts of excuses as to why something can't be done. It has never been easier to be successful in business than it is now. There are thousands of business opportunities, interest rates are low, consumer confidence is at an all time high and people want to spend their money. My advice is don't wait for the next big thing, it is here now so grab it before the next clever entrepreneur does.

What advice would you give to an aspiring entrepreneur who wants to get started in a business of their own?

Get started now! Take action, don't just talk about it. There is nothing worse than hearing someone talk about their great ideas but never actually doing anything about them. Talk is cheap so get out and get moving.

Once you have started your business, get educated. Join networks, there are plenty of groups where business people come together and share ideas, and for women the Australian Businesswomen's Network is awesome. If there are no business networks close by try to find a mentor that will give some guidance, and read some books on the subject. There are also great magazines such as *Dynamic Small Business Magazine* and *Working from Home*, which offer ideas and interviews with business people.

If you have no idea what to do then try the Telstra website and find out about the finalists and winners in the Telstra Business Woman of the Year Awards. Having been a finalist in 2004, I met some of the most amazing women who are all itching to pass on what they know. Be brave, call one of them and I guarantee if you have a number of targeted questions and don't waste their time, you will find them to be very helpful.

It is best to do something that you are passionate about, then the rest will fall into place. If you love what you do and it doesn't feel like work then you will succeed.

How do you balance running a business and having a life?

Balance is an essential part of running a successful business. Without time out you become a workaholic and not much fun to be around! I gain my sense of balance through exercise. Coping with the stress of business is easier when you're fit and your body rewards you by bouncing back quickly. It's hard to be your best when you are exhausted. My outlet is a long swim or a surf ski. For recreation, nothing beats a few days away in the bush, hiking with friends and camping overnight in a place where there are no mobile phones or computers. Adrenaline sports get me going too, and a week skiing is the best thing to calm my stress levels.

When I was building my business I didn't take holidays for years. I saw it as a mark of pride – 'I work so hard I don't have time for holidays' – how wrong and stupid I was. Now I love my holidays and my weekends. They're filled with sporting events and time with my family and dogs.

What are some of your personal and business goals for the next five to ten years?

There are plenty of goals ahead that I am preparing to take on. Recently I have purchased a commercial property with a business partner that is now a restaurant. My partner is a very successful restaurateur and our goal is to find another property and do another fit out.

I am currently a board member for two not-for-profit organisations and I'm gaining experience in the responsibilities that office carries, which I would like to use in other industries. I have also become involved with Opportunity International (OI), a wonderful organisation seeking to address the issue of worldwide poverty through providing loans for poor entrepreneurs in third world countries. In November 2004, I travelled with a group of businesswomen to Bali and Kupang (West Timor) and saw the work of OI first-hand and the difference those small loans make to the quality of life for whole villages. I know there is plenty of work for me to do as a volunteer for OI and my aim is to make a significant difference to the lives of those in poverty.

Suzy visiting a village in West Timor during an Opportunity International (OI) Insight Trip.

The next few years will also see plenty of physical challenges, as achieving ultimate fitness is my goal. My family is always a priority and I intend to spend more time with my parents as they get older, ski with my sister who lives in Canada and visit the Gold Coast as often as possible to see my older sister and my nieces and nephews.

FREE BONUS GIFT

The 'Secrets Exposed' series has offered a FREE BONUS GIFT valued at $14.95 to all readers of this book…

52 Best Ever Business Quotes – Contained in this document are 52 business insights from some of history's greatest thinkers. Featuring names such as: Benjamin Franklin, Jan Clazon, John F. Kennedy, Richard Branson and Bill Gates, you'll be motivated, educated and inspired. Topics include: leadership, customer service, negotiation, creativity and much more.

Simply visit the website below and follow the directions to download direct to your Notebook or PC.

www.SecretsExposed.com.au/female_entrepreneurs

TANYA HAMERSFELD

" If you have a great idea, share it and solicit feedback – don't hold it tight to your chest. I have yet to meet a paranoid entrepreneur who is successful. The successful ones share their dreams and aspirations, and bare their souls. "

TANYA HAMERSFELD

Tanya Hamersfeld was born in Montreal, Canada. Her family moved to Australia and settled in Adelaide when she was still a baby. Tanya holds a Bachelor of Arts (majoring in Psychology) as well as other qualifications specific to the training industry.

Tanya launched her company from home with the start-up capital of $10,000 while she was still at university. Within eight years Corporate Training Australia (CTA) had become one of Australia's largest training companies. Today, it has a presence Australia-wide. Its clientele reads like a Who's Who of business, including: Nike, Myer, JR Duty Free, Ernst & Young, AMF, Metricon, Harris Scarfe and the Mitre 10 group to name a few.

Tanya personally supports numerous charities including UNICEF, Lighthouse Foundation, Mirabel Foundation, Canteen, and UIA, and encourages group social conscience within her organisation. The team is involved in a variety of charities.

Tanya's successes have been recognised when she was named finalist in the 2002 and 2003 Telstra Business Woman of the Year Award, and 2003 Ernst & Young, Entrepreneur of the Year Award.

Today, Tanya is enjoying her business more than ever. She says the initial growing pains have passed and the company has found its niche in the market. Tanya is married to Leonard who also runs his own business and who is a great source of advice and assistance. The couple live in Melbourne and are expecting their first baby – although some would say that Tanya's first baby is CTA and this is baby number two!

When did you and your family first realise that you had an entrepreneurial flair?

Most of the people in my family, including my parents, have their own businesses. I'm from a background where it is part of our culture to eat together at least once a week. My brother and I learnt a lot around the dinner table and I think I got my entrepreneurial spirit from the conversations that naturally occurred there. I continue to learn today at my husband's family dinners where there are also a disproportionate number of people with their own businesses.

No one in my family ever said anything to me like, 'You have entrepreneurial talent', but what did happen was they helped me to identify the areas in which women were already achieving success. We found that it was in human resources and training, and this helped me in my decision to study organisational psychology at university.

What was your first significant business venture and what did you learn from it?

My current business would be my first significant venture; it's called Corporate Training Australia (CTA). I started it in 1996 as a sales training company in South Australia and it now has offices operating in all the major cities in Australia.

The business has taught me a lot, and I am still learning every day, but in particular I have learnt to take risks and that you can't afford to just cruise along. You have to keep striving to get to the next level because business is always moving and changing, and you need to be moving in the right direction too.

In the beginning, what were some of the business skills you were lacking and what did you do about it?

66 So instead of trying to conquer all of my skill shortages, I compensate for them... **99**

I had many weaknesses, some of which I still possess. For example, I didn't know much about finances and I am still not strong in the financial side of the business, but I have a very competent finance team and my external accountant sits on my board as well.

I think the key is to find people who have the skills that you lack, and together you can achieve much more. So instead of trying to conquer all of my skill shortages, I compensate for them by having a great team, which leaves me free to focus on what I'm best at, which is selling and developing new course material.

What is the biggest mistake you've ever made in business and what did you learn from it?

I've made so many mistakes that I don't know where to begin, but it's the same for everyone. It's tempting to just push mistakes aside and move forward, yet it's much smarter to take the time to analyse why they occurred and to create a plan that will help you avoid them happening again. Progress *breeds* mistakes – the more new ground you cover, the more likely you are to make them. I've learnt that by having good mentors you can avoid some mistakes by listening and taking their advice.

If I were to single out my most significant mistake it would be that I used to say 'yes' to every client request. We went from being a training organisation to a company that offered recruitment and mystery shopping, both of which require completely different skill-sets and have completely different sales cycles. I took my eye off the main game. We have recently shed those two services from our offering and as a result sales have increased and we've become much more profitable.

Why do you believe that teamwork is such a vital part of business success?

If you don't have teamwork, you don't have a business. It can't be all about you, it has to be about what you can achieve as a group. No doubt you've heard the saying, 'There is no *I* in Team'? Well, businesses have found that the key to successfully accomplishing projects is often through the development of teams. Whereas in the past, teamwork tended to only be used for special projects, now it is often the norm to work in teams every day. Effective teamwork has become an essential element in the success and survival of a business. But team building is not always easy to accomplish, this is how we do it:

- Training sessions on teamwork with activities that highlight the importance of working as a team.
- Weekly departmental meetings which set targets and action lists that people must report back on.
- Fun projects that are worked on collaboratively.
- Lunch, snacks or drinks together at least one Friday per month. We order out and sit around the table discussing what's going on in the business.
- Celebrate group successes publicly.

Achieving true collaboration is a problem that plagues companies because in the real world individuality is rewarded more often than team participation. To overcome this, managers must be able to develop ways for people to grow as individuals as well as in teams.

Why do you love the word 'enthusiasm' and how do you use it in your business?

The word 'enthusiasm' originates from the Greek word 'ethous', it originally referred to someone who is 'inspired by God' – and you can't get more powerful than that! We set ourselves a challenge whenever we go to present to a client to say either, 'I'm excited!' or 'I'm pumped!' because we know that enthusiasm is contagious and that's our secret weapon!

Our enthusiasm creates a certain 'vibe' in our office, which a lot of our clients notice and compliment us on. Our team cares about each other and the impression we make, and we work together to create massive enthusiasm. This attitude has resulted in a hands-on management approach, combined with a belief in empowering all employees, which has resulted in a unique corporate culture endorsing sound business principles and personal development, while having a social conscience.

Are you fazed by others who try to copy your business ideas?

I always tell my team, 'As long as our competitors are copying us, we are on the right track!' And fortunately, this is exactly what has happened to us ever since our inception. We were the first to offer one-on-one training to retailers and it was a hit due to the tight wage percentages they operate on. We have been the first with many initiatives in our industry and I find it very flattering when competitors copy us. It's an extremely empowering feeling for our team to be ahead of the rest. Let's face it, you only try to emulate people whom you admire; you only try to plagiarise material that you think will help you to gain something; you only copy people who are leading the way. It's not something to be afraid of, and I would much rather be the one being copied than doing the copying.

It's been said about recognition that 'Babies cry for it and grown men die for it'. What are some of the things you do to recognise and reward your staff?

I nurture a healthy, open environment that encourages communication through meetings, emails, social gatherings, workshops and an annual awards night. I also issue a monthly statement to everyone highlighting the top performers and the 'Team Member of the Month'. Everyone receives this very well, in fact they wait for it to be published and whenever I miss a deadline I always receive friendly reminders!

What can businesses do to attract higher calibre employees?

You must remember that *people* are the bottom line of any business. Your people are the ones who guarantee the customer experience. They are the ambassadors of your business and if they are happy you can achieve great things.

In order to attract quality people you need a quality environment that is supportive of creativity, innovation and flexibility. People want to feel valued and encouraged to come up with new ideas that have an impact on the organisation.

Most people spend more time with their co-workers than they do with their families, and for many people the workplace is a surrogate family – a place where they look for support, encouragement and appreciation. The extent to which employers provide this type of atmosphere can be a good determinant of how successful they will be in reducing staff turnover.

It also helps if you have a successful company that is achieving great results in the marketplace. People like to work for the winning company because it makes work more exciting.

Surprisingly, many of the reasons why employees leave their jobs have little to do with money. They often leave because of a human factor, such as conflict with management, broken promises, lack of appreciation, support or direction. And sometimes it's nothing to do with the employer at all, such as a need to be geographically closer to their families.

66...we know that enthusiasm is contagious and that's our secret weapon! 99

Whatever the reasons, employers need to understand them and work to minimise their effects.

When it comes to the business, why don't you like making too many decisions?

I am faced with the reality of needing to remove myself from making many of the day-to-day decisions and placing trust in my team. It is just not practical for me to make all of the decisions that the company faces. And I know that I will lose good people if I don't relinquish some of this responsibility to them. I believe in empowering my staff, and by doing so, I give them a sense of commitment and ownership, which in turn allows for the exploration of research, ideas, innovations and suggestions – and that's what helps to give CTA its edge.

What is one of the funniest things that has ever happened to you in business?

I once had someone apply for a job by walking into the office and singing their résumé to me! They were very out of tune and very loud, which made it particularly funny. It obviously made an impression on me, as I like uniqueness. Apart from that, I try to put a humorous spin on most things. We have a motto in our offices, 'If you haven't laughed at least once today, then the day is not complete'.

Have there ever been times when you wanted to give up, and if so, what got you through?

I have never wanted to give up. Everyone experiences tough times but they just make you enjoy the good ones even more. Sometimes when I do complain, my husband asks me if I want to give up and the answer is always a resounding *no way!*

When you have a passion that borders on obsession, it's nearly impossible to ever feel like you want to give up. The concept is alien to me. Challenges motivate me, I like to see if I can rise up to them, and I like to set myself new goals all the time. I'm never satisfied. When I achieve a certain goal, I'm always planning my next step.

I also now have a responsibility that extends beyond me. I have a team of people who rely on this company for their source of income. And I have a large number of women working for me who earn equal to, or more than, their spouses. So no matter how big the personal challenge is, I have a lot of great sources of inspiration and many motivating factors that contribute to my will to continue.

I also think that having your own business offers freedom. This is particularly relevant to women. I have a number of female friends who hold quite senior positions in large corporations and it's much more difficult for them to juggle family commitments. When it's your company, you have the freedom to find lateral solutions to work/life balance.

Even if I do momentarily think about giving up it raises the question, 'What would I do?' And I can never think of a better alternative, so I get back to business and move on.

> **❝ I don't want to work with a team of robots who can do 10,000 keystrokes per minute – how boring! ❞**

What is the most important thing you have learnt about succeeding in business?

I used to think that good businesses were based on good ideas but that's not entirely true. The key is in the implementation. If you have a great idea, share it and solicit feedback – don't hold it tight to your chest. I have yet to meet a paranoid entrepreneur who is successful. The successful ones share their dreams and aspirations, and bare their souls. It's only once you articulate your vision that people will want to become involved in helping you to make that vision come to fruition.

Another thing I have learnt is that people tend to do business with people they enjoy spending time with. So I constantly try to form new connections by meeting with prospective clients face-to-face. It's so tempting to just sit at your desk and send emails all day but you lose the human element. We have recently implemented 'Computer-Free Days' where we're not even allowed to switch our computers on. Instead, we call our clients, drop by and have a coffee with them, or handwrite a card or note to them. It keeps our workplace personal and fun. I don't want to work with a team of robots who can do 10,000 keystrokes per minute – how boring!

Why do you promote charity and a philosophy of giving back to the community?

I have come from a family where giving was considered the natural thing to do. When you work in a business that is constantly growing and you continuously set yourself new goals to achieve, it can be easy to lose sight of the fact that there is more to the world than just monetary gain. I think that charity and contributing to those in need puts our lives into context and reminds us that there is more to life.

Our team votes on a new charity every quarter that we donate money to. Usually, on the day that we make the donation we wear silly hats or all have lunch together. I love times like this, when we can bring our team together for a noble cause and remind ourselves that there are things that are bigger than us out there. We all need to remember that so we don't become egomaniacs!

I also believe that everyone has a role to play in building strong, active communities. Many businesses, large and small, already recognise this by pursuing social responsibility programs, which benefit their employees as well as the 'good cause'. Many people go on to get involved with local groups outside of work and feel that volunteering improves their interpersonal skills and careers.

Who are the mentors that have inspired you and what important lessons have you learnt from them?

I have many mentors and I also have a board of directors who take a keen interest in my business and serve to guide me.

Of course, my dad has been my most significant mentor, and continues to be. His advice is always practical, and he gives me advice on day-to-day things, which most mentors don't have the time for.

More recently, my husband has become one of my most influential mentors. He has a successful company of his own and a wealth of experience. He also has a real flair for marketing and is highly creative, so he looks over my proposals and helps me with my presentations.

The advice I get from each of them is in different areas where their expertise lies, so I feel like I am getting a very balanced view and have both sides covered because of their different experiences. In return, I help both of them with the development of job descriptions and training strategies for their businesses, so it's a good trade.

What do you think are some of the essential characteristics of a successful entrepreneur?

The habit of hard work – Starting a company is hard work; don't let anyone kid you about that. What I believe is that unless you *already* work hard you should not start a company.

Motivation to achieve – In almost every case, successful entrepreneurs are people who are highly motivated to achieve. They tend to be 'doers', people who make things happen, and they are often competitive. Many researchers have concluded that the most consistent trait found in successful entrepreneurs is the sheer will to win. They don't want to come in second or third, they want to come in first.

Street smarts – Shrewd or sharp might be better words. We all know owners of some very successful businesses who were lucky to even finish high school, yet they always seem to make the right moves. Call it common sense, instinct, whatever you want, but successful entrepreneurs seem to have intuitive good judgment when it comes to making complex business decisions.

Nonconformity – Entrepreneurs tend to be independent souls, unhappy when forced to conform or toe the line. They find it difficult to work for others and want to set their own goals. So many famous nonconforming entrepreneurs spring to mind such as Richard Branson, John Ilhan and Richard Pratt.

Strong leadership – Starting a new company can be a harrowing experience, full of uncertainties and risks. Successfully bringing an organisation through these trying periods requires a lot of leadership skills.

Calculated risk-taking – Contrary to popular opinion, entrepreneurs do not take excessive risks. Through careful product and market selection, creative financing, good team building, and thorough planning, the real risk of starting a new business can be minimised. In the world of small businesses, optimism is truly cheap and high-risk takers fade fast.

Reverse gambling – Almost without exception people who start companies are not gamblers. They are attracted to situations where success can be determined by applying their personal skills rather than by chance. They prefer that their destiny be determined by hard work and conscious decision-making, rather than by the roll of the dice.

What are your top tips for becoming a successful entrepreneur?

Firstly, I need to respond by saying I don't view myself as one yet; it is my aim to eventually become a successful entrepreneur. Starting a business is one of those huge, life-altering events. You need to think of it as a marriage – it takes the same depth of commitment and desire. You are going to be living with your business 24 hours a day, 365 days a year. And like with any relationship, if you want your business to be successful, you're going to have to work at it. It's going to have its ups and downs and surprises. But if you're the right type of person, with a solid plan, starting your own business can be the most satisfying, exhilarating experience of your life.

It's important to understand that the success of an entrepreneur is not measured by how much education he or she has had, or by how many years of experience are under his or her belt. An entrepreneur's success is measured by their achievements.

If anyone can succeed in business, what do you think holds people back from becoming successful entrepreneurs?

Fear of failure and the consequences associated with failure, or a lack of confidence. There are a few inhibitors to success in my opinion; laziness is the worst one of all. One of my friends who opened a retail outlet comes to mind. He is a smart man, but he

66 Entrepreneurs tend to be independent souls, unhappy when forced to conform or toe the line. 99

was never there, he was always out having coffee leaving the casual staff looking after his business. He wasn't there to oversee the business and identify areas for improvement. And needless to say, his business is no longer around.

Another inhibitor is people who do not think laterally. We come across obstacles every day in any job and it is the business owner's responsibility to help staff overcome them and find alternatives. If someone takes 'no' for an answer, or accepts an obstacle without challenging it, then it will be much more difficult for them to succeed.

What are some of the ways people can go about deciding what type of business to get involved in?

You have to be passionate about what you do. There is no point starting a cosmetics company if you don't love beauty products! Passion is the ingredient that gets you over the line every time. People who say to me, 'I want to start my own business', but don't know what field they want to get into confuse me. Those who say, 'I have an idea, I know the field and have researched the market to see what is out there' are the ones I really enjoy spending time with.

Innovative entrepreneurs are often at the forefront of their industry so they hear the words, 'It can't be done' quite a bit. They alter their path if the criticism is constructive and useful to their overall plan; otherwise they disregard the comments as pessimism. The best entrepreneurs know that rejection and obstacles are a part of any leading business and they deal with them appropriately.

Is there a significant quote or saying by which you live your life?

I think my favourite quote would be one by (John) Calvin Coolidge, who said:

'Nothing in the world can take the place of persistence. Talent will not; nothing is more common than unsuccessful men with talent. Genius will not; unrewarded genius is almost a proverb. Education will not; the world is full of educated derelicts. Persistence and determination are omnipotent. The slogan 'press on' has solved and always will solve the problems of the human race. No person was ever honored for what he received. Honor has been the reward for what he gave.'

If you had your time over again what would you do differently?

I don't know. I recently saw the movie *The Butterfly Effect*. It was about a man trying to change his past and yet not liking the results each time. I'm too scared to comment on how I would change things because it would mean that I would not be where I am today – and I like where I am and how I got here.

I'm very grateful for my life. I really enjoy the connections I have with the people in my team at work, with my friends and with my family. My business continues to challenge me and I find that very invigorating. I have made mistakes but I'm not sure that I would want to trade them for other mistakes.

What are some of your personal and business goals for the next five to ten years?

When I first started my business, I did so with the intention of one day being able to deliver the company's service offerings on a national basis. With our acquisition of another business under out belt and offices in Sydney, Adelaide, Brisbane, Hobart and Perth, I am closer to achieving that goal.

I would also like to create an environment that is truly family-friendly. While I love my business, my family and friends clearly come first. I believe that professional success can be attributed to maintaining excellent personal relationships. When people ask me how I separate my business from my home life, I get very confused – I don't think that they *need* to be separated, but they do need to be well integrated in order to achieve balance.

I once asked one of my senior managers to bring her family in to work so that they could see her beautiful office and understand how important their mum's role is in the business. They seemed very proud of mum and now they will be more supportive if she has to stay back late occasionally. In order to keep fostering this family-friendly environment, my goal is to have an in-house crèche. We are one step closer to this as we invite our trainers to bring their young children in for our fortnightly meetings. The kids occupy themselves with paper and coloured pens while we brainstorm new improvements for the business.

SONIA AMOROSO

66 To have consumers respond to that marketing – well, I imagine it must feel something like what a performer feels when they get a positive response from the crowd – it's incredibly rewarding. 99

SONIA AMOROSO

Sonia Amoroso was born in the early 1970s to Italian immigrant parents and grew up in the inner western Sydney suburb of Five Dock.

She studied communications at university, majoring in advertising, which gave her the tools to go on to write, design and manage some of the most successful direct marketing campaigns in Australia.

Following a chance meeting with Peter Nicholas, who would become her business partner, Sonia founded Cat Media Pty Ltd. While many people think that Cat Media is simply a marketing company, it in fact owns two major umbrella brands, Naturopathica and Skin Doctors Dermaceuticals, and markets almost 40 sub-brands including household names such as FatBlaster, Hair No More, Menoeze, Horny Goat Weed, Vein Away, Perfect Pout and the cult skin cream, Relaxaderm.

From practically no start-up capital, Cat Media has become Australia's fastest growing health and beauty company, with an annual turnover of more than $32 million. Sonia's success is due in part to her personal passion for natural health and beauty. She is completely hands-on in her company and even though she now employs more than 100 staff she is still very much involved in everything from research and development, to marketing. Sonia's ability to create innovative and attention grabbing marketing campaigns using a unique and aggressive 'hybrid' style of marketing has given her company a distinct competitive edge, and enabled it to grow and expand with incredible speed.

Cat Media has offices in Sydney, Melbourne, New York and London and exports to more than thirty countries. The company and Sonia herself have been recognised with multiple prestigious awards for achievement both in Australia and internationally.

What were some of the challenges you faced growing up with immigrant parents?

Being a first generation Australian growing up in the 1980s was definitely a little challenging. I believe we are the only generation of children to have grown up in what I call a cross-cultural time warp. When our parents left Europe in the 1950s and 60s, life was simple. Traditional values were everything, cultural ideas about women and their place in society were very strong, and our parents left their homelands with these values and belief systems intact. Meanwhile, social change was happening around the world at a faster rate than at any other time in history, but in the immigrants' view it was Australia that was different, they didn't realise that the same changes were taking place in their homelands, so they kept their traditional ways and enforced them on their children.

What that meant was while we were at home, we lived in pre-1960s Italy, and away from home (which was really only school as I wasn't allowed to do anything else!) we lived in 1980s Australia. I lived with many restrictions that my Anglo Saxon friends did not have, so I always felt different or left out – there were no sleepovers or days out with friends. One small blessing was that I grew up in the very Italian Sydney suburb of Five Dock, so I had many neighbourhood friends who were in the same position as me. This experience made me the person I am today. Not only because it gave me a moral and ethical grounding that no experience in the business world could ever shatter, but also because it gave me the strength of character that I would need in business.

Although I was always a little rebellious, the oppressive nature of my culture, particularly when it came to the role of women, really brought out the strong-minded woman in me who would not be told what to do. It gave me a real problem with authority, which led me to relentlessly question why that authority was in a position to tell me what to do: 'I can't go to the school dance this Friday? Why not?' 'Why' and 'why not' became questions that I asked constantly – why should my career be dependent on a superior when I am clearly more capable? Why can't a woman take

> **❝ I had an epiphany and I knew that I would never work for someone else again. ❞**

her life and her career into her own hands? Why can't a person be destined for greatness just because she is a woman?

This simple, childish question became a precursor for my future and the answer was always the same: there was no reason. There is nothing and no one that can stop you from achieving your goals. It's one of the most powerful lessons I have ever learnt and I have my background to thank for it.

Why did you choose to study a degree in communications and what are the most important things you learnt from it?

Before going to university, I worked for a couple of years and was unfortunate enough to have two sexist bosses in a row (what do you know, it wasn't just an immigrant attitude!), and that compelled me to take my life and my future into my own hands. I had an epiphany and I knew that I would never work for someone else again. My rebellious nature and problem with authority served me well to propel me into an education which would give me the tools I needed to be able to work for myself.

I chose communications originally because of my love of writing. At the time I didn't know that writing advertising copy would be my true love, it just made sense to me that with writing I could always work for myself – whether it be as a freelancer or a self-published author, the goal was always to be autonomous. The communications degree certainly provided me with the tools I needed. I started the course with the intention of majoring in journalism, but when I took an advertising class out of interest, I loved it so much that I dropped journalism and went head first into advertising.

The great thing about the course was that it was so practical. Obviously you need to have a creative side, but to add to that I learnt how to produce an ad from start to finish – in any medium. I learnt how to use desktop publishing programs to produce print ads. I learnt how to use video production equipment to edit and produce TV ads. I studied photography and wrote and created radio ads. I was equipped with all the tools I needed to create any type of advertising I chose. But most important of all, I learnt that I had an inherent talent for writing words and creating concepts that sell. I was very fortunate to learn this early on as it is one of the most important rules in business – *play to your strengths*. I credit that course with helping me understand what my strengths are.

Where did you meet your business partner Peter Nicholas and what made you decide to start a business together?

I met Peter at a Student Union dance. Peter's brother Alex (who is now our general manager) was the president of the union and the organiser of the dance – you never know where you are going to meet the people who will help you change your destiny! Peter and I had a lot in common. Most importantly, we shared a passion and talent for marketing. Peter was a devoted student of direct marketing and I was passionate about all types of advertising – including the diametrically opposed 'brand advertising'. We realised that if we pooled our talents we could create amazing things. It's strange, but one thing we shared was an unfaltering belief in ourselves and in each other. It's quite unusual to identify that so early on but the synergy was so strong we just knew it was too powerful to turn our backs on. We both wanted the same things and knew that we could create opportunities for each other that we would not be able to achieve on our own. We still call each other 'the dynamic duo' and I still believe there is a little bit of magic in the merging of our dreams.

Of all of the different types of businesses you could have created, why did you choose natural health and beauty?

In a word: passion. Peter and I both love the 'wellness' industry, particularly the anti-ageing element. When we first decided to go into business, we embarked on a number of different projects, one of which was a

> **66** At the time, onlookers thought we were one hit wonders – they were in for a big surprise! **99**

research project. We were going to write a book on cosmetic plastic surgery and its alternatives – an area of great interest to both of us. At the time, new cosmetic anti-ageing ingredients were entering the market which were said to have a dramatic effect on the skin. We were sceptical, but we had small batches of creams made up by a formulating chemist and gave them to volunteers to trial for 30 days. What happened at the end of the 30 days astounded us and set the stage for our future business. We expected the women trialling the products to come back reporting lovely moisturising properties, but nothing much more, so we were shocked to find them begging us for more. The creams had made such a dramatic difference to their skin over such a short period of time that we knew we were onto something.

There was a huge gap in the market for a clinical strength skincare brand. We didn't realise at the time how far ahead of the market we were. The book project was shelved and Skin Doctors Cosmeceuticals was born.

I am a big believer in natural therapies – they changed my life. The year we started I was struck with the Epstein-Barr virus and it left me with chronic fatigue and recurring infections. It was seriously debilitating and I had no one to turn to. Western medicine could not tell me what was wrong, every test came up normal and yet I was constantly unwell. It was only through alternative medicines that I found relief.

It is extremely rewarding to have a business that has the goal of helping people as its foundation. I think the first time that really hit me was the day we received a letter from a lady who was taking our Menoeze supplement. She told us the tragic story of her two near death experiences as she was flown by air ambulance to hospital due to a reaction to HRT. She believed her life to be over. Then she started taking Menoeze and she described in her letter how it had changed her life, or rather how it had given her life back. It was heart wrenching and I think we knew from that point on that this industry is where we always want to be.

What was your first product and how did you get it off the ground?

Our first product was called Vein Away. It was a topical treatment for spider veins and broken capillaries and it's still in our product portfolio today. We started to sell using a direct response ad – it was a simple print ad with a coupon and a free call number at the bottom. We only had about $700 at the time and everyone asks us how we managed to do that with no real budget – well, that's the beauty of being able to create your own advertisements. We somehow managed to get an account at a major publishing house in Sydney, which enabled us to place a small ad. I was still at university at the time so I had access to the production facilities and created the ad myself.

The response was phenomenal. We knew we were onto a winner so we took the money we made from that ad and reinvested it into more. Then we took those earnings and reinvested them and so on and so on. The campaign was so successful that within six weeks we had made Vein Away a household name – a result that was unheard of! Because it was becoming a brand so quickly, people were going into their pharmacies and asking about it, which really opened the door for us to get into retail. At the time, onlookers thought we were one hit wonders – they were in for a big surprise!

You have a number of different companies, brands and sub-brands under the Cat Media umbrella. What are they and what do they do?

We don't have a normal, or rather, a simple company structure. We are quite unusual in the way we do things – we had to be to make an impact in an already saturated market. Cat Media develops, distributes and markets health and beauty products currently under four different brand names: Skin Doctors Cosmeceuticals, Naturopathica, Kamouflage Cosmetics and the newest addition, Macquarie Pharmaceuticals. Each of these brands carries its own sub-brands under our marketing philosophy of *'product is king'* (as opposed to the more traditional approach of the brand being king).

- *Skin Doctors Cosmeceuticals* is a line of clinical strength skin solutions. We call them solutions because they are 'problem specific', that is, they are developed to treat specific problems. We don't do fluffy or generic moisturisers, our aim is to have a solution for every skin problem that a woman may experience in her life – from unwanted hair, to spider veins, to acne, to wrinkles and everything in between. Skin Doctors Cosmeceuticals carries sub-brands such as Relaxaderm, Potent-C, Ingrow Go, Antarctilyne and many more.

- *Naturopathica* has a similar philosophy. We were the first ailment-specific nutriceutical brand. Naturopathica products are complete and comprehensive solutions to common ailments. It carries some powerful sub-brands, many of which are category leaders such as FatBlaster, Menoeze and Horny Goat Weed.

- *Kamouflage Cosmetics* is a fun line of quirky cosmetic products, which includes the popular Jungle Bronze and Liquid Jewels sub-brands.

- *Macquarie Pharmaceuticals* is our newest addition. It is serious complementary healthcare and is also ailment-specific. However, it's slightly less mainstream than Naturopathica and has more of a medicinal edge.

Your FatBlaster product has achieved record-breaking success. What were the steps you went through to take it from the initial concept to owning a staggering 76 per cent of the weight loss market?

The marketing campaign behind FatBlaster is a perfect example of how important it is to have a USP (Unique Selling Proposition). If you are going to compete in a saturated market, or even in a market dominated by one or two major players, you cannot compete on the same playing field. You have to set yourself apart, that is, you have to have a point of difference. The weight loss market was pretty saturated when we came on the scene, but there was no real innovation and everyone was pretty much doing the same old thing. Our philosophy was different.

The first step was to bring a unique product to the market. While everyone was offering single ingredient supplements, we took all of the ingredients shown to have an effect on weight loss, researched the perfect synergy and dose, and put them all into one pill. That was the birth of FatBlaster. Our first point of difference was that we had a multi-ingredient formula. It sounds simple now, but no one was doing it at the time. Another point of difference was our marketing. It was different on every level, from our advertising to our packaging and point of sale concept. The difference in our advertising was obvious, it was aggressive, benefit-driven advertising, featuring long copy that really communicated the benefit of the product to the consumer.

The packaging was something else. FatBlaster was launched in the early days of Naturopathica and we had a very limited budget for point of sale displays, so we made our packaging into the point of sale – everything from the name of the product, to the use of photos on the pack made the product an advertisement in itself. At that time, no one was using photos on their packs, it just wasn't done, in fact people thought that we were mad and didn't hesitate to tell us so. But this unique technique really made an impact at the point of purchase. Hence, we stood out from the crowd.

The result was that FatBlaster became Australia's number one selling weight loss product in its first year. It was also single handedly responsible for growing the weight loss category in pharmacies by 100 per cent in its first year on the market. And, it was the first and only complementary health-care product to ever win the prestigious AJP Health Product of the Year Award, beating established brand names such as Nicorette, Nurofen, Panadol and Zyban. After five years it continues its stronghold on the market with an ownership of between 70 and 80 per cent of the category.

What are the advantages and disadvantages of selling your products via pharmacies and health food stores, as opposed to directly to the consumer?

Well, of course you make less money when you sell through a retailer because they have to make their margin too, but the advantages certainly outweigh the disadvantages.

For our business and the way we market our products, the channels are very complementary. Selling direct helps us to pay for part of the advertising, which means we can place more advertising. Placing more ads grows the market in retail, and the retail presence gives the brand credibility and visibility in a very different way to advertising. People see the ads, and even if they don't buy right there and then, the message is rein-forced at a retail level – and boom – the advertising kicks in and the purchase is made.

Most people are more comfortable buying from an established retail outlet rather than via mail order. But it works both ways. Being in retail has a positive effect on direct response advertising. Having the credibility of a long-term relationship with customers in retail grows the brand recognition, as well as brand loyalty and trust. That trust, which is now well established, makes people feel more comfortable about buying direct, which again means that we can buy more ads and so the circle continues.

How have you been able to expand your products into more than 30 countries?

Simply by being in an industry that helps to satisfy some basic human needs: the need to feel good (health), and the need to feel good about one's self (beauty). That message translates across all cultures so there is a demand for our type of products all around the globe. Of course, there is also more competition, but we have stayed true to our philosophy and it has worked for us.

Why are you so determined to conquer the highly competitive North American market and how are you going to do it?

The USA is the 'holy grail' of consumer culture. Just like the song about the consumer epicentre of America says, 'If you can make it there, you'll make it anywhere!' It's the most challenging of all markets, but if we make it, well, *then* you can ask me if I am happy with our success!

66...no one was using photos on their packs, it just wasn't done, in fact people thought that we were mad...**99**

We are in a growth phase at the moment – there is so much more that we want to achieve, and breaking into the American market has always been one of those things. There is a highly emotional element to that goal, because the US is where we were first inspired and where we learnt a lot of our marketing techniques. But there are two other reasons why it is so important to me personally. First, because it is such a hard market to succeed in and people are constantly reminding me how many Australian companies have met there doom there, I feel we really have something to prove and I've never been one to back down from a challenge. And second, success in the American marketplace has a wonderful marketing term attached to it, 'the trickle-down effect'. Americans are seen as opinion leaders in consumer culture, so if a brand is successful there, that success trickles down to other global markets. It will set us on the path to becoming a truly global brand.

Earlier this year we started selling in a few thousand GNC outlets across America. More recently, we have launched in hundreds of department stores throughout the US. We have positioned ourselves as 'affordable prestige' or 'masstige' and we have the most distinguished of neighbours – our counters are in the elite company of Chanel and Estée Lauder. We are following the same growth model in the US as has been successful in Australia: supporting our products with aggressive advertising, but staying within set budgets to achieve organic growth.

Even though your business already has a lot of great products, you still have a whole division dedicated to research and development, why is that?

One of the biggest sins in any business is to remain stagnant. In order to survive, you need to be able to move with the industry or the industry will run you over and leave you behind. To be truly successful, you need to aim to not just survive but to be an innovator. Because the health and beauty industry is science-based, things move at record speed. Every single second there are new discoveries and developments, so it's vital that we keep abreast of changes. We position ourselves as cutting edge, so we have to be ahead of the trends. It is important to us to be the very first to come out with a new technology.

We want to be the 'Coca Cola' of our industry – the first to market, and always the market leader. This gives us the power to create demand for a product, then to create new categories, which is what we are best at. In *creating* the category, you are in the enviable position of owning it. That's what we aim for with every new product launch. I suppose if we were happy with the level of success we've achieved so far, this wouldn't be as vital. But we still have such a long way to go. I'm often asked if I always thought I would be so successful, but the funny thing is that you are constantly re-evaluating your definition of success, so what I might have considered successful when we first started, is very different to what I want to achieve now. As far as I'm concerned, we still have a long way to go.

They say you have pioneered a distinct 'hybrid' style of marketing. What is it and why does it work so well?

Put simply, it's the merging of two diametrically opposed styles of marketing – direct response and brand advertising. Both are incredible forms of communication, but both have their limitations. Brand advertising is limiting in its nature and requires a lot of money behind it to make it work. It's also not very good at communicating benefits with consumers – I could go into why but that would take a book of its own! Direct marketing is far more effective at selling product and communicating benefits – it is our first love and we continue to run direct response advertisements to this day. We took elements of both forms of advertising and in doing so, brought the direct response advertising style into a retail environment.

The reason it works so well is because it has the appeal of the brand and the communicative quality of direct response

> **66** ...if a brand is successful there, that success trickles down to other global markets. **99**

ads. These ads are made to sell product, no other reason (and believe it or not, there are other reasons why ads are created!), that's why they work.

What are some tips you can share on how to write better advertising campaigns?

I have one tip: write them yourself. Don't go to an advertising agency. Quite often they are more concerned with their own corporate image and will create ads that are artistic or creative – but won't necessarily *sell* your product or service. No one knows your product or business like you do, so how can you expect anyone else to be able to communicate your uniqueness in the same way that you can? Look, there is another tip in there: make sure you communicate your USP (Unique Selling Proposition). It sounds so basic but it's surprising how many businesses just don't get how important it is. You need to tell people exactly why they should choose you above your competitor down the road.

What is a typical day in the life of Sonia Amoroso?

There is no 'typical' day in my life, that's what makes it so interesting. My day could include anything from appearing on morning television shows to planning ad campaigns; writing TV or print advertisements; attending management meetings; planning new product lines (or developing new products for existing lines); testing products (that's the fun part); meeting with suppliers, clients or the media; doing interviews; photo shoots; producing ads and corporate video material for training; tradeshows; planning advertising schedules; planning events; developing international markets; liaising with major international buyers (lots of late night conference calls); working with our design department on ads, posters, brochures and point of sale; developing new packaging concepts; dealing with government compliance issues and the list goes on and on. Every day really is very different from the previous one – and there is never a dull moment!

What do you think are some of the essential characteristics of a successful entrepreneur?

Most true entrepreneurs have one common quality, and that is an ability to identify opportunities and assess risks. However, the clincher would have to be their ability to *take risks*. I guess you would call it *vision*. All successful entrepreneurs possess that vision.

What are your top tips for becoming a successful entrepreneur?

1. Be passionate about what you do – If you don't love it, you won't stick to it.
2. Know your USP (Unique Selling Proposition) – If you don't know why people would choose your product or service, how will they?
3. Take risks when you believe in something – Just be sure you assess and/or minimise the risk first.
4. Understand your strengths and weaknesses – Focus on your strengths and align yourself with experts that specialise in your weak points.
5. Learn to be a great leader – Great leaders have vision and the ability to inspire that vision in others. Everyone you deal with will react or perform based on what you put out there. That includes your staff, your suppliers, your bank and potential investors. Even the general public and your customers are all waiting to be inspired by you!

If anyone can succeed in business no matter what their background or circumstances, what do you think holds people back from becoming successful entrepreneurs?

66 It sounds so basic but it's surprising how many businesses just don't get how important it is. 99

While someone's ethnic or financial background has nothing to do with their potential to succeed, there are personal qualities that can either propel a person forward, or hold them back.

> **66** ...there needs to be an understanding of the simple entrepreneurs' equation: risk = reward. **99**

For example, a woman who has all the right ingredients to be a huge success may not even try because she was brought up to believe that she should raise a family and be a stay-at-home mother. Or a man who was brought up living hand to mouth may decide that job security is more important to him than risking it all and living his dream. And some people simply might be shocked by the workload and dedication that is required to run your own business, and just give up.

I believe at the centre of all of these things is the one true thing that holds people back: fear. Running your own business means taking a big leap of faith, and it's simply not for everyone. It *is* hard and it *does* mean giving up the security of being an employee. It also means sleepless nights and seemingly endless days. No nine-to-five anymore. No being able to just switch off when you walk out of that office. An entrepreneur is working 24 hours a day.

Having said that, the rewards are more than ample. Even if all you do is make a living – you're a great success. Think about it. How many people get to make a living out of something they love doing and not having to answer to anyone? Chances are, if you love doing it, then you're probably very good at it, and that's the real key. Whatever it is that you love to do, it's likely to be a core strength, but if you don't understand what your strengths are, how can you make a business out of them?

It's never as simple as, 'I'm going to go into business'. There needs to be a reason. There needs to be vision. There needs to be passion, and there needs to be an understanding of the simple entrepreneurs' equation: risk = reward. There is no reward without risk. That's a frightening prospect, but the truth is if it were easy everyone would be doing it!

What do you love most about business?

The thing I love most about business is the autonomy it allows me. I enjoy being a leader. I enjoy the creativity of doing things our way and not having someone else dictate the way it should be done. I enjoy breaking the rules and being successful against all odds. I know one of the most important things to both Peter and myself is that we really can both say, 'I did it my way'.

I love the industry that we are in, and I love my work within that industry. To have two great passions fulfilled in the one business really is a dream come true. Planning marketing campaigns doesn't feel like work to me, it's a labour of love. And to have consumers respond to that marketing – well, I imagine it must feel something like what a performer feels when they get a positive response from the crowd – it's incredibly rewarding. If I had to sum it up in one sentence, I think it would go something like this: I love 'loving' what I do, earning a living from it, and helping people at the same time. I am truly blessed.

If you had to start over again with nothing, what would you do?

I would do exactly what I did the first time around. I would identify a passion – an industry that I would love to be in (you can't be bored *and* successful) and I would assess its marketability, that is, how big is the demand? Who are the competitors? And what can I offer that is different?

I would then test a very small marketing campaign. If that was successful, I would reinvest those earnings into more marketing, and if that was successful again, I would reinvest again, and so on and so on.

If I had nothing, I would avoid taking a large amount from an equity partner. That simply makes the risk much greater. I would prefer to take calculated risks and grow a business on positive cash flow.

FREE BONUS GIFT

The 'Secrets Exposed' series would like to offer you a FREE BONUS GIFT valued at $9.95 to all readers of this book…

The Prophet by Kahlil Gibram – This text (mentioned by Amy Lyden) stands as one of the most widely read books of the twentieth century. Through a series of 26 poetic essays, its iconic writer captures the essence of life and shares profound understandings for the moment. Recreated in eBook format, it's yours to read and pass on to friends.

Simply visit the website below and follow the directions to download direct to your Notebook or PC.

www.SecretsExposed.com.au/female_entrepreneurs

Carol Comer

CAROL COMER

66 I just love what I do. When I am working late into the night because I have been at Mckenzie's swimming sports that day, I'm not complaining about working. What I do is not really 'work' it's a huge load of fun and so fulfilling! 99

CAROL COMER

Carol Comer was born in 1964 and grew up in the small country town of Thames on the Coromandel Peninsula in New Zealand. While she did very well at Thames High School, she was keen to embark on a business career, and chose to join the workforce rather than go on to university.

After establishing a successful career in sales and marketing, Carol started High Impact Marketing Limited after she had her daughter, Mckenzie. She was looking for an alternative that would enable her to have fulfilling roles both as a mother and as a businesswoman.

Starting from the basement of her home, High Impact has grown to become a multimillion-dollar business that exports promotional products all around the world for clients such as Burger King, Coca-Cola and Air New Zealand. High Impact has won seventeen international awards for its creative and innovative product solutions.

Carol was one of three Kiwi entrepreneurs to take on three Aussie entrepreneurs on the NZ television production *The Money Game*, and she has been profiled in *The New Zealand Herald*, *North & South* magazine, *Her Business Magazine* and *The Kiwi Effect* business success book. She regularly conducts motivational speaking for business and school groups.

Today Carol lives with her husband Rob and daughter Mckenzie, between their house on Great Barrier Island, Auckland and their newly acquired home at Mermaid Beach on the Gold Coast.

What made you decide to go into business for yourself?

I had been very much the career woman in the corporate world; I loved my job and worked the normal corporate hours of 7.30am to 6.00pm. When my daughter Mckenzie was born, it was a delightful surprise and I wanted to have the best of both worlds – to be the best mum I could be as well as to have an interest in business.

I had seen many 'successful' people work too hard at the expense of their children and families, only to end up losing it all, so it simply wasn't an option for me to go back to the long and somewhat inflexible hours that the corporate world required. Choosing to start High Impact was really about me creating an opportunity for myself through which I could have real time with my daughter as well as a business life.

Why did you choose to do something in the marketing and promotions industry?

I had been working in the promotional advertising industry for five years when I fell pregnant with Mckenzie, prior to that I had been in sales and marketing for twelve years – and I loved it. I couldn't think of a more inter-esting, creative industry to be in. I have a real passion for it, and it's very important to me to do something that I am passionate about – I couldn't sell nuts and bolts, or toilets for example – no disrespect to the nuts, bolts and toilet industries!

Where did you get the initial capital to start the business and what did you spend it on?

I borrowed $70,000 from the bank, which I spent on a car, mobile phone, desk, computer, logo design, stationery and business cards. The balance went into the business as cash flow.

> 66 I have seen some very successful husband and wife teams...and I have seen some complete disasters. 99

Finding a great bank manager is essential to the success of your business. We keep our bank updated with quarterly reporting and let them know well in advance if we need an extension on an overdraft. Banks do have their very conservative rules, however the more they understand and are a part of your business, the more supportive and helpful they can be.

Once you laid the foundations for the business how did it grow?

In the first six months I read a fantastic book by Michael Gerber called *The E-Myth*. This book has been, and continues to be, one of the major contributing factors to the success of High Impact. I built my entire business on the foundations of this book.

My intention from day one was always to go global. I knew that I only had so many hours in the day, and I also knew that it took the same amount of hours to confirm an order for 5,000 caps as it did an order for 500,000, so I wanted to get the maximum results from the time I invested. We started working with New Zealand companies and then approached their Australian branches based on the success of the New Zealand promotions. In just eight years we're now exporting to eighteen countries around the world, including India, the Philippines, Hong Kong, Taiwan, Korea, Singapore, Japan, Tahiti, New Caledonia, Fiji, Rarotonga, Samoa, Belgium, the UK and the USA — all with a team of just eleven people.

We also have a 'can do' attitude toward business. We take the time to find out what our clients really want and we make it happen. For example, one client in Taiwan wanted us to deliver FIS (free into store), so we flew to Taiwan to find out what we needed to do to make it happen. We met with the client, freight and customs agents and just did it. Our attitude is that nothing is impossible. Sure, from our base here in New Zealand we can manufacture toys in China and sell them into Taiwan!

What is the biggest mistake you've ever made in business and what did you learn from it?

The biggest mistake I made was not facing reality soon enough. It's too easy as a very positive, enthusiastic person to believe that everything will turn out just as you planned. And usually it does, however when it doesn't and you must face the reality of the situation and make a decision it can be easy to procrastinate and bury your head in the sand. I have learnt to face reality in this way and to make better decisions quickly and move on.

What's it like being in business with your husband?

Rob is a 50/50 financial partner, however he has very little to do with the day-to-day running of High Impact. He was a fireman for eighteen years and has been in the police force for the past two, so although he would probably like to, he doesn't have time to work in the business. I have seen some very successful husband and wife teams, particularly where each person's role is very clearly defined. And I have also seen some complete disasters, especially when there are overlapping roles, uncertainty around responsibilities and an unfair balance of workload. Personally, I wouldn't like to work full-time with my husband and I'm sure he wouldn't like to work full-time with me!

Was it difficult to juggle the demands of a start-up business with a very young daughter?

It wasn't difficult 99 per cent of the time because I was incredibly disciplined with my time management and I had my schedule planned almost to the minute. It would consist of:

6:00am	Gym
7:30am	Wake up Mckenzie, have breakfast and get dressed
9:00am	Drop Mckenzie at pre-school
9:00am-3:00pm	Work, client visits and calls (I focused on only doing things that had to be done during the business day, everything else I would leave until later in the evening.)
3:00pm	Pick up Mckenzie from pre-school
3:00-7:00pm	Spend time with Mckenzie (and Rob if he wasn't working or windsurfing!)
7:30pm	*If Rob is at home* *If Rob is at work*
	Check emails, do urgent tasks Work until 10.00-11.00pm
8:30pm	Rob and Carol time

One per cent of the time it all turned to custard of course! Once, I had an urgent call from an overseas client and had to close Mckenzie in her room, screaming for my attention, while I took the call out in the backyard. I felt so awful about that, but I'm sure I'm not the only mum trying to juggle work and motherhood that has ever done something like that.

Now, if I need to call a client and I have Mckenzie with me, I'll sit her down with some food or in front of a cartoon, and make the call. We have answering machines and I use them when I need to. Most of our clients and suppliers are parents too and they completely understand that I am not always available between 3.00pm and 5.00pm.

When I am away overseas on business, I often work eighteen hours a day so that I don't have to be away from my family for as long. I would much rather work eighteen hours a day and be away for six days, than only work twelve hours a day and be away for nine days.

What is your strategy when it comes to employing and managing staff?

When I'm looking for new staff, attitude is everything. A person could have all the experience and qualifications in the world, but if they don't have the right attitude, or if their values are not congruent with the values of our company, then they are not going to be right for us. To make sure we find the right people, our pre-employment process is very important. Comprehensive job descriptions are reviewed to determine the skills required, recruitment specialists are contracted, prospective candidates are thoroughly checked and interviewed, and personality test results are considered to make sure the successful candidate will fit into the team. Before we make any final decisions, candidates are invited to meet with our staff (without me present) so that everyone can ask questions and get to know each other.

My management style is one of encouragement, empowerment and autonomy. I encourage my staff to think and act by trusting and empowering them to achieve their objectives. Their roles are quite autonomous, but if they are unsure about something, my door is always open.

We believe our people *are* our business so we invest in our people. Last year we invested $10,000 to bring an American promotional products expert, Cliff Quicksell, to New Zealand for a one-day training session. The first half of the day was with our staff and for the second half of the day we invited a group of clients to join us for a very worthwhile training session.

Every month we hold a luncheon focus meeting at which all employees are encouraged to share open communication. This is a great opportunity for interaction between everyone in the company. At this meeting, staff can vote for who will receive the monthly 'warm fuzzy' award, a soft plush purple donkey with a $50 note around his neck. We also update everyone on the company's achievements and direction. This fosters the entrepreneurial culture of High Impact – it's a place where people enjoy working and where they know what's going on.

> "...who will receive the monthly 'warm fuzzy' award, a soft plush purple donkey with a $50 note around his neck."

High Impact's Mission Statement is: 'To have fun, successful partnerships which consistently exceed expectations'. This was developed with our employees to reflect our ethics in how we deal with people both *inside* and *outside* the company.

What is a typical day in the life of Carol Comer?

Here's what I did today:

8:00am	Arrive at work, check emails, make final preparations for our sales meeting, wrap a small gift for our creative manager who worked particularly hard last week.
8:30am	Lead our morning sales meeting and discuss a new marketing promotion to gain new merchandise accounts.
10:00am	Answer emails, set up a meeting with our public relations agent to discuss our twelve-month PR plan, sign some expense cheques, view some new product samples from the USA.
11:00am	Meet with our operations manager to discuss US rates, forward cover, balances, cash flow, sales budgets, and profit and loss for 2006.
12:00pm	Lunch (leftovers from last night) and answer emails.
1:00pm	Spend a few minutes with my husband Rob, before he starts his afternoon shift at the police station.
1:15pm	Complete agenda for tomorrow's training session with a new strategic partner who will work with us on new creative promotional campaigns.
2:00pm	Meet with an account director to discuss new budgets for 2006 and for an update on her trip to Australia last week.
3:00pm	Discuss new High Impact merchandise range with creative manager.
3:30pm	Leave work to pick up Mckenzie.
4:00pm	Take Mckenzie to gymnastics class.
4:35pm	Check emails from home office.
5:30pm	Pick up Mckenzie and back home to prepare dinner.

6:00pm	Mckenzie and I have dinner and start on the homework for this week.
7:30pm	Read Mckenzie one chapter of an Enid Blyton book before bed.
8:00pm	Relax with a coffee and finish these questions! I'll probably work until 11.00pm tonight and watch half an hour of TV to relax before bed.

What do you love most about business?

I love the way High Impact allows me the flexibility to spend quality time with my daughter and to be there for her school events and holidays. I love the thrill of the chase in business – chasing new ideas, new clients, the best manufacturing partners and new markets. And I love the opportunities that High Impact allows me to give to people. I love seeing my staff grow and develop. I love supporting charity events. I love seeing our manufacturing partners' businesses grow, and I love seeing our clients' businesses grow.

Have there ever been times when you wanted to give up, and if so, what got you through?

Yes, there have probably been about three times when I could have seriously given up. Business is tough, much tougher than I imagined it would be. One of those three times I thought, 'If this is what business is about then I'm just not tough enough for it!' But where there's a will, there's a way. When I was in a position where I felt I had nothing more to give, I just had to dig a little deeper. My attitude is to just not give up. I feel the need to find a way and get on with it! One of my teachers wrote on my fourth form school report that I had a 'dogged determination'. I didn't quite know what that meant at the time, but I believe that my dogged determination is what got me through those dark times. And I guess only three dark times in eight years is not too bad!

> 66 I thought, 'If this
> is what business is
> about then I'm just
> not tough enough
> for it!' 99

What are some of the ways you help your clients to stand out from the crowd with their promotions?

The most effective place to start is with a specific brief that defines the objectives of the promotion. We'd ask questions such as:

1. What is your company about? Describe your brand and values.
2. What is the primary objective of the promotion?
3. Are there any other objectives?
4. Who and how many people make up the target market?
5. What do you want to communicate to this target market?
6. When and where will this promotion take place?
7. What is your budget?
8. What is the timeline?
9. How will the promotion be executed and delivered?

You can either use a promotional marketing company to develop a promotional concept based on the brief or even brainstorm with a few friends or colleagues. I have seen some awesome results come from brainstorming with a few friends over a glass of wine!

Why do you believe that creativity and innovation are so important to business success in the 21st century?

Business can be really ruthless – clients are less loyal and margins are being sliced left, right and centre, so companies must know (and make sure they let their clients know) what their leverage is in order to survive. Often, because there are so many competitors who can all do basically the same thing, your leverage is in creativity and innovation. Clients are always looking for the latest and greatest thing. They are looking for suppliers that really help them with their business and provide proactive and innovative solutions that will grow their sales.

To identify your leverage, ask yourself these questions:

- What does our company do that others in our industry don't or can't?
- What would encourage a new client to come to us?
- How do we make sure we keep our clients?
- Where can I learn, and what can I study to ensure that we keep up-to-date with trends around the world?

You must always be thinking of better ways to do business because what *was* your leverage last year, could have been copied by your competitors this year. When a business stops being creative and innovative, the business stops.

A very large percentage of what we create and manufacture for our clients is new and cannot be purchased anywhere else in the world. For example, the Looney Tunes toys we produced for Hungry Jack's in Australia could only be obtained by buying a Hungry Jack's Kid's Meal in Australia. These toys won two Gold Awards at the Australasian Promotional Products Awards, and they are a perfect example of what High Impact can create – they were highly collectable, interactive, fun and most importantly our customers loved them.

A promotional campaign for Hungry Jack's that won
two Gold Pyramid Awards at the Australasian
Promotional Products Association Awards in 2004.

What are some low-cost ways that businesses just starting out, or without big budgets, can tell people about their product or service?

Word of mouth is always the most effective promotion. Encourage your existing clients to 'spread the word' and maybe offer a small incentive if they introduce a new client to you. Belonging to industry organisations where you can network and meet new people is also a very effective way of getting your business out there.

When marketing your business, it's always good to have a clear objective of who your specific target market is and what results you are aiming for. And rather than placing a half page ad in a newspaper that your target market may not necessarily read, research and identify twenty new potential clients and market directly to them. It might cost $20 to deliver a marketing piece to each of the twenty potential clients, but if it gives you seven appointments which lead to four orders then it's a very successful result. And, it will probably end up costing a lot less than placing an ad in the newspaper.

What prompted you to set up a representative office in Hong Kong?

With our exports around the world it was essential that we have a representative Hong Kong office, as our shipments leave Hong Kong for delivery to many of our clients. The office conducts pre-shipment inspections to ensure that everything is perfect with the goods and documents prior to export. It's also great to have assistance when we encounter any communication difficulties or production challenges.

What do you think are some of the essential characteristics of a successful entrepreneur?

Every successful entrepreneur has a dogged determination to succeed. They are committed and focused, and pursue their business with enthusiasm, self-motivation and confidence. They have a certain drive and leadership about them which makes them stand out in a crowd. The best attribute that an entrepreneur possesses however, is the ability to get back up again after being knocked down. Too often the 'average' person just gives up after a couple of trials and tribulations.

What are your top tips for becoming a successful entrepreneur?

1. Believe in yourself and have the courage to just do it.
2. Surround yourself with positive, encouraging, motivated and like-minded people, and stay away from negative people.
3. Employ the services of the best bank manager, accountant, financial adviser and coach – you can't afford not to.
4. Listen to your customers – they will tell you what they want.
5. Care about the little things – do they really matter? *Yes*!
6. Never lose your focus.
7. It's all about attitude.
8. Enjoy what you do, and do it with passion.

What are some of the ways people can go about deciding what type of business to get involved in?

First, decide what you enjoy in life – what is your passion? Maybe it's fishing, diving, cooking or travelling. Whatever it is, you should pursuit it. Do something you love and do it because you want to, not because you want to make money. I know of businesses that were started solely to make money, but the business owners quickly lost interest when they didn't return instant results. High Impact has never been about the money. I started it to allow for a balance of motherhood and business, and also because I just love what I do. When I am

> **❝ I know of businesses that were started solely to make money, but the business owners quickly lost interest... ❞**

working late into the night because I have been at Mckenzie's swimming sports that day, I'm not complaining about working. What I do is not really 'work' it's a huge load of fun and so fulfilling! I am not saying that businesses don't need to make money, they do, that's how they grow and employ staff, what I am saying is that if you love what you do, the money will follow.

Apart from business, are there any other asset classes that you invest in and why?

I like to invest in property. We have invested in both residential and commercial properties and both have proven to be very successful. There are some wonderful books and seminars on investing in property which are a good place to start.

Have you slowed down a little in recent times or are you as busy as ever?

I'm as busy as ever! At different times I have slowed down but the result has always been that the business slows down too. Entrepreneurs must lead by example. They must retain their passion and focus, work the longest hours in the company and be the driver. I have never seen a business grow and develop while the entrepreneur is slowing down. I would assume that the only way this could happen would be if the entrepreneur replaced him or herself with a manager. But no one has the same passion and interest in the business as its creator and owner.

How has your business helped you on a personal level?

I have grown and learnt so much with High Impact. It has pushed me way out of my comfort zone and led me to achieve things that I didn't even know were possible. It has also taught me so much about people, partnerships, challenges and celebrations.

The personal satisfaction that comes from having worked so hard and being awarded seventeen international awards with eleven fantastic staff, who actually work for *me*, is quite unbelievable. It's a feeling I cannot quite describe.

It brings me back to my beginnings, to when I worked until 4.00am to get a deal done, or when I got on a plane and visited seven countries in five days, or when I have seen my staff reach their own personal objectives – these memories give me such a feeling of satisfaction.

High Impact has also helped my staff to grow too. It's my goal with all my staff that when they do leave me one day, they'll leave with a feeling of 'Wow, what a great experience, fantastic company and inspirational boss!'

What techniques do you use to help you achieve your goals?

I love reading business, motivational and success books and attending seminars. I'm always reading something. I love hearing about other people's success stories and learning from them. It's also good to hear about other people's challenges too because it's so beneficial to know what can go wrong before it does.

I am a real writer of goals. Every year I set personal, professional, family and financial goals. I refer to them as often as possible, if not once a day then at least once every two days, and each month I measure how I am going and what I need to work on.

ELIM CHEW

66 I love the constant change and the excitement that the fashion world can give you... It can be a challenge keeping up with the trends, but I like the fact that it keeps you guessing and keeps your adrenaline pumping. 99

ELIM CHEW

Emil Chew was born in Singapore in 1966. After finishing school she trained as a hairdresser in London.

In 1988 Elim founded 77th Street, which now has thirteen stores and has revolutionised the streetwear fashion scene in Singapore. In 2004, 77th Street became Singapore's first retailer to set up a shopping mall in The People's Republic of China with a 400,000 square foot underground shopping complex at Xidan Cultural Centre in Beijing. Elim's other business ventures include Ethics Apparel menswear.

Elim lends her expertise, experience and time to various youth organisations in Singapore. She founded The Young Entrepreneur Mastery (TYEM) with partner Adrian Lim to instil entrepreneurial skills in young people, and the Get A Life membership program which offers benefits and privileges in fashion, entertainment, lifestyle, education, sports and arts to its 77,500 members. In 2004 she launched a book for youth titled, *My Voice*, featuring 77 real life experiences written by youth from all walks of life. All proceeds from *My Voice* go toward the funding of life skills, entrepreneurial and creative skills workshops run by TYEM.

With Elim's sharp business acumen, 77th Street became the first fashion retailer to win the prestigious Singapore Promising Brand Award – Most Distinctive Brand in 2004. Her personal accolades include receiving the Young Woman Achiever Award. and Leadership and Mentoring Award 2003, the Montblanc Businesswoman of the Year award in 2002, and being named Most Promising Businesswoman of the Year by the Association of Small and Medium Enterprises (ASME) in 2001.

Today Elim lives mainly in Singapore and is actively involved in her church. She cites Pastor Kong Hee as the biggest influence in her life for sharing with her biblical principles that have guided her in her professional and personal lives.

When did you and your family first realise that you had an entrepreneurial flair?

I think my family and I influenced each other. My family is made up of my mum, my sister Sulim, my brother Chris and my god-sister Sam. They have been my biggest mentors throughout my life, and each of them helped me in one way or another to discover my entrepreneurial spirit. For example, from when we were young, my siblings and I would trade stamps with each other and sell small items such as stickers and greeting cards at school for a good profit.

My teachers noticed that I had a flair for business and many people, especially my church pastor, Reverend Kong, commented that they could see me going places. They were all inspirational to me in a way that I believe has helped me get to where I am now.

What was your first significant business venture and what did you learn from it?

At the age of 21, I trained as a hairdresser in London with many different salons including Vidal Sassoon, Toni and Guy, and Jingles. From those experiences, I gained enough confidence to open my own salon, Elim Emanuel Hair and Beauty Salon and Training Centre. We built up a strong support base of loyal clients and increased the number of salons as we grew into a successful chain.

What I learnt from that experience was business opportunities are always there. If you hear opportunity knocking on your neighbour's door, open *your* door and invite him in for a cup of coffee – your neighbour is probably watching TV with the volume turned up high, and didn't hear him knocking. Later, they'll wonder why opportunity only ever knocks on their neighbour's doors and not their own.

In good times and bad there are success stories – you just have to know how to identify and seize opportunities when they come along.

> **66** The $15,000 fee I received for the event went straight into the start-up capital to open my first 77th Street outlet. **99**

What made you decide to start your current business?

When I came back to Singapore from London about twenty years ago, I saw that there was a gap in the fashion scene, and I thought it was a niche that I could fill. At that time, fashion in Singapore was either very high-end or very low-end; street fashion was almost unheard of – unthinkable even, given its outlandish connotations – especially to Singaporeans who were very conservative at that time.

I had the opportunity to be a hair stylist for a fashion show as part of an international conference for a renowned company, and this was the catalyst I needed to start 77th Street. The $15,000 fee I received for the event went straight into the start-up capital to open my first 77th Street outlet.

Where did the name '77th Street' come from?

'7' means God created the world in seven days, and it also means completion and perfection, so 77 seemed to be the perfect business name to me.

What are your top tips for running a successful retail business?

1. Choose something that is difficult for others to copy. Whether it's because highly specialised skills are needed, or because it's expensive to get into, choose something that has a natural obstacle to being copied and you'll eliminate most of your competition before they even get started.

2. Choose an area that you are very proficient in and you'll always be ahead of your competition because you'll know what is going to happen next, what you need to do to get ahead, and where you can innovate to give you a competitive edge.

3. Always model yourself around what the best people in the industry are doing, and then do it even better than them.
4. Never take advice from those who are worse off than you. If they were good at what they do, then they'd be better off than you. If you take advice from people that are worse off, you'll just end up exactly like them.
5. Every cent counts, so keep a close eye on your finances.
6. Train your staff well to not only satisfy customers, but to delight them.

What are some of the ways in which you deliver excellent customer service?

Wow, to explain it all would take a three-day seminar! In a nutshell, we really go the extra mile for our customers, even the unreasonable ones. They will know what you've done for them and they will talk about it to their friends, family and colleagues.

What is 'Get A Life' and how did you get over 77,500 people to join?

Get A Life was created to reward our customers for their loyalty and as a mechanism to get their feedback. Through it, we can ascertain who our regular customers are, what their spending patterns are and what each individual likes. I believe it is essential that you communicate with your customers and keep in touch with them regularly in a warm and friendly way – so if you are a member of Get A Life, you will not go unnoticed.

The program has weekly contests and offers free tickets to movies, concerts, parties and other prizes such as the latest electronic gizmos and gift vouchers. On top of that, customers or 'Streeters' as we call them, also get discounts from many famous youth-related merchants; you can go to www.77thstreet.com to see the range of places that offer goodies. Because the program is aimed at youth, it is vibrant, cool and hip to be a member – hence we have 77,500 members and it is still growing.

We also often collaborate with schools. One good example is a joint project we did with the Institute of Education to set up a 77th Street Retail Training Centre in ITE College East. This centre will provide students with deeper insights into the fast-moving retail sector and gear them up to meet the challenges of the industry. We also extend our Get A Life membership program to all ITE students.

You have now established an entire shopping mall in the world's largest market, China. How did that come about?

Simply, the opportunity came along and we took it. The mall is a milestone for us, progressing from being a retailer into property management. And as it is something new, we have had a lot of challenges to overcome. We intend to duplicate the mall in other parts of China and around the world. In 2004 June, we opened the 77th Street Plaza, the first underground shopping centre in the heart of Beijing, Xidan Culture Square and the whole mall is designed for youth, just like 77th Street. By 2006 September, we will set up in Song Jiang/Shanghai.

In the beginning, what were some of the business skills you were lacking and what did you do about it?

When we first started, we were almost completely devoid of fashion industry experience; everything we did was based on instinct and what we just thought would work. At first, it was a very difficult journey and we had to go through a lot of trial and error, which was extremely painful at times.

Looking back, the biggest mistake I made was placing my trust in people too easily. I thought everyone would act from a place of integrity, just as I did. I'm not saying that you should be cynical and not trust anybody, but act with caution and remember that some people will take advantage of you if you're not careful. I've learnt to make better judgment decisions when it comes to people's character.

What do you love most about business?

I love the constant change and the excitement that the fashion world can give you. Fashion is ever changing and fast, and what is in today, maybe passé tomorrow. It can be a challenge keeping up with the trends, but I like the fact that it keeps you guessing and keeps your adrenaline pumping.

A benefit of my particular field of business is the interaction I am able to have with young people today. It's a tremendous opportunity to be able to nurture and influence them to have good values and to go on to make their own contribution to society when they're older. They, in return inspire me with their strength, energy and passion.

What were some of the challenges you had to overcome on the journey to achieving your personal and business goals?

People always told me that I would have no personal or quality time if I took up a business of my own. Everyone was so pessimistic and at times I found myself believing them. I now see how wrong they were. I do have quality time, I enjoy my work and the fruits of my work. And if you enjoy yourself at work, then it also becomes your personal, quality time. It helps that the people I work with are like a second family to me. My staff are a godsend, without them 77th Street wouldn't be what it is today.

Have there ever been times when you wanted to give up, and if so, what got you through?

Sure, there are always ups and downs and it can be tempting to give up, sometimes even I have been a victim of this. But the thought of giving up terrifies me, it would mean that I have failed. It would also mean

> **"**...we opened the 77th Street Plaza, the first underground shopping centre in the heart of Beijing, Xidan Culture Square...**"**

that everything I have been trying to build for all these years would crumble the day that I give up. Not only does that affect me but it would also mean disappointment for all of my customers, staff and the people who look up to me.

At these times, when you stop to look at the bigger picture you can see how much of an affect you are going to have in a negative way if you did give up – and you can see that if you just keep going, what a positive effect you will continue to have. This should be enough to get you through any tough times.

If you had to start over again with nothing, what would you do?

I started with nothing, so it is my firm belief that I could easily do it again, especially because I now have a more advanced knowledge. However this time, I would be more astute when it came to finances as it is very important to be good with accounting and financial systems in order to grow a business well.

What advice would you give to an aspiring entrepreneur who wants to get started in a business of their own?

There are many things that an aspiring entrepreneur has to keep in mind. First of all, they need to assess whether they really have what it takes – the entrepreneurial mindset. Every successful entrepreneur has mindsets and habits which are uncannily similar.

I believe just about every entrepreneur has a compelling reason to start their business. So you have to find the purpose that drives you to take action to achieve what you want. If you say, 'I want to *try* doing business', then it's better that you don't because trying alone is not enough. You must have a doggedness and determination to succeed.

You should also have a little bit of experience out in the workforce. This will also give you access to mentors who have experience in the field that you want to start in. Model yourself after successful businesspeople. You can also learn from those who don't succeed so that you don't fall into the same pitfalls by realising and learning from their mistakes.

Assess your strengths and weaknesses and find out what you can do best. In areas of weakness, find partners or team members who are strong and work with them.

The last thing is don't give up, succeeding is about persistence. A successful businessperson has dreams and visions, but also the perseverance to make those dreams a reality.

What is the most common mistake that new business owners make?

They think that they know all there is to know about their business, but that cannot be. It is a lifelong journey of learning and adaptation. Things change and will always continue to change.

For example, you might think that you can whip up a better tasting hamburger than McDonald's, so you start a hamburger rival to compete with them. But if you fail to realise that there are so many more things to do in your business besides being able to cook a delicious beef pattie, then you will fail.

Can you tell us about The Young Entrepreneur Mastery (TYEM)?

I established The Young Entrepreneur Mastery (TYEM), to help instil an entrepreneurial mindset in the young people in schools, polytechnics and universities. The training programs run by TYEM, which include life skills, entrepreneurial and creative skills, can help youth to embrace life and career choices with purpose and confidence.

We also launched our first youth-related book, called *My Voice*, in February 2004. It is a book that provides youth with a platform to share their inner thoughts and innermost secrets. It is a compilation of 77 voices from the

" Quite simply, it's the people that make a good company successful. "

souls of youth from all walks of life. *My Voice* is supported by Ministry of Community Development, Youth and Sports (MCYS), South East Community Development Council (CDC) in collaboration with Radio UFM 100.3FM and Drama Box (Theatre Company). All proceeds from the sale of *My Voice* go to the funding of training programs run by TYEM.

Dale and Elim in her conference room, with proof in the background that Elim is one of Singapore's most admired personalities.

How do you manage multiple businesses and personal projects all at the same time?

I have an excellent team who are cross-trained and each individual is very efficient in their area of work. Quite simply, it's the people that make a good company successful.

I am very fortunate to be in the position where I can work with my family; people I love and trust. My sister Sulim scopes out new opportunities and new markets, and my god-sister Sam is also very dedicated to the area of merchandising.

Through your career, what is the most important thing you have learnt about business partnerships?

Have a very clear shareholders' agreement drawn up, leaving very little room for disputes. Choose partners who can contribute in their area of expertise, not just cash, thereby enabling you to gain from other people's strengths and experience. Also, partners must believe in the same vision and values as you do, and want to make the vision a reality as much as you do.

These criteria are crucial as partners usually argue about issues when business turns bad – and even more so when business is booming! So it's critical to put in place mechanisms to avoid these conflicts right from the beginning.

What do you think are some of the major cultural differences between Asians and Westerners? Do you have any advice for doing business with Asians?

In a nutshell, Westerners are more direct and to the point when it comes to business, whereas Asians need some warming up and time to develop trust and confidence. Sometimes Westerners' forthrightness may come across as being rude and insensitive, which it is not intended to be. On the other hand, an Asian's way of doing things may come across as evasive and dishonest because of too much politeness. For example, when presented with a gift, an Asian will first decline saying, 'Oh, you don't have to do that' a few times so as not to come across as being greedy, but they will still accept the gift, so it may portray some element of being hypocritical.

Also, Asians do not open gifts immediately, unlike Westerners, in front of the giver thereby conveying respect to the giver and again not wanting to come across as being greedy. However, the Westerner may feel slighted because it may seem to them that the Asian is nonchalant about the gift and is not being appreciative.

I know there are a number of good books available on this subject. So if you are planning to travel or do business in a foreign country, I highly recommend some further reading. Believe it or not some very big business deals have been lost because of tiny cultural misunderstandings.

In what ways have your spiritual beliefs and biblical studies affected the way that you run your businesses?

My Christian background influences all aspects of my business, from instilling values, to the business's vision and the way I conduct dealings with people. For me, the bible is my code of conduct and my business manual. And for every serious decision, my family, my senior staff and I will seek the advice of CEO – God. We always pray before major decisions are made.

At the end of your career if you could be remembered for one thing, what would it be?

As someone who has lived happily and done my fair share for the betterment of society. I want to be remembered for touching as many souls as I can, and have many people remember me for showing them that there is always light at the end of the tunnel.

KATRINA ALLEN

66 I now put my children first, at the end of the
day they are much more important than my
business. Having my own business is lovely
as it provides me with a great lifestyle, but if
I didn't have happy children, I wouldn't
see the point. 99

KATRINA ALLEN

Katrina Allen was born in Melbourne in 1967. She grew up in Brighton in an entrepreneurial environment with a supportive loving family.

Katrina completed one of Australia's most acclaimed graphic design courses at Swinburne University in Melbourne. Prior to finishing, she landed her first job with Farman Foley Gill. She then worked for several agencies, finishing her ten years at M & C Saatchi as a senior art director and collecting some 50 industry awards along the way.

Over time, frustrated with the agency process and at not having complete creative freedom, Katrina set about her own creative projects. She has published two books, *China Plate = Mate*, a book of rhyming slang which was bought by the Ink Group and made into a calendar, and *Twinkle Twinkle*, a photographic book on animals in nursery rhymes.

Having briefly tasted creative freedom, Katrina started to look for a business opportunity of her own. She found the opportunity she was looking for in the unlikely field of feminine hygiene products. Through market research Katrina found that many women were unhappy with the bright, floral packaging and flimsy cardboard boxes that most tampon manufacturers use. So she set about developing packaging that was discreet and that would securely contain tampons in the most crowded of handbags: De jour was born.

Today, De jour is stocked in Coles, BI-LO, Priceline, Woolworths and most independent supermarkets and pharmacies. The company accounts for six per cent of the $80 million feminine hygiene category, and Katrina's aim is to arrest at least ten per cent from the big brands.

Today, Katrina takes pleasure in being the mother of three small boys. Whilst Katrina enjoys having her own business, she loves being able to combine the joys of a loving family life.

When did you and your family first realise that you had an entrepreneurial flair?

Looking back, I probably first discovered that I had entrepreneurial talent when I was about nine or ten; I was always looking for ways to make money. First, I bred white mice which my father helped me to sell to the zoo, pet shop and local school. After that, my friends and I made Christmas decorations that we sold to our families. And I also used to buy lollies at the corner shop and sell them to the kids in our street for twice the price!

Right from those early days my father has always helped me in business, and pretty much every other area of my life. He taught me the most important lesson that I have ever learnt – that there are many ways to skin a cat! Never ever give up, there is always another way to look at a problem.

Having failed art at school how did you manage to score a place at Swinburne University in one of the most acclaimed graphic design courses in Australia?

Probably because I had the 'gift of the gab', and perhaps even more importantly, because I was persistent. I had been to Open Days while I was in Years 10, 11 and 12, so when it came time to have my admission interview, they knew exactly who I was. I firmly believe that you can negotiate anything as long as you know what you want and can show the right people how keen you are, and I think they saw that in me.

How did you land your first job in advertising?

I was in my final year of graphic design at university, it was around July and I knew that in November everyone would be applying for jobs. I also knew that I wasn't the strongest student in my class so I began to think about how I would stand out when it came time for us to look for work. I decided to get started early, so I went out looking for a job in August

> **❝ I learnt how pitches are put together, how to win business, what dazzles clients, what works and what doesn't. ❞**

with my folio only half complete. I remember all the other students were shocked because no one else had thought of taking their folio out 'til November. No one had told us that we couldn't do that, it was just what everyone thought, so no one did it. I was offered a job at Farman Foley Gill and they held it for me until I completed my course.

Why did you feel that you were so prepared to run your own business?

I believe that working as an art director in a number of different advertising agencies was the greatest learning experience of my life. I worked with many major clients such as Qantas, McDonald's, CUB, National Australia Bank, Elle Magazine, Witchery, National Foods and Pura Milk, and I learnt a lot about different businesses, how they work, and how they do things.

I had to make lots of client presentations, so I had the opportunity to enhance my presentation style, and I learnt a lot about pitching for new business. I learnt how pitches are put together, how to win business, what dazzles clients, what works and what doesn't. I also learnt how to work with clients in relation to timings and deadlines. As well as these practical skills, I learnt about costings, budgeting and pulling a job together. On the media side of things, I learnt how to run advertising campaigns, about branding and marketing, and how to target a specific audience.

In short, my experience in advertising taught me enough for me to feel prepared to run my own business and it was probably the best thing I could have ever done.

What was your first significant business venture and what did you learn from it?

My first significant business venture was creating a book. It was published through William Heinemann publishing and it was called *China Plate = Mate*. I had a photographer help me with it, but I was the person running the show, and I felt that if I could publish a book I could do anything.

That experience ignited my passion for business. I come from a very entrepreneurial family and was always told that it is good to have your own business and that you can make more money working for yourself than for someone else. I also knew that one day I wanted to get married and have kids, but I wanted to be able to earn my own income as well. Being able to have the flexibility to take holidays and spend time with my family was one of the main reasons why I wanted to start my own business.

What led you to the feminine hygiene market, an already well-established industry?

In my research of the market, I saw that there wasn't much in the way of plain and discreet packaging, which is something that I knew would appeal to women since tampons are something that we generally like to keep plain and discreet! I did market research via a questionnaire to about 600 women, and their responses convinced me that I was on the right track. I saw the opportunity and decided to create De jour tampons as the 'Calvin Klein' of the tampon market.

The great thing about this market is that demand will always remain constant. Women are not going to stop having their period, and they're never going to stop needing tampons. The fact that this is such a stable market was one of the key deciding factors for me to get into this business.

In the beginning, what were some of the business skills you were lacking and what did you do about it?

The one major skill I lacked when I started De jour was in the area of finance and accounting. In the beginning I wasn't interested that side of the business, but I have gradually learnt to become really good at reading profit and loss statements and have become very hands-on with all my credits and debits. I still have my bookkeeper do all the GST stuff, but I write every cheque so that I know every dollar that comes in and goes out of my business. I realise now that finance isn't that difficult at all, it's just about how much money you are getting in and how much money is going out – it's that straightforward.

What is De jour's Unique Selling Proposition (USP)?

Our USP is that De jour tampons is the only brand that comes in discreet charcoal grey and silver zip-lock bags. We are the only company in the world that does that. The benefits are that they won't fall out into your handbag, which is a common problem for many women, and that they are discreet. Most tampons come in either colourful boxes or plastic packaging that has a tendency to tear so the contents spill everywhere.

The original idea for the packaging was plain but sophisticated charcoal grey and silver boxes, the zip-lock bag actually came about later, after I saw Glad® bags in the supermarket – something just suddenly clicked and De jour's USP was born.

You used both your own money and a bank loan to get De jour off the ground, but you say that it was not a risk. Why is that?

I actually spent very little getting De jour off the ground as I was able to do all the design work myself and pull together the research and presentation. It wasn't until I got my first order from Coles that I actually had to outlay any money. So there was no real risk because I already had a firm order. It was still nerve-wracking though, I remember saying to my father, 'My God – I've had to order this full container of tampons' – there are about two million tampons in a container – and part of me wondered what I would do with all those tampons if the order fell through. Dad said, 'Don't worry, you can always sell them to your friends', this is typical of my dad's way of looking at things, and he made me laugh.

Did your experience in advertising help when it came to pitching your product to Coles and BI-LO? And what are your top tips for successful business presentations?

Absolutely! Having been an art director, I constantly had to present creative ideas to our clients and I gained a huge amount of experience in this area. So when it came to the crunch, I knew how to pull a great presentation together.

My presentations were completely different from anything that the buyers had ever seen before because I approached it from an art director point of view, rather than from a marketing department perspective. They saw my brand as innovative and different, and they recognised that the packaging would be a hit with consumers.

My top tips for successful business presentations are:

1. Make sure your presentation is simple, clean and easy to understand.
2. Make sure it looks different or does something unique.
3. Make people remember your product. One of the things I did was leave my product samples in beautiful silver boxes, and when I came back to see them again later people would always comment that they still had the silver box. Now I leave all my products in very large zip-lock bags which relates to my brand and is something that people always remember about me.

What is the most important thing you have learnt about branding?

66 The most important thing I've learnt is to not try to be all things to all people. 99

The most important thing I've learnt is to not try to be all things to all people. You need to accept who you are as a brand, what you stand for, what you believe in, take the share of the market you know, and be happy with that. Once you try to become everything to everyone, your brand means nothing. It would be like Louis Vuitton suddenly deciding to do low-cost suitcases for $20. That would devalue the brand enormously. The reason people want a Louis Vuitton is because it represents prestige. Likewise, if I suddenly came out with brightly coloured packaging, I would be just like everyone else.

I like my brand to represent a modern, sophisticated woman who wants something that is sleek and stylish. I am not after consumers who want something bright and colourful, they're not my audience. So, remember who you are – that's the most important thing about branding.

Your company has been featured countless times in all forms of media. Do you have any tips for how to get free publicity?

Obviously, you need to let the media know what you are doing and it's really important that you have something they will be interested in talking and writing about – you have to give them a story that they can work with.

Initially, my story was that De jour were the first tampons to come in zip-lock bags, and we've been able to maintain media interest over time by becoming involved in other issues and creating new angles. For example, we got media coverage for being the only brand that places health cards in its packaging, then we got coverage because we began the 'No to GST on Tampons' campaign, and we've also had coverage about the success of the business itself. It's important to constantly be active in creating different angles for public interest.

What is the most important thing you have learnt about succeeding in business?

You need to be very thorough, you need to have a meticulous system for responding quickly to requests, reporting back and keeping people up-to-date with where you are at. You also need to keep your eye on the big picture and where your business or idea is going. You may not necessarily have all of the detail, but you do need to be able to see the end game.

What advice would you give to an aspiring entrepreneur who wants to get started in a business of their own?

I have only two words: hard work. An entrepreneur has to do a lot of it, and surround themselves with people who are smarter than they are who can work hard too.

It's really important to research the business you are thinking about going into, as well as the market, to see if there's a big enough opportunity. I would suggest speaking with other entrepreneurs to see what skills they have brought to their businesses and what they think sets them apart from their competitors.

Running your own business is really tough and it takes a certain type of person to be able to do it. A lot of people think you'll have more time to do whatever you want, and although this may be true after a certain number of years, you still have to put in a lot of effort, especially in the beginning. And at the start, many people who run their own businesses don't make as much money as they did when they were getting paid a salary and it's hard to not get discouraged by that.

> 66 I was a workaholic and worked my butt off for ten years. And I'm not interested in doing that again... 99

My advice to anyone is to be very careful and to make sure that you understand and have made allowances for every circumstance you might face in your business. Don't become discouraged because you're not earning packets of money or expect that it will be easy from the beginning, because you'll be in for a shock. And don't worry if it's not all happening today. I worked for ten years in an advertising agency and was 31 before I started my business. It doesn't have to start straight away, and sometimes it's good to get experience working for other people and learning how other businesses operate.

What is the most common mistake that new business owners make?

I think the most common mistake is unnecessary spending. People go off and buy a whole lot of new things that they don't really need and don't have the money for. I mean, my desk is so old – but I know of so many new businesses that go and buy all this flash equipment and furniture – unless you have to do that to create an impression for your clients, it's not something I would be doing.

Another mistake is when new business owners think it's going to be easy. Working for yourself doesn't mean you clock on at 9.00am and finish at 5.00pm, it means your business is on your mind all day and all night. I can't count the number of times I've woken up at 3.00am trying to solve problems within my business. When you are the person bringing in the money and paying all the wages you can't just switch off.

What were some of the challenges you had to overcome on the journey to achieving your personal and business goals?

One of the greatest challenges initially was that I had come from working in a large advertising agency where I was used to having a lot of people around me, being very creative and having lots of interaction. Then suddenly, I was working on my own and starting a business. I found it really difficult, especially on Friday afternoons not having anyone to go to lunch with, or to get a drink with after work. I had a hard time learning to enjoy my own company and motivating myself to come to work every day.

Also, not really having had any experience, I found the whole supermarket process quite a challenge. I didn't understand how it all worked, for example, fees, structures and terms. If I had understood more, I would have been a little savvier and probably wouldn't have paid out so much money.

I also sometimes find it challenging to not take things personally. When I lose business or a company wants to take one of my products out of the range, I can sometimes feel really disheartened and emotional. I'll mull over it for few days and try to look at other positive things that are happening within the business, and after that I'm able to look at situations clearly again and think of ways to solve the problem and get my products back on the shelves.

It is very common for people to become consumed by their businesses and turn into workaholics. How have you avoided buying into this philosophy?

I did that in advertising, I was a workaholic and worked my butt off for ten years. And I'm not interested in doing that again, in fact I believe it would be a mistake.

These days I am interested in being happy, healthy, having a good marriage and spending time with my children. I don't want to miss out on their childhoods. I want to spend time with my friends, weekends with my family and be home by 5.00pm to see my children.

Do you think that anyone can become a successful entrepreneur?

No, not everyone should be in their own business and not everyone can become a successful entrepreneur. It requires certain qualities in a person, it's just like not everyone can be an Olympic sprinter, most people don't have the skill-set for it.

If you had to start over again with nothing, what would you do?

If I had absolutely nothing, I would probably go back and become an art director at an advertising agency again. I would wait until I had earned a sizeable amount of money, and then try again.

I would probably also reverse all the mistakes I made the first time around. There are a few things that I would do differently if I had the chance. One would be to call my company De Jour Sanitary Products right from the very beginning instead of the original name I chose, which was The Woman's Room. I would also like to have been a little savvier on the 'No to GST' campaign that I started. I should have got a PR company involved with me so I could have had more exposure because I was the first person to inform the public that we were going to have a tax on tampons. It was a huge issue for four or five weeks and yet none of it was credited to me and I probably really missed out on a big opportunity.

How has having children affected you personally and in running your business?

I now put my children first, at the end of the day they are much more important than my business. Having my own business is lovely as it provides me with a great lifestyle, but if I didn't have happy children, I wouldn't see the point.

In terms of running my business it just means I have had to become more organised. I run my life to a clock, working in half-hour blocks. I bring my little ones into the office one day a week and they just fit in with me. If I have to go home for some reason, I can. If I need to stay home or take them to a class because one of their grandmothers can't take them, then I do.

What are your top tips for becoming a successful entrepreneur?

1. Surround yourself with people who are smarter than you.
2. Understand the market really well.
3. Understand your competitors.
4. Go with your gut feeling.
5. Put your family first and your business second (but make sure your business does come second, not third or fourth).
6. Think about your mentors and ask yourself what they would do in different situations.

If you can't find a mentor, how else can you get inspiration?

Read books about great business people, athletes or people who have done wonderful things. I have read books on Ray Kroc who started McDonald's at the startling age of 56, Howard Schultz who started Starbucks, Helene Rubenstein who started her cosmetics brand back in the early 1900s, and Lance Armstrong who survived cancer and went on to win the Tour de France a record seven times. I have also gone to seminars and conferences to hear speakers who have been inspirational.

As I always say, you can always learn something from someone else. Even if you spend an hour with someone or read an entire book and only take one thing away, my gosh, that is one thing you didn't know before that can help you to grow your business, and that's important!

KRISTINA NOBLE &
SIMONE BABIC

66 Being in business is a great exercise in personal growth as it always challenges you on multiple levels. For us, it comes down to the fact that we believe we are effective at making the right decisions. 99

KRISTINA NOBLE & SIMONE BABIC

Kristina, born in 1971 and Simone, born in 1974 are sisters who grew up in the Melbourne suburb of Glen Waverley.

Kristina completed a Bachelor of Economics and Graduate Diploma in Accounting at Monash University and began her career in the IT division of accounting firm, Grant Thornton. Simone studied a Bachelor of Science at Melbourne University, with a focus on communications and information exchange at a time when the internet was in its infancy. The sisters' interest in IT and the use of technology in business, together with the emerging opportunities presented by the internet, were the catalyst for starting Citrus, an online marketing agency.

Through sound management, flexibility and a firm eye on the future, the agency survived the infamous dot-com boom and crash. Citrus specialises in business-to-consumer applications, and has a distinctive flair in delivering outstanding websites integrated with a range of results-driven online marketing solutions.

Kristina and Simone see it as their responsibility to give back to the community through business and Citrus sponsors several foundations and charities.

Both Simone and Kristina are married (Kristina to Peter Noble, Citrus's CEO), and both live in the bay side suburbs of Melbourne and enjoy travelling, spending time with their family and of course, building businesses!

When did you and your family first realise that you had an entrepreneurial flair?

As far back as we can remember we were helping out with different parts of Dad's business. Our tasks ranged from writing Christmas cards and wrapping champagne bottles in our younger years, to writing the monthly invoices a little later on. Dinner conversation regularly included discussions about the business and some of the daily pressures that Mum and Dad were dealing with.

It was an exciting and dynamic family and one that we thoroughly enjoyed being a part of. We were always on the go, and everyone had to pull their weight and contribute to the running of the household. Saturday was the day for chores and all of us would work together to wash the cars, mow the lawns, scrub the verandahs and so on. It was extremely bonding and set the foundation for our thinking; we all work together and back each other up.

We were raised with a very clear understanding that hard work was a key to success and with the very distinct message that you never give up – it was something like, 'persistence beats resistance'. And we were encouraged to start our own business, so with this goal in mind we finished our university degrees and did just that!

Whose idea was it to start a business within the IT industry and why the name 'Citrus'?

Simone was studying information communications at the University of Melbourne and six months before she finished her degree she suggested that it might be time for us to start thinking about what business we were going to get into. The 'internet' had just started emerging as a buzzword in the newspapers and there was an almost nervous energy about how this unknown medium was going to revolutionise business. She had some limited exposure to the concepts behind the internet in her course, and

> 66 It was important that the name reflected more of an agency feel rather than just a web production house. 99

although they were quite theoretical it was enough to convince us that this thing was worth investigating a little further.

At that time I was working with the chartered accounting firm, Grant Thornton, in the IT department. My role was to help people understand technology and how it could be applied to their businesses to increase efficiencies, particularly in the areas of accounting and business systems. I'd worked with about 60 different companies across numerous industries and there was one common denominator – companies were not taking technology seriously, and more importantly, they didn't understand how it could impact their bottom line. I started developing a real excitement around the possibility of working with a new technology such as the internet to make a difference to companies' performance.

Simone and I started having some in-depth discussions around how this might work. At the tender ages of 21 and 24, these discussions were a lot less in-depth than we thought at the time, however coupled with our enormous energy and excitement it was more than enough to get us started.

Naming the business was great fun. We started by working out what our business stood for, what our image would be and how we wanted to be perceived. Words such as 'fresh', 'dynamic', 'unique' and 'bold' were at the top of the list. It was important that the name reflected more of an agency feel rather than just a web production house. We had sufficient foresight to see that our industry was going to be ever-changing, in fact that was the only thing we could be sure of, that it would change radically and often! So we chose a name that had a positive feel, that embodied our brand values, that would not pigeonhole us as a specific type of business – and of course, one that we both loved. That's how Citrus was born.

At what point did you realise that you needed additional staff?

We realised that we needed staff because there was just far too much work for us to handle. Not only that, but we soon realised there were some skills that neither of us had, such as programming. We started by outsourcing the programming but the costs were just too prohibitive and we realised that we'd have to bring it in-house. This was a really interesting time, it was difficult to conduct an interview with someone and find out if they were suitable for the job when you only had a very limited understanding of what they actually did. The first programmer we hired came in as a temp for two weeks and as it turns out she has been with Citrus for more than five years!

How did you survive the dot-com crash of 2000 and what did you learn from that experience?

There were two main reasons why we survived. The first was that we worked closely with some key clients that we were making a real difference for. They valued us and the results we were producing for them, and because of that they weren't swayed by the media hype. The second was that we were running a tight ship. Financial planning was high on our priority list and we always ensured that cash flow was good.

Needless to say it was a steep and invaluable learning curve. Being in such a fluid industry means that we need to constantly watch for trends, identify where we fit and how we are going to get where we want to go. At the bottom of the crash we launched a new division of our business – online marketing. This was a very courageous move as we had to bring in specific skills, train existing staff members and invest in new technology. But it has paid off. Online marketing now comprises well over 50 per cent of our total business revenue and we see it as a major growth area.

What's it like being sisters and working so closely together?

We can only say that being sisters has worked to our advantage on every level. We are extremely close and think alike in many ways but we challenge each other too. We share the same vision, the same commitment to one another, and we know each other so well. We each have a huge amount of respect for the other and it is a pleasure to be able to realise a vision together.

The essence of our business relationship is communication. It works so well because we can speak freely about anything and everything and that has helped us to guide and transition the business since its inception.

Why do you think it's important to separate yourself from the day-to-day running of the business?

Being able to get a perspective on the business is critical to ensuring that it flourishes. When you are immersed in the day-to-day operations, it's difficult to gain an objective view on what is best for it or in which direction it should be heading. We have had the experience many times when we've been able to see an issue with clarity after an extended period of time away from the business. We also have regular strategic planning days where we workshop the direction of Citrus and what the next twelve months to two years may hold, and this has always provided us with a very rewarding way of moving forward.

In the early years it was difficult to find the time to do this, or to even place it high on the priority list because there were so many day-to-day things that demanded our attention, but now we make regular time to meet and discuss the bigger picture. In fact we do this at least once a month in addition to annual holidays, which double as strategic planning sessions. At the end of each holiday invariably we will have come up with a fantastic idea that just seems so obvious in moving the business forward. So it's important to take this time out from the business because it keeps your ideas fresh and objective.

Many business owners are content to leave the financial and legal aspects of their businesses to others, why do you believe it is so important to have a thorough understanding of these areas?

These are areas of your business that you need to pay attention to and get right. Make sure that you know and understand as much as you possibly can. At the end of the day you are liable for all decisions made, not your accountant or lawyer, they are simply providing professional advice. And don't assume that they are always right, ask questions and make sure you have enough information to make informed decisions.

On the financial side, know your numbers and set specific financial goals. Create a month-by-month projected financial plan that is broken up into your revenue streams, direct expenses and overhead expenses, tallying up to a profit and loss calculation. Have the twelve-month projection on the same worksheet with a total for the year. Track this every two weeks, entering the actual figures into the column next to the month you are in. It will give you a very quick and easy way of following your business activity, including revenue streams that are or aren't performing well, what is happening with your expenses and overall profit/loss. You can also start to see patterns from month to month and it gives you an indication of where you need to be focusing your energy. Toward the end of the year you can compare your estimates with actual data and use this information to formulate your plan for the following year.

Create budgets for all expenses too and ensure that these are communicated to the different departments of your business. This will help to keep your spending under control. You must know where every dollar is going out of the business and why.

On the legal side of things, become what we call a 'legal eagle'. Go over all contracts you need to sign with a fine-tooth comb. This is not an area to be lazy in. Many

> 66 So it's important to take this time out from the business because it keeps your ideas fresh and objective. 99

people never read the fine print, but you must read every term and condition carefully if you are putting your signature to it. Don't be afraid to question clauses or to propose changes that suit you and your business better. If in doubt have your lawyer take you through the contract.

What do you love most about business?

We love the fact that it allows us to be creative. Having your own business means that the final decision, and responsibility for that decision, rests with you. This is such an empowering experience because it means that you are creating what you think is right for the staff, for the clients, for the suppliers and for everyone who touches your business. Ultimately, the business is a reflection of your choices. The other aspect of this is that it gives us freedom. Not only in the sense that we can make our own decisions about what to do with our time, but also the freedom to direct the business.

If anyone can succeed in business no matter what their background or circumstances, what do you think holds people back from becoming successful entrepreneurs?

Business is generally a mystery to most people. They look at successful businesspeople and think that they must have a hidden talent or something special about them. The biggest lesson I learnt very early on in business was that entrepreneurs are just normal people and once I'd realised that, I thought 'If they can do it, so can I'. By being involved in entrepreneurial networking groups you get the opportunity to meet other entrepreneurs which continually reinforces the fact that they are just normal people doing their thing and facing the same challenges that everyone does.

It all comes down to the way you think about yourself and what 'mind power' you have to back yourself. What I mean by that is that you have to believe in your vision, what your business is about and that you are capable of bringing the whole thing together. Being in business is a great exercise in personal growth as it always challenges you on multiple levels. For us, it comes down to the fact that we believe we are effective at making the right decisions. We make decisions with conviction and clarity and as a result it provides leadership and direction for our entire team.

I guess the key difference is that business people have steep learning curves all of the time as they constantly strive to retain a competitive edge and stay ahead of the market. If they don't, the business won't survive. There are therefore some characteristics that do make entrepreneurs and their businesses appear mysterious, but be assured that with some hard work and smart thinking you can learn and achieve anything.

Have there ever been times when you wanted to give up, and if so, what got you through?

The dot-com crash was a very difficult time not only because it challenged the day-to-day operations of our business, but also the underlying validity of the internet as a viable business tool. When everything you read and everyone you spoke to said it was a fad and that it was over, it was really difficult to be in the business with any conviction and to believe in what we were doing. Companies literally stopped spending money on their websites, budgets were pulled and there was this overall sense of relief that they didn't have to deal with this unknown medium anymore.

We had a number of meetings to determine what our next steps would be. Financially we were in reasonable shape as we had a few clients that understood the value of the internet and were convinced that it wasn't going anywhere – back then they would have been seen as visionaries! But we were forced to look at the core and work out if we still believed in the internet, even if everyone else didn't. We decided that we did, and invested funds into starting our online marketing division. This was difficult at times but also extremely rewarding.

> ❝ Companies literally stopped spending money on their websites, budgets were pulled. ❞

What is the most common mistake that new business owners make?

The most common mistake is that new business owners don't put enough thought into where they are going with their businesses. By that I mean developing strategic plans and making sure that those plans are followed diligently.

For those who are just starting out, a plan is the best way to really make a difference to the business quickly. It's a very intense time when a business first starts and generally new business owners get caught up in the detail of what is happening and forget about the bigger picture. This is a problem because the months just keep rolling by and if you are not meeting your strategic objectives you will go nowhere.

What are some of the ways people can go about deciding what type of business to get involved in?

A great way to determine possible business opportunities is by looking at different industries and identifying what interests you. Above all, you have to be interested and inspired by what you are doing. Once you have determined this, it is a good idea to start attending networking functions in the industry of your choice. The single biggest way to generate opportunities is by talking to people and learning about the industry. I have always found this is the most effective and interesting way to learn and it never ceases to amaze me how much people have to offer and how willing they are to share information. Once you start to refine your ideas about your business, I recommend that you try to make appointments with some business owners in the industry of your choice to ask them about their experiences.

What advantages do you believe women have over men in business?

The main area that being women has helped us is with our staff. We have always fostered the view that our team are the most important component in the ongoing growth and development of Citrus. We have invested a lot of time and money in staff development and culture. All of our staff have been encouraged to do self-development courses funded by the company. We have even had meditation courses conducted by external people at our premises. We spend one-on-one time discussing challenges in the workplace, and whenever a challenge arises we perceive it as an opportunity and create an environment where everyone can share and grow from the experience.

What do you say to people who think it is too late to get into business and fear they've 'missed the boat'?

It's never too late! Many entrepreneurs choose to continue to be involved in business at some level for the rest of their lives because it is just part of who they are. Artists love to paint – entrepreneurs love doing business, it really becomes a creative outlet. There are people in the business world who reach retirement age and decide to give it a go, only to return and start a new business from scratch at the age of 60 and over. It's all a state of mind, if you believe it is too late then that will be a barrier that stops you and we would suggest that a shift in attitude is well overdue. You need lots of energy, drive, ambition and passion.

How do you balance running a business and having a life?

This is probably the single most important thing we have learnt over the years. Being self-confessed workaholics with unlimited passion, enthusiasm, loads of energy and very high standards was our personal cocktail of disaster. We wouldn't undertake anything unless we knew we could throw ourselves into it 100 per cent and give it our best shot. Plus, we had a touch of the 'I work the hardest out of everyone I know' syndrome. All of this meant that we would sacrifice our personal needs for the sake of getting the job done. This isn't sustainable if you want to live a balanced life, and these are some of our tips for journeying out of this attitude:

Reap the Rewards Along the Way – One of the most important things in business is to put yourself first and reap the rewards as you go. This makes it all worthwhile and motivates you through the tough times. For example, if you choose to be in business because it represents a certain level of freedom for you then it's important to exercise that freedom. You might take a long lunch, book in a massage or take a long weekend. Or, if you choose to be in business to make money then reward yourself with a payrise, bonus or dividend as soon as the business can afford it. Whatever your reasons for being in business, whether material or otherwise, make sure you get the rewards along the way.

I see so many people in business who don't take annual leave for years, or pay themselves next to nothing and run themselves into the ground. Yes, there are periods when we must do these things, but if it's ongoing then you risk burning yourself out. The other issue is that often these behaviours and attitudes create the culture of your organisation, which opens up a big can of worms in the long term.

Draw the Line Between Work and Play – Another important factor is living a balanced life. It's really important to have a life outside of your work and to understand that you are not your business, the business is an entity unto itself. Making sure that you spend time with family, friends or doing whatever you like doing is very important.

[Kristina] I remember making a conscious decision to not work on Saturdays (after having worked every Saturday for years). It was a tough decision to make because I was losing the benefit of a full day in the office without interruptions. And for some reason I also felt guilty about it, but I made the break and it's one of the best decisions I've ever made. I now spend time with family and friends on Saturdays which is personally far more rewarding.

Mind, Body, Spirit – Another part of work/life balance is nourishing your mind, body and spirit. Whether it's in the form of training, yoga, meditation, taking vitamins, camping, reading, going to a dance party, doing self-development courses, playing with your kids, undertaking physical challenges 'Richard Branson-style' – whatever your thing is, make sure you make the time to do it. It nourishes your soul, unclutters your mind and makes you more productive when you are working.

It's a case of understanding that there is always going to be something left on your 'to do' list and that you'll never get everything done. You need to accept it, and trust. Know that rewarding yourself and having a good work/life balance means that both you and the business will be in better shape as a result.

What is the most important thing you have learnt about succeeding in business?

Probably the single most important thing we've learnt is to be able to relate to people on all levels. This involves the ability to really listen to people when they are speaking and to be able to cut through to the core issues, even when they aren't being communicated effectively. Anyone can learn how to manage cash flow or to set up systems and processes, but being able to relate to people is a massive advantage in business. If you really listen, drop your defences, put yourself in the other person's shoes and communicate with them on that basis then any people-related issues will be resolved quickly and effectively. The other side of this is to be able to communicate whatever you have to say clearly, directly and effectively.

Next, you need to learn how to steer the ship in tough times and constantly think outside the square. Having a resigned attitude in business is a major disadvantage. A big challenge is learning how to constantly create better situations for your business. Some of the things that have helped us to attain a different perspective on our situation include:

- Travel – This gives you physical and mental distance from your business, allowing fresh ideas to be generated. It often happens automatically, you'll be lying on a beach and an idea will pop into your head and quickly turn into a real brainwave.
- Thinking courses that open your mind – Go to www.schoolofthinking.org, founded by Michael Hewitt-Gleeson and Edward de Bono, and enrol in a free virtual short course that will change your thinking patterns and broaden your mental capacity. There are many other materials available, go searching and see what jumps out at you.
- Pretend you are sitting on the couch at home watching your situation on television – What would you tell the person to do?

Who are the mentors that have inspired you and what important lessons have you learnt from them?

Our parents have been the main mentors in our lives. It's great to be able to talk openly about business issues, knowing that your mentor really does have your best interests at heart. And being able to discuss both personal and professional issues with them is a major plus. They are both inspiring leaders in their own right and offer more support than one would think possible. We speak with them several times a day and have dinner or breakfast with them several times a week. They have an amazing approach where they listen and give their opinion, but never force it. They also have a deep respect for us and understand that the final call is ours. They allow us to learn from our own experiences without interfering and provide ongoing support where we need it.

These are some classic learnings that they have passed on to us, and that we will no doubt pass on to our own children:

- Nothing is impossible.
- Be an honest business person.
- Always treat people equally.
- Work hard, play hard.
- Do anything to support your family.
- Family comes before business.
- Don't take things too seriously; retain your sense of humour.
- You are in business to make money.

What are some of your personal and business goals for the next five to ten years?

Our future plans are to:

- Open up new business streams in areas that interest us.
- Have kids at some point – This is one of the biggest issues facing career women today. The balancing act of having a career and children is very challenging both personally and professionally. The benefit of being in your own business though is the ability to have flexible hours and the means to pay for help.
- Travel extensively for business and pleasure – This is something we both love and would like to maximise over the next few years. We do quite a bit of travel at the moment, however with plans to expand the business and start families, the balancing act will become even trickier.

FINAL THOUGHTS

Having just re-read this book for probably the tenth time, we both continue to be deeply inspired and moved by the messages it contains – more so in many ways than we were by the *Secrets of Male Entrepreneurs Exposed!*, which was launched a few months ago (no offence guys!).

Once again it's the stories that seem to connect, and the personalities that become like real-life mentors and guiding lights on the journey. It's interesting over the last couple of months, during our own times of reflection and decision-making, we've been catching ourselves asking, 'How would Sandy handle this situation?' or 'I know how Margaret would respond here', and even, 'I bet Kristina's desk doesn't look like this!' If it hasn't already, it will begin to happen for you too, the more you re-read the chapters and begin to integrate each person's ideas and philosophies.

Know that despite the title of this book, there really is no great secret to business success. As this book demonstrates, all the information you will ever require to succeed is freely available, as long as you have the drive, courage and 'smarts' to actively seek out what you need to know.

As we have both personally discovered, the real driver of success in business (and in life) is simply *implementation* – the ability to apply, put into practice, and take action on the things you hear and read. With this in mind, perhaps the best thing that you can do right now is re-read each of the chapters, and with a notepad and pen by your side, write answers to these two questions:

- What are the three most important things I've learnt from this chapter?
- How can I implement these lessons into my business/life, starting today?

Go on give it a try, after a few short weeks you'll be amazed at the impact it will have.

In closing, remember this: 'Nobody can go back to the beginning and make a brand new start. But everyone can start from now and make a brand new end', so begin on your path now! Don't wait for circumstances to be just right, because they may never be. And don't worry that you don't know enough, because you never will. Just make a start and continue learning as you go.

Remember that the moment you start moving forward, making progress toward your goals, challenges will rise up to test you. It's almost as if life is asking you: 'How badly do you want to achieve your dream?' Ask yourself this question right now, so that when the challenges come, and they most certainly will, you'll be prepared with the answer.

We trust that you've enjoyed this book. It has been a real honour to work with these wonderful women and share their stories. Take the ideas to heart, put them into action and remember to enjoy life along the way.

DREAM BIG!

Dale and Katherine Beaumont

P.S For anyone either looking to go into business, or already in business, we recommend also reading *Secrets Of Male Entrepreneurs Exposed!* where you'll find even more brilliant ideas and inspirational stories from other successful entrepreneurs.

P.S.S We love receiving letters or emails from people who have been inspired by something shared in one of our books, so please contact us with your tales of inspiration.

How To Claim Your FREE Bonus Gifts
Valued Over $147

Some of our contributors have generously offered FREE bonus gifts for all of our readers. Here are some of the things you'll receive simply by visiting our website:

FREE GIFT # 1 ($47.00 Value) Secrets to MEGA Business Success – Having struggled in small business for many years, Sandy Forster finally discovered the secrets to success and went on to create a number of businesses, generating millions of dollars without spending a cent on advertising! In this special transcript from one of Sandy's LIVE events, she shares her complete uncensored story and how you can explode the success of your business. Certainly a must-read!

FREE GIFT # 2 ($29.95 Value) Kirsty's Tips to Business Success – Having become a self-made millionaire at the tender age of 23, in this e-book Kirsty Dunphey shares 21 powerful tips to maximise your business success and create a happy life. Learn how to turn obstacles into opportunities, how to find your life's purpose, how to become financially savvy, and how to create long-lasting relationships.

FREE GIFT # 3 ($47.00 Value) Millionaire Visualisation – In this special 35-minute audio product, Sandy (with music) will guide you step-by-step through a powerful visualisation experience designed to unlock your inner wealth. You'll discover what makes your heart sing and how to see your future with more clarity to attract greater levels of abundance into your life.

FREE GIFT # 4 ($30.00 Value) Live Interviews with Margaret – This transcript of several live radio interviews takes you up-close and personal with businesswoman, wealth strategist and best-selling author Margaret Lomas. Packed with practical information on investing and purchasing positive cash flow properties, you'll also learn the '20 Must-Ask Questions' before acquiring any piece of real estate.

FREE GIFT # 5 ($14.95 Value) 52 Best Ever Business Quotes – Contained in this document are 52 business insights from some of history's greatest thinkers. Featuring names such as: Benjamin Franklin, Jan Clazon, John F. Kennedy, Richard Branson and Bill Gates, you'll be motivated, educated and inspired. Topics include: leadership, customer service, negotiation, creativity and much more.

FREE GIFT # 6 ($9.95 Value) The Prophet by Kahlil Gibram – This text stands as one of the most widely read books of the twentieth century. Through a series of 26 poetic essays, its iconic writer captures the essence of life and shares profound understandings for the moment. Recreated in eBook format, it's yours to read and pass on to friends.

Simply visit our website and follow the directions to download your free gifts:

www.SecretsExposed.com.au/female_entrepreneurs

About the Authors

Dale Beaumont

Dale Beaumont was born in Sydney in June 1981. Growing up, he participated in a number of sports and at the age of nine was selected for the elite NSW Gymnastics Squad. Training 34 hours per week, he soon learnt the value of discipline, hard work, having a coach and most importantly, delayed gratification.

After six years of intensive training, Dale changed his sporting focus to competitive aerobics so that he could spend more time on his studies and pursue other interests. In 1998 he became the National Aerobics Champion and the youngest Australian to compete at the World Aerobics Championships, where he placed eighth.

After finishing high school, Dale began attending various personal development and success seminars, where he learnt from people such as Jim Rohn, Michael Rowland, Bob Proctor, Robert Kiyosaki, John Maxwell, Brandon Bays, Brad Sugars, Mark Victor Hanson and many others.

At the age of 19, together with good friend Brent Williams, Dale wrote his first book titled *The World at Your Feet,* and co-founded Tomorrow's Youth International, which now runs educational and self-development programs for 13 to 21-year-olds in four countries. Dale has been featured on the *Today* show, *Sunrise*, *Mornings with Kerri-Anne*, as well as in countless newspapers and magazines.

Most recently, Dale has been hard at work developing the 'Secrets Exposed' series, to bring together the very best material from hundreds of Australasia's most successful people. With more than twenty books planned for the next three years and an up-coming seminar series, Dale is now a sought-after speaker on topics such as: start-up business, networking skills, book publishing, internet marketing and generating publicity.

Dale lives in Sydney with his beautiful and very supportive wife, Katherine. With a baby next on the 'to-do' list and lots of international travel plans, Dale is looking forward to the challenges ahead, and to spending more time enjoying life.

For more information about Dale's workshops and educational materials, or to book him as a guest speaker at your next conference or event, please visit: **www.DaleBeaumont.com**

Katherine Beaumont

Katherine was born and raised in Newcastle. As the eldest of four children she quickly learnt to look after herself and keep entertained by reading lots of books.

After graduating in naturopathy with the Australian Traditional Medicine Society Award, Katherine worked her way from the ground up in the health food industry. Proving her talents and passion, Katherine was headhunted for the role of national sales and marketing manager for an Australian vitamin and supplement company.

Thriving in her role, Katherine was promoted to general manager. She travelled around Australia introducing new products to the market, writing articles for magazines and running health seminars, routinely putting in an 80-plus hour workweek. When her father became terminally ill, the reality of corporate life and what it was doing to her was quickly put into dramatic perspective.

To redefine her purpose, Katherine joined up with her best friend (and partner in mischief) Jo, to expand her naturopathic clinic and work on other health concepts. Katherine also turned to her other love, personal development, where she met Dale. The pair were married in a romantic ceremony on the beach at sunset in Hawaii, fulfilling yet another of Katherine's childhood dreams.

Today, Katherine and her husband own several companies, including a successful Network Marketing business which has given Katherine the opportunity to call her time her own, and to help others do the same, as well as speak to tens of thousands of people on health. Outside of business she still loves reading (especially about Ancient Egypt) and travelling to exotic hide-a-ways.

About Our Contributors

We would again like to say a huge 'thank you' to the amazing women who have helped to make this book possible. Some have their own books and other educational products – for more information, contact them directly.

Sue Ismiel – Life Source Group
Address: PO Box 8303 Baulkham Hills NSW 2153
Phone: (02) 8850 9444 Fax: (02) 8850 9400
Email: customerservice@lifesourcegroup.com Website: **www.LifeSourceGroup.com**

Joanne Mercer – Joanne Mercer Footwear
Address: PO Box 330 South Yarra VIC 3141
Phone: (03) 9866 1900 Fax: (03) 9866 1313
Email: info@joannemercer.com.au Website: **www.JoanneMercer.com.au**

Sandy Forster – Wildly Wealthy Women
Address: PO Box 362 Moolooaba QLD 4557
Phone: 1300 133 249 Fax: (07) 5493 9650
Email: info@wildlywealthy.com Website: **www.WildlyWealthy.com**
Book: *How To Be Wealthy FAST*

Sonia Amoroso – CAT Media
Address: PO Box 5311 Sydney NSW 2001
Phone: (02) 8295 3333 Fax: (02) 8295 3444
Email: tbooth@catmedia.com.au
Website: **www.SkinDoctors.com.au** and **www.Naturopathica.com.au**

Margaret Lomas – Destiny Financial Solutions
Address: PO Box 5400 Chittaway Bay NSW 2261
Phone: (02) 4351 0380 Fax: (02) 4351 0379
Email: info@destiny.net.au Website: **www.Destiny.net.au**
Books: *How to Make Your Money Last as Long as You Do, How to Create an Income for Life* and *A Pocket Guide to Investing in Positive Cash Flow Property*

Katrina Allen – De Jour Sanitary Products
Address: 286 Chesterville Road Moorabbin VIC 3189
Phone: (03) 9555 1318 Fax: (03) 9555 4048
Email: feedback@dejour.com.au Website: **www.dejour.com.au**

Suzi Dafnis – Pow Wow Events International
Address: PO Box 122 Rosebery NSW 1445
Phone: (02) 9662 8488 Fax: (02) 9662 8611
Email: info@powwowevents.com.au Website: **www.PowWowEvents.com.au**

Kirsty Dunphey – M&M Harcourts
Address: 187 Brisbane Street Launceston TAS 7250
Phone: (03) 6331 5111 Fax: (03) 6331 5100
Email: kirsty@harcourtstasmania.com.au
Website: **www.HarcourtsTasmania.com.au** and **www.KirstyDunphey.com**
Books: *Advance to GO – Collect $1 Million* and *Made In Australia*

Sue Whyte – Intimo Lingerie
Address: 2 Meaden Street Southbank VIC 3006
Phone: (03) 9645 9939 Fax: (03) 9699 7255
Email: intimo@intimo.com.au Website: **www.Intimo.com.au**

Tanya Hamersfeld – Corporate Training Australia
Address: 643-647 Glenhuntly Road Caulfield South VIC 3162
Phone: 1300 666 480 Fax: (03) 9523 1066
Email: inspired@ctra.com.au Website: **www.ctra.com.au**

Suzy Yates – Bay Street Mediaworks
Address: 66 Bay Street Ultimo NSW 2007
Phone: (02) 9212 4335 Fax: (02) 9281 9811
Email: suzy@baystmediaworks.com.au Website: **www.baystmediaworks.com.au**

Kristina Karlsson – kikki.K
Address: PO Box 107 Albert Park VIC 3206
Phone: (03) 9645 6346 Fax: (03) 9645 6932
Email: info@kikki-K.com.au Website: **www.kikki-K.com.au**

Amy Lyden – Bow Wow Meow
Address: PO Box 1818 Bondi Junction NSW 1355
Phone: (02) 9369 2666 Fax: (02) 9387 5437
Email: info@bowwow.com.au Website: **www.BowWow.com.au**

Carol Comer – High Impact Marketing
New Zealand Address: PO Box 68 721 Auckland
Australian Address: PO Box 75 Mermaid Beach QLD 4215
Email: carol@himpact.com.au Website: **www.HighImpact.cc**

Shelley Barrett – ModelCo.
Address: PO Box 201 Double Bay NSW 1360
Phone: (02) 8354 6700 Fax: (02) 8354 6777
Email: info@modelco.com.au Website: **www.ModelCo.com.au**

Elim Chew – 77th Street
Address: 21 Serangoon North Ave 5 #w03-01
Ban Teck Han Building Singapore 554864
Phone: + 65 6482 1377 Fax: +65 6481 8507
Email: enquiries@77thstreet.com Website: **www.77thstreet.com**

Kristina Noble & Simone Babic – Citrus
Address: Level 5, 100 Albert Road South Melbourne VIC 3205
Phone: (03) 9681 5333 Fax: (03) 9682 5586
Email: info@citrus.com.au Website: **www.Citrus.com.au**

Other great titles now available

Secrets of Male Entrepreneurs Exposed!

In this book you'll discover...

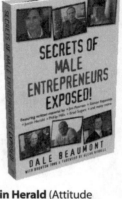

- How to come up with your multimillion dollar idea
- Creative ways to raise hundreds of thousands in capital
- How to build and lead a champion team
- Unique marketing ideas that will explode your profits
- Master techniques to influence people and sell your ideas
- What it takes to get media exposure and loads of free advertising
- How to package and franchise your business to go global

Featuring written material by...

Jim Penman (Jim's Mowing) • **Siimon Reynolds** (Photon Group) • **Justin Herald** (Attitude Clothing & Intimidate) • **Phillip Mills** (Les Mills International) • **Tom Potter** (Eagle Boys Pizza) • **Brad Sugars** (Action International) • **Tim Pethick** (nudie Founder) • **Douglas Foo** (Apex-Pal International) • **Michael Twelftree** (Two Hands Wines) • **Domenic Carosa** (destra Corporation) • **Jim Zavos** (EzyDVD) • **Craig Lovett** (Cleanevent International) • **Glenn Kiddell** (VitaMan Skincare) • **Trevor Choy** (Choy Lawyers) • **Carmelo Zampaglione** (Zamro) • **Andrew Ward** (3 Minute Angels)

Secrets of Property Millionaires Exposed!

In this book you'll discover...

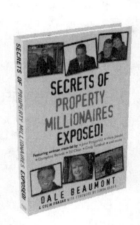

- The essential qualities of all top property investors
- All the various property strategies and which one is right for you
- How to make money whether the market is going up or down
- Master negotiation techniques that will save you thousands
- How to structure your portfolio correctly to minimise tax
- How to use partnerships and joint ventures to explode profits
- Expert tips on market trends and future growth areas

Featuring written material by...

Hans Jakobi (Australia's Wealth Coach®) • **John Fitzgerald** (Multimillionaire Investor) • **Craig Turnbull** (Author, Speaker & Mentor) • **Patrick Bright** (Leading Buyers' Agent) • **Dymphna Boholt** (Asset Protection) • **Sam Vannutini** (Renovations Expert) • **Edward Chan** (Taxation Specialist) • **Gordon Green** (Residential & Commercial Investor) • **Peter Comben** (Property Developer) • **Rick Otton** (Vendor Financier & Wrapper) • **Gary & Jenny Leather** (Husband & Wife Duo)

To order your copies online and SAVE, visit

...or coming soon

Secrets of Young Achievers Exposed!

In this book you'll discover...

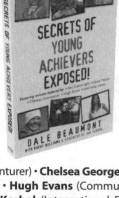

- What it takes to become a real success
- How to know what you want to do with your life
- How to get motivated and stay motivated
- How to overcome criticism and discouragement
- What all super-achievers have in common
- How to reach the top of any career, *fast*
- How to turn your dream into reality

Featuring written material by...

Bec Cartwright (Actor & Singer) • **Jesse Martin** (Young Adventurer) • **Chelsea Georgeson** (Pro Surfer) • **Amy Wilkins** (TV Presenter & Fitness Coach) • **Hugh Evans** (Community & Aid Worker) • **Ilona Novacek** (Leading Model) • **Ben Korbel** (International DJ) • **Stephanie Williams** (Ballet Dancer) • **Tim Goodwin** (Aboriginal Activist) • **Simon Tedeschi** (Concert Pianist) • **Torah Bright** (Pro Snowboarder) • **Jeremy Lim** (Singaporean Ambassador)

Secrets of Great Public Speakers Exposed!

In this book you'll discover...

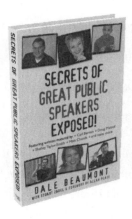

- Why the ability to communicate in public is critical to career success
- What all successful speakers have in common
- How to overcome fear and project confidence to your audience
- How to plan and structure a presentation for maximum impact
- How to use the right type of humour and have your audience in stitches
- Simple techniques to communicate subconscious messages
- What it takes to make $1 million a year as a professional speaker

Featuring written material by...

Doug Malouf (Speaking Coach) • **Shelley Taylor-Smith** (World Champion Athlete) • **Carl Barron** (Leading Comedian) • **Matt Church** (Top Corporate Speaker) • **Catherine DeVrye** (Best-selling Author) • **Billy Graham** (Boxing Champion) • **Gavin Blakley** (Former Toast-masters President) • **Ron Tacchi** (Founder of Speaker Seeker) • **Wayne Berry** (Australasia's Leading Sales Trainer) • **Robyn Henderson** (Networking Expert) • **Ron Lee** (The Corporate Ninja) • **Peter Sheahan** (Youth Speaker) • **Candy Tymson** (Gender Differences Expert) • **Michael Rowland** (Personal Development Speaker) • **Amanda Gore** (Aussie Speaker in USA) • **Chris Rewell** (Image Consultant)

www.SecretsExposed.com.au

Contributors Wanted For Future 'Secrets Exposed' Books

Yes, you can now be involved in the creation of a number of other exciting titles in the 'Secrets Exposed' series, including:

Australian Celebrities	Inspiring Leaders
Film Actors	Great CEOs
Sales Professionals	Sporting Heroes
Small Business Owners	NRL Stars
Music Icons	Marketing Gurus
Stock Market Millionaires	Weight Loss Champions
AFL Stars	Aussie Exporters
Christian Achievers	Personal Development Coaches
Great Team Builders	Soccer Stars
Profound Parents	Winning Franchises
Aussie Sporting Legends	Powerful Women
Big Business Tycoons	PLUS MANY MORE…

You can help to share the secrets of Australia's most successful people by nominating a contributor, and you'll be credited in the 'acknowledgements' page of that book!

To nominate a contributor for any of the above works, or to suggest another 'Secrets Exposed' title, please send your ideas in writing to:

Dream Express Publishing
PO Box 567
Crows Nest NSW 1585
Australia
Email: info@SecretsExposed.com.au

Discover The Amazing Success Behind Australia's Leading Educational and 'Life-Skills' Program for Teenagers and Young Adults

After five years and more than 7,300 thrilled participants in four countries, your teenager NOW has the opportunity to experience the highly acclaimed 2½ day advanced life-skills seminar *'Empower U'* . . .

- Do you feel that your teenager could be achieving more, but can't seem to get them motivated?
- Do you want to give them the *best* education possible?
- Do you want them to have every means at their disposal to live a happy, successful and rewarding life?

Then you need to discover WHY thousands of parents agree that the 2½ day *'Empower U'* program is the best decision you can make for your son or daughter's future…

In a fun, teenager-friendly environment, Dale Beaumont and Brent Williams will reveal the very same motivation and high-achievement secrets that propel the world's top performers to success – and that are already working wonders for thousands of kids across Australia. Secrets that your child will learn and apply to their life immediately. Secrets we've made so simple to understand and use that you will notice *immediate improvements*.

At *Empower U* your child will become so motivated, so focused, and so determined to succeed that they could well become a super-achiever in a very short time. Your child will walk away from *Empower U* with total *belief* in their own abilities and absolute *certainty* that they can achieve anything they want. Plus, they will have a 'toolkit' full of specific strategies they can use to convert their desires into tangible, real-world results - starting right away!

It doesn't matter whether your child just needs some friendly encouragement or a total 'attitude overhaul', *Empower U* will give them the belief, tools and strategies they need to get moving in the right direction.

"I am so glad that a friend told me about Empower U. My daughter attended almost two years ago at the age of fourteen. She is now seventeen and more motivated than ever. I think the most amazing thing about her experience is that it was not just a one-off. They have supported her the whole way and that has been just terrific."

Peter Stacey   *(Father of Jessica)*

"My two daughters attended the Empower U program. One excited, one sceptical. The change in both of them is truly amazing. I am now such a big fan and I just hope that more people take the chance on this that I did. Because then they will see what I now see."

Tura Lechminka   *(Mother of Alana and Kathryn)*

Whether it's more motivation, improved attitude, better exam marks, a savings plan, landing a great job, or just a more open family relationship … you will see results *FAST!*

To enrol your son or daughter into the next *Empower U* program simply give us a call or check out our website…

Tomorrow's Youth International

1300 732 782

www.TomorrowsYouth.com.au